Ulrich Becker (Ed.)

Esperanto
in *The New York Times*
(1887 – 1922)

Esperanto
in
The New York Times

(1887 – 1922)

✤

Edited by
Ulrich Becker

✤

Mondial

Mondial
New York

Ulrich Becker (Editor):

Esperanto in *The New York Times*
(1887 – 1922)

Copyright © 2010, Mondial

Translation of the Introduction: Eve Hecht

ISBN: 978-1-59569-169-9

Library of Congress Control Number: 2010928505

www.mondialbooks.com

Contents

Introduction i

1888 1
1897 9
1901 11
1902 12
1903 15
1904 27
1905 37
1906 38
1907 46
1908 66
1909 125
1910 134
1911 149
1912 166
1913 180
1914 186
1915 190
1916 198
1917 208
1918 211
1919 214
1920 214
1921 220
1922 228

Index 257
Bibliography 267
Internet Links 271

Introduction

This book is an entertaining look back at the beginnings of the Esperanto movement in the US and beyond, opening a window into contemporaneous accounts on the pages of a world-renowned newspaper – from the first mention in 1897 of a call by the author of Esperanto for reactions to his plan for an international language, and on to the passionate defense of the achievements of Esperanto and the contribution of its speakers to international understanding in readers' letters from 1922.

Several years ago, the *New York Times* opened its entire archive to the public. While the reprinting of articles from 1923 onward is quite costly, under US law, publications up to the end of 1922 are in the public domain, i.e. they may be reused free of charge.

As a result, we have included in this volume all the articles that could be found in the *New York Times* archives that mention such keywords as "Esperanto," "Zamenhof," or "Samenhof," etc. and that fall within the period from 1887 (the year in which Esperanto was first publicized) to 1922, with only a few exceptions: For one, the first article in the book elucidates the planned language movement *before* Esperanto became known in the US; on the other hand, numerous irrelevant articles, in which "Esperanto" is solely the name of a racehorse or a ship, have been mostly – although not always – left out.

Thus, while the collection of articles is also a treasure trove for historians, it should be regarded cautiously as a historical assembly of facts. Then, as now, many journalists were quick to publish half-truths or falsities as fact and to promote negligible items to headline status.

The book is supplemented by an appendix containing an index of the names of persons mentioned in the newspaper articles, a short bibliography, and a collection of links to reliable information on Esperanto on the Internet. These links may also be accessed directly at *www.mondialbooks.com/nytimes*.

Some of the articles in this collection reflect aspects of the history of the Esperanto movement quite vividly, among them the ongoing disputes of Esperantists with representatives of other planned language projects, particularly Ido; the adulation of the author of Esperanto, L. L. Zamenhof, his influence on the community of speakers, and his death; the early persecution of Esperanto, such as the banning of the Russian Esperanto League for "espionage" (after its president, Postnikoff (Aleksandr Postnikov), had been sentenced to, in the *Times'* words: eight years of "penal servitude"; the fruitless efforts to get the League of Nations to officially recognize the language, etc.

In many articles, we find odd anecdotes about Esperanto and the Esperantists: about marriage proposals made to Zamenhof at the World Esperanto Congress in Geneva in 1906; about the sensational visit of a "good looking young apostle" of Esperanto from Switzerland, Edmond Privat, to the US; about a "very old Esperanto family"; about "Esperanto, Chief of the Black Hand"; about the hundred students who pulled Zamenhof in a carriage through the streets of Antwerp; about the efforts to rename the USA as "Usonia" ("Usono" in Esperanto means "USA"); about the tragic love affair, and its end in violent death, of two Esperanto speakers, and much more.

Many passionately-written letters from readers illustrate the ups and downs, the successes and conflicts of the Esperanto community, as well as its perennial, sometimes effective, but more often fanatical disputes with the skeptics outside their ranks.

These first 35 years of the history of Esperanto seen from the vantage point of the *New York Times* show how Esperanto gradually became established in the US and in the world, carried on the high hopes of its early, idealistic proponents. In contrast to these aspirations, pragmatism has replaced idealism for the majority of the hundreds of thousands of Esperanto speakers in the world today: Esperanto is the international language of choice for a large group of people from almost all of the world's countries, who are unwilling to accept the enormous pressure of the major languages, and the continuing destruction of the many "minor" languages and cultures, and who wish to use a neutral language for their international contacts.

In 1922, when enthusiasts tried to introduce Esperanto to the League of Nations, an opponent of the language used the pages of the *New York Times* to grumble:

> "Even an endless chain of interpreters is better than this pallid tongue which has no past, no memories, no rich, terrible and beautiful associations, which has been taught by no mothers and lisped by no babes, which has never been loved and made immortal by the poets, for whose song and meaning and music men have never died and have gone gladly to battle."

But today, in the year 2010, when we look back on the history and the achievements of Esperanto, this assessment and these arguments appear rather weak:

After more than 120 years, no one can claim that Esperanto is devoid of a history or a past.

- Today we can read reminiscences by and about the pacesetters of the Esperanto movement at the end of the 19th century.
- We hear and read of the disputes between the proletarian and the bourgeois Esperanto movement in the 1920s and 30s in a politically-turbulent Europe, and of the fight against the ban on Esperanto during the Third Reich and in the 1950s in Eastern Europe.
- Today we marvel at the small but growing band of "native speakers" of Esperanto: spouses who come from different cultures and who do not have an adequate mastery of their partners' languages, speak only Esperanto with each

other and raise their children in Esperanto-speaking households.
- Esperantists today quarrel over whether the many poets who approach Esperanto with a creative bent are making the language too colorful and confusing, and damaging its structural regularity, or whether they are in fact enriching the language.
- And, alas, Esperantists will never forget those labeled as traitors by Hitler and as cosmopolitans by Stalin, who died in ghettos, concentration camps, and gulags, or were silenced by firing squads.

Perhaps in 1922 it was still acceptable to accuse the author of Esperanto of naïveté and to predict that his dream would be stillborn.

But a speech community that survived the chaos of those times, both world wars and the Cold War of the 20th century, and in fact emerged from them even stronger; a speech community that, in an age of Americanization of the world, seeks to bring the values of the smallest cultures and languages to the consciousness of humanity and claims that only a neutral language as the international and interethnic language can keep them alive, cannot possibly be as weak and useless as many of its uninformed opponents would like to pretend.

*   *   *

The notations marked by asterisks at the end of some articles are those of the book's editor, not those of the *New York Times*.

Outdated and no-longer-used spellings of the names of places and persons are included unaltered, while errors in quotations in Esperanto have been tacitly corrected.

About planned languages and Esperanto

A planned language is a human language the development of which originates in a consciously-designed and planned language project. As a rule, it is intended to facilitate international communication. Other names are international language, artificial language, auxiliary language, etc. There is only one fully-functioning planned language, Esperanto. In addition, there are a series of planned semi-languages (i.e. planned language projects that for a short historical period were used somewhat extensively, such as Volapük, or others, that existed over a rather longer period, or still exist, but with only a small number of speakers, such as Ido or Interlingua) and a great many planned language projects that truly never got beyond the planning stage.

Ludwik L. Zamenhof, the author of the Esperanto language, grew up in the polyglot city of Bialystock, at the time part of Czarist Russia, and now a part of Poland, where he experienced the altercations between the various ethnic groups. Since he viewed the lack of a common tongue as one of the causes of such conflicts, he began work to develop a language that would be simple and that could be learned as an interethnic language to supplement existing languages.

When Esperanto first appeared in 1887, the planned semi-language Volapük had already passed its peak. The disappointed proponents of Volapük either turned away from planned languages in general or switched to Esperanto, which was considerably easier to learn.

Today Esperanto is spoken on all inhabited continents, by several hundred thousand people – some estimates even put the number of speakers in the millions. It is used in almost all areas of human activity, and its vocabulary continues to grow in a controlled manner. Original and translated literature, theater performances, an extensive range of journals and publications, professional organizations, many cultural and religious associations, radio broadcasts, tourism, hundreds of international conferences and festivals each year and more, are a regular component of the life of the international community of Esperanto speakers.

Ulrich Becker

Some Rivals of Volapük*
That are not Likeley to Supplant it

Prof. Bauer's Spelin** and Prof. Bell's World-English***—
The Study of Volapük in the United States

All Volapükia is again agitated, not by dissensions this time, but by speculations as to proposed innovations, alleged improvements, and suggested substitutes for the new language. A temporary truce has been patched up between Prof. Schleyer, the creator of Volapük, and the International Academy, but the crust of peace is so thin that the smoldering quarrel may burst forth into flame again at any moment.

Within the past few months several new candidates for popular preference have appeared, the inventors of which and their friends are waging a lively little warfare in behalf of their bantlings, only the echoes of which have as yet been heard in this country. The most important of these contemporaneous devices, and by far the most dangerous rival thus far encountered by Volapük, is called Spelin. It is the work of Prof. George Bauer, a native of Croatia, a Province of Austria, and Professor of Mathematics in the Realschule of Agram. He is an old Volapükist—in fact, was one of the first to acquire the new language, and frankly confesses that but for the preliminary work of Prof. Schleyer he would never have thought of building Spelin. It is a superstructure, based on the same principles as Volapük, but more logically and philosophically carried out. Prof. Bauer's effort loses nothing by the modest way in which it was put forth. It was launched in the form of an essay, in which the writer, without making any attempt to propagate it, invited criticism from Volapükists and linguists generally. In this country avowed and proficient followers of Schleyer commend the improvements made by Bauer, but are not yet prepared to complicate the situation by deserting the standard of the German priest. An examination of Spelin by one even slightly versed in Volapük will show that it is a natural step toward the evolution of a universal language as easy

SPELIN

A UNIVERSAL LANGUAGE

BY

PROF. GEORGE BAUER.

OF AGRAM, AUSTRIA.

A condensed translation from the German with an introduction

BY

CHAS. T. STRAUSS.

NEW YORK:
PUBLISHED BY CHAS. T. STRAUSS.
1889.

as it is progressive. The alphabet contains two letters less than Volapük, and there is a decided diminution in the matter of inflection. Spelin certainly does express an idea more briefly and with less monotony of termination than Volapük. Its brevity and simplicity are powerful factors, and, as the change from Schleyer's language is in the nature of an improvement and not of a substitution, hesitating Volapükists will openly advocate the adoption of Spelin, although many secretly favor it and are assimilating the new ideas contained therein. All the American students with whom the writer has come in contact concede that had Spelin and Volapük started even the former would have been the choice of cultivated linguists in all parts of the world; but they also maintain that it doesn't follow that a system which appeals to linguists on account of its beauty, symmetry, and simplicity will become the most popular medium of communication with the masses. The question involved, therefore, is whether Spelin can overcome the great advantage in time and publicity possessed by Volapük. American linguists generally do not believe that it can, but there is some difference of opinion on that point, and time alone can determine whether Spelin will prove to be a natural and permanent graft on the Schleyer tree. At all events, the essay of Prof. Bauer is worth examination by all who are interested in the development of a universal language.

Prof. George J. Henderson of London is the author of an ambitious attempt to supplant Volapük. His idea is not entirely original, and does not seem destined to die of anything else than inanition. Lingua, suggested by him, is simply old Latin deprived of its inflection and supplied with a modern grammatical system, new words being adopted for modern ideas. As a whole it is tangled and cumbrous. The main defects are its irregularity, lack of brevity, and difficulty of acquirement.

American authors are likewise busily engaged in the production of aids to the student of Volapük. Dr. Klas August Linderfelt, Librarian of the Milwaukee Public Library, is the author of a Volapük method and the prospective author of a dictionary. Mrs. Bauer of Walla Walla, Washington Territory, has published a grammar, and Col. Charles E. Sprague, Secretary of the Union Dime

Savings Bank of this city, is the author of a hand book, the latter having already exhausted several editions. Five hundred unbound copies of the Colonel's work, lying in Alexander's bookbindery, were destroyed in the *Century* Company's fire. Dr. M. W. Wood of the United States Army will issue his Volapük-English dictionary within a few weeks.

The most ambitious step, however, has been taken by Prof. Alexander Melville Bell, father of Alexander Graham Bell, of telephone fame. The complexity and impracticability of his proposed system are a great and disappointing surprise to his friends, his past achievements warranting the expectations of much better things from him. Prof. Bell has a world-wide reputation as a phonetician, and his well-known invention, "Visible Speech," was of incalculable benefit to deaf-mutes. This "Visible Speech" consists of a scientific alphabet for all languages in which the form of the character indicates the precise action of the vocal organs in producing the equivalent sound, such as labial, dental, nasal, &c.

Being asked for a critical opinion as to the merits of Prof. Bell's new "World English," Col. Sprague recently said: "In the light of his previous achievements, I certainly expected that Prof. Bell would in some measure have solved the universal language problem by forming a new English which would be adapted for international use. But he has done nothing of the sort. His 'Visible Speech' was a much more praiseworthy effort. By means of it I was enabled to acquire the power of imitating the sound of a saw passing through wood, a trivial accomplishment of which I could never before become master. The 'Visible Speech' proved to be of the highest value to Prof. Alexander John Ellis in developing and illustrating the early English pronunciation. Prof. Ellis is himself an expert Volapükist, and will no doubt be greatly disappointed in this last effort of Prof. Bell's 'Visible Speech,' however, was away over the heads of the people, and could never have gained recognition as a universal language. In 'World English' Prof. Bell has merely added one to the 50 or 60 attempted phonographic alphabets of English. He assumes that with a photographic alphabet English is by no means the greatest difficulty to be overcome. Aside from all questions of spelling, there yet remains the almost insuperable obstacle of the idiomatic use, choice, and arrangement of words. An English letter from a foreign gentleman of education is almost invariably well spelled, but, if he has learned the language from books only, the arrangement and construction of his sentences are most ludicrous. Prof. Bell's idea is that we shall continue to spell as at present, but that, in communication with foreigners, we shall spell phonetically, thus reforming the language where it doesn't need it. His alphabet contains 43 characters, 19 of which are different from the ordinary Roman letters, and 16 of the 19 are, either entirely or in the acceptance given them, new to the standard writing of all languages in the world. If two concurrent methods of spelling English are to be maintained, as suggested by Prof. Bell, namely, a historically spelled literary style and a phonetic style, foreigners will inevitably use the former, and to call the latter 'World English' will not make it so. A foreigner who only wanted to correspond would more easily learn 'literary' English in the first place."

The writer was then shown printed specimens of Prof. Bell's "World English." Without having even glanced at the alphabet he at once read a long paragraph rapidly and intelligently. Perhaps the clearest idea of its character can be conveyed by describing it as "shortened longhand." Any reporter who is not a stenographer would make almost identical "notes" in following a public speaker. Almost every telegrapher in the land uses the same sort of phonetic spelling for conversational purposes on the wires. This means of communication consists mainly of consonantal spelling and arbitrary abbreviations. Prof. Bell, however, supplies the missing sounds by means of the added letters. The Steno-Telegraphic Code, devised by Walter P. Phillips, is "World English" in embryo, and antedates Prof. Bell's candidate by several years. The limitations of the new system seem to be a rapid method of communication (written only) between English-speaking persons, for a conversational knowledge of the language seems to be a prerequisite. As a whole, therefore, Prof. Bell has suggested nothing novel except 16 new letters of the alphabet.

The spread of Volapük in the United States is claimed by its advocates to be gradual and satisfactory. The far West and the extreme South seem to have the infection of its most virulent form. Washington Territory proudly claims the honor of having established the first Territorial association of Volapükists in America. This has given the funny men of the press opportunity to pun on Walla Walla, and similar eccentric nomenclature of the extreme Northwest. A gentleman who purchases from an agency all clippings referring to Volapük finds his mail freighted with two or three line jests of greater or less capacity for producing frenzy concerning the new language. But the clippings show that there is a really widespread and extending interest in this country concerning Volapük, and a sincere desire for accurate and comprehensive knowledge concerning it. Thus, Prof. F. A. March's article on the subject in the June *Forum* has been reprinted, in whole or in part, in every section of the United States. Not a few newspapers and periodicals have established Volapük departments, where lessons after the plan of the Westminster Sunday school lessons are given. In many towns where Volapük has obtained a footing, Volapük sociables, at which no other language is permitted to be used, have become a popular diversion shared by young and old alike.

In this city the progress has not been great. New-Yorkers are hard to interest in matters not immediately available and profitable, and the introduction of the new language here has been up-hill work. Col. Sprague's class has suspended sessions for the Summer. At the last meeting (the twelfth lesson) the exercises were conducted entirely in Volapük, not a word of English being spoken.

In the early part of August Col. Sprague will deliver a lecture and conduct a class in Volapük in the Summer School of Languages of the Chautauqua University. The Colonel views the possible published reports of these lectures with some degree of apprehension. Said he to the writer: "If I am misquoted in New-York, how much more liable are my utterances to be misreported elsewhere. For instance, this paragraph is yet going the rounds as an alleged extract from my address before the Metropolitan Stenographers' Association: 'Charles E. Sprague, author of a handbook on Volapük, is quoted as expressing the opinion that Volapük is too artificial to become universal.' What I really did say was that 'no language can become absolutely universal. An international language must necessarily be an artificial one.' Here is another complete misconception of a fact: 'The declination of a leading scientific study (the Philological Society of London) to participate in the projected congress is not encouraging to those who are interesting themselves in the spread of the universal language.' Now, the truth is that the invitations to an international congress were issued by the American Philosophical Society, the object being to devise and agree upon a language to supplant Volapük. The Philological Society of London, apparently believing that Volapük was good enough for present purposes, declined to accept the invitation to send delegates to such a congress. Their action was, therefore, rather a quasi-endorsement of Volapük than a blow at its progress and diffusion. I hope, however, to be spared misrepresentation during my Summer lecture season, and shall take every precaution against it."

After a careful review of all the evidence it seems fair to conclude that although the United States was the tardiest of all the progressive nations to bestow attention on Volapük, its acquirement is now regarded in this country as a valuable linguistic accomplishment, whether or not it ever becomes an approximately international means of communication. It is a diverting study, especially easy to one who already has some knowledge of Latin, French, German, and English, and has now passed far beyond the ridiculous stage.

Published: July 27, 1888

---

* Volapük: "World language," auxiliary language project by Johann Martin Schleyer, published in 1879.

** Spelin: An auxiliary language project based on Volapük. Created in 1886 or 1888 by Georg Bauer from Zagreb.

*** World English: A modified, simplified English created by Alexander Melville Bell (approx. 1888).

In a well-written little pamphlet that comes all the way from Grodno, Russia, somebody named L. SAMENHOF reveals that he, like so many other people, has been worrying about the world's need for a universal language. Incidentally, he also reveals that he has invented a new language called "Esperanto," which he presumably regards as well calculated to repair the misfortune that befell the human race, according to the legend, as a result of an attempt to prove the possession of an architectural audacity equal to its astronomical ignorance. M. SAMENHOF does not sing the praises of "Esperanto," however, but, after rehearsing in pellucid French the dire losses and endless inconveniences arising from diversity of tongues, and after telling again the long-familiar advantages there would be in an international language, if people could only be persuaded to select and learn one, he tells in detail of a scheme by which the choice at least may be made. He asks everybody who is interested in this great subject to send him a short article, in no matter what language, stating the writer's views and the idiom whose selection he advises. These essays M. SAMENHOF purposes to publish exactly as received and in three volumes—price, 6f. each. Suspicious persons will shy at this point, and think they see in the plan merely an ingenious device for making money out of that portion of the public which has visionary ideas on the language question. Such does not seem to be the case, however, as the sum demanded is hardly large enough to cover expenses. Be that as it may, each contributor to the volumes is asked, after reading his own and the other articles, to fill out and send to Grodno a blank form, stating whether he thinks an already existing language, living, dead, or artificial, and, if so, which, should be made the international one, or whether an entirely new language should be constructed. The result of this vote will be published, and M. SAMENHOF thinks the most difficult part of the task will have been accomplished. Perhaps so. At any rate the scheme has interesting features. If it is carried out, and if the majority of participants cast their ballots in favor of English as the world's language for science and commerce, the adoption of that tongue for those purposes, which is inevitable anyway, may be appreciably hastened.

Personal

In a well-written little pamphlet that comes all the way from Grodno, Russia, somebody named L. SAMENHOF reveals that he, like so many other people, has been worrying about the world's need for a universal language. Incidentally, he also reveals that he has invented a new language called "Esperanto," which he presumably regards as well calculated to repair the misfortune that befell the human race, according to the legend, as a result of an attempt to prove the possession of an architectural audacity equal to its astronomical ignorance. M. SAMENHOF does not sing the praises of "Esperanto," however, but, after rehearsing in pellucid French the dire losses and endless inconveniences arising from diversity of tongues, and after telling again the long-familiar advantages there would be in an international language, if people could only be persuaded to select and learn one, he tells in detail of a scheme by which the choice may be made. He asks everybody who is interested in this great subject to send him a short article, in no matter what language, stating the writer's views and the idioms whose selection he advises. These essays M. SAMENHOF purposes to publish exactly as received and in three volumes—price, 6f. each. Suspicious persons will shy at this point, and think they see in the plan merely an ingenious device for making money out of that portion of the public which has visionary ideas on the language question. Such does not seem to be the case, however, as the sum demanded is hardly large enough to cover expenses. Be that as it may, each contributor to the volume is asked, after reading his own and the other articles, to fill out and send to Grodno a blank form, stating whether he thinks an already existing language, living, dead, or artificial, and, if so, which, should be made the international one, or whether an entirely new language should be constructed. The result of this vote will be published, and M. SAMENHOF thinks the most difficult part of the task will have been accomplished. Perhaps so. At any rate the scheme has interesting features. If it is carried out, and if the majority of participants cast their ballots in favor of English as the world's language for science and commerce, the adoption of that tongue for those purposes, which is inevitable anyway, may be appreciably hastened.

Published: May 26, 1897

An International Language

From Harper's Weekly.

A circular has been widely distributed which sets forth the need of an international language, especially adapted for use in the publication of works of scientific value or of especial interest to scholars. It is thought, reasonably enough, that if an agreement could be reached as to what language, whether one now in use or a new one, is fittest to serve as a means of communication between the nations, it would save an immense deal of time and trouble and be a universal convenience.

As a congress of all persons interested in such an agreement is impracticable, it is proposed to discuss the subject by letter, and every person who has views about it—whether he prefers adopting an existing language for international use or inventing a new one—is requested to write them out and send them to Mr. L. Samenhof, Grodno, Russia. The plan is to print all the essays received in a book, a copy of which is to be sent to each contributor, who shall then vote, also by letter, for the plan he prefers. The scheme is not necessarily impossible of execution, provided that due funds can be procured to carry it out, but only exceptionally hopeful persons will expect important results from it.

Published: July 25, 1897

Wheelmen's Own Lingo

They Tour So Much that They Are Adopting a Universal Language

From The London Express

"Esperanto differs from Volapük in that it is intended to be merely an auxiliary language common to all nations rather than a universal language supplanting the existing ones."

So said Mr. O'Meara, the manager of the correspondence bureau of the Cyclists' Touring Club, to an Express representative yesterday.

"It would be useful to cyclists, because they go abroad a good deal, but it would be useful to all. The Touring Club de France have taken it up, I imagine, because they are energetic people who would be the first to take up such a novelty. The language is also being taught in American academies.

"Roughly Esperanto has been created in the main by taking roots common to all languages, and adding distinctive terminals to show whether they are being used as nouns, verbs, and so on.

"Theoretically, all the principal languages have been drawn upon equally, including Latin and Greek, but there is really a preponderance of Russian and Slavonian roots. That is probably because Dr. Zamenhof, the inventor, is a Russian. He is a doctor of medicine, and published his language in 1887.

"The chief defect of Esperanto is that there are four participles, as in Russian, whereas two, as in other languages, would have sufficed.

"The grammar consists of about twelve simple rules — to which there are no exceptions. People could learn it without the least difficulty. How long it took them to become proficient Esperantistoj — speakers of Esperanto — would depend upon the extent of their European vocabulary.

"I think the language is practical, but it would have to be taken up by everybody, and the different nations would have to refrain from making different variations."

Here is a specimen of Esperanto:

Jam longe mi volis la adreson de la persono en la urbeto X. Serĉante en la Adresaro de Esperantistoj, mi kun ĝojo trovis vian adreson, kaj mi rapidas uzon el tiu ĉi trovo.

This is the literal translation:

Already for a long time I wished to have the address of a person in the town of X. Searching in the Directory of Esperantistoj I with pleasure found your address, and hasten to make use of this discovery.

Published: June 1, 1901

Welfare of the Blind

The Work of the International Brussels Congress— The Braille System Criticised

The International Congress for the Amelioration of the Lot of the Blind, which has just concluded its sittings in Brussels, brought together representatives of the principal countries of the world, many of them being well-known specialists in the cure and treatment of the blind. The debates of the conference were of a thoroughly practical nature, and brought out many useful points in connection with the education and general treatment of the blind.

... The next matter of importance which occupied the attention of the congress was that of a system of "shorthand" for the blind— the advantages and inconveniences of its employment. This discussion was of an essentially technical character and gave rise to considerable divergence of views. The principal object was the creation of a system of stenography that excluded the defects of the Braille system of writing. The latter process is very slow, both as regards reading and writing; it demands a large quantity of paper and is very expensive; a book printed in Braille costs twenty-four times that of a book in ordinary type. Many different suggestions were made in this connection, but as the question embraces a whole study in itself it was decided to appoint a technical committee to examine the matter. The same committee has been requested to examine the possibility of the employment of the Esperanto system by the blind. ...

Published: September 7, 1902

Failure of Volapük

Not a Success Though Most Practicable for a Universal Language

The opening up to trade of remote regions and the extension of civilization among barbarous people have called the attention of scientists to the need of a universal language which all may understand. There are to-day hundreds of different languages and dialects spoken in the four quarters of the globe. No one has mastered them all, and few persons, comparatively speaking, know any other tongue than that of their parents. Those to whom a knowledge of the principal languages is essential are travelers, merchants engaged in foreign trade, and professional linguists.

A universal language—one that may be written and understood by all the human family—has been the dream of linguists for a hundred years. Various artificial languages have been invented to answer this purpose, the most notable being the "Esperanto," devised by Prof. Zamenhoff of Moscow, and "Spelin," by Prof. Bauer, of Agram, Croatia. Both failed to become popular. As the result of the experiments that have been tried from time to time in this direction, it has become the general opinion that the world will not take up any artificial language until it is fully adopted by the English-speaking nations.

"The attempt made to establish Volapuk as a universal language has, I am sorry to say, been a failure. Despite the efforts made by some of the leading linguists to create wide interest in the subject, the experiment did not result as we had hoped it would. The failure was due to the fact that the percentage of those who really need to know several languages besides their own is not yet sufficiently large to insure the success of a universal language."

Volapuk was the most practicable artificial language that had been devised for the purpose. It was invented by the Rev. Johann Martin Schleyer of Constance, Germany, a celebrated linguist, and he worked out the vocabulary and other details more thoroughly than most of his competitors, so that it was an actual language in working order. It was found to work all right in practice, but not enough people could be found who were willing to devote their time to its mastery to make it a success.

The trouble was that Volapuk was from fifty to a hundred years ahead of its age. I am satisfied that some such universal language, greatly improved upon, perhaps, will one day be adopted by the leading peoples of the earth.

The Volapuk experiment was the most notable ever tried, either here or abroad. Thirteen years ago, when it was at the height of its popularity, no less than 265,000 persons had become familiar with the speaking and writing of Volapuk, and 130 societies had been formed for its propagation. While it was strong in Germany, Austria, Spain, France, Italy, Sweden, and Denmark, in the United States there were only 6,000 students of the new language.

Perhaps the chief reason why Volapuk was not taken up more extensively here was that our young men had not the patience to master a language that was not then in general use. They felt that French or German or Spanish was much more practical, and therefore much more desirable.

Charles E. Sprague in
The Washington Times.

Published: October 19, 1902

Esperanto's London Boom

When Dr. Zamenhof, a Polish M. D., was eight years old his mind began to be troubled at the confusion of tongues in and around his native village, which is near Warsaw.

Later on, to enable the people of four or five different nationalities, who were his neighbors, to indulge in mutual intercourse, he set himself to the construction of another language, which he hoped might one day become cosmopolitan.

He called the new tongue "Esperanto," which, to the 80,000 "Esperantists" now scattered over the world, means hope. The language has many little strongholds on the Continent, at least one in England—at Keighley, Yorkshire—and a society for its study has just been formed in London.

Mr. Felix Moscheles has been elected President, Mr. J. O'Connor Vice President, and Mr. W. T. Stead Treasurer, and a room in Mowbray House has been placed at their disposal, where gratuitous lessons will be given every Monday evening from 5:30 to 6:30.

"Esperanto" is said by its adherents to be so simple that eight hours' study will enable a man to read any "Esperanto" book with a dictionary of 800 words.

The two great peculiarities of the language are its invariable terminations in "o" for nouns, "a" for adjectives, and "e" for adverbs and its system of word-building, by means of which from one root word—such as "sano," meaning health—fifty other words can be constructed.

An Esperantist, who was interviewed yesterday, said "Esperantu esperanto sukcesos," which means, "Let us hope it will succeed."

London Mail.

Published: February 8, 1903

Mr. Alden's Views

A New International Language—News of Kipling—Forthcoming Books

...

London, Feb. 11.—London is somewhat interested, judging from the comments of the press, in the new international language called "Esperanto." So far as I have been able to learn any facts about the new language, it is a great improvement on Volapük, which was preposterous from beginning to end. Volapük was not a simple lex, and simplicity is the one thing which is required, if we are to have an international language. Esperanto is far simpler, and to that extent is an improvement on Volapük, but it still is very far from being an ideal language in point of simplicity. Most people fancy that Arabic is a difficult language, and so it is, owing to certain peculiarities in it which are quite unnecessary. But in its main structure Arabic is simplicity itself. A new international language based on Arabic and pruned of the eccentricities of Arabic would meet a great want. It does seem absurd that all the world should have to learn eight or ten separate languages when one simple language would meet all the necessities of daily intercourse. Probably Esperanto will go the way of all other experiments of the kind, and will be soon forgotten, but the inventor is at least entitled to the credit of having grasped the idea that simplicity should be his aim, and although he has not been entirely successful in carrying out this idea, he has made an effort in the right direction.

...

Published: February 21, 1903

International Language

The New York Times Saturday Review of Books:

Your London correspondent is slightly astray in speaking of Esperanto as the "new" international language. I possess a grammar of Esperanto sent to me eleven years ago. The language was invented by a Russian, Dr. L. Samenhof, in 1887. Volapük, devised by J. M. Schleyer in 1879, reached its high tide in 1890, and dropped into disuse because it had too much grammar and the vocabulary was constructed on an impractical principle. Beginning with Dr. Samenhof, a number of erstwhile Volapükists have constructed international languages, basing their vocabulary on the enormous number of words which resemble each other in the principal modern languages, and giving a strong preference to the Latin side. By far the best of these is the "Idiom Neutral*," mainly due to Voldemar Rosenberger of St. Petersburg. In this all the good features of Volapük and Esperanto are preserved, and the objectionable features of both are eliminated. The bad points of Samenhof's language are that it requires certain special characters for printing, has an accusative case, and the verb is not simple enough.

The following is a sample sentence in English and the three artificial languages:

English—Scientific books published in this language can be read by everybody in the original.

Volapük.—Buks nolavik pebüböl in pük at kanoms pakapälön fa alim in rigad.

Esperanto.—Libroj sciencaj publikigataj en tiu ĉi lingvo povas esti legataj de ĉiu en originalo.

"Idiom Neutral."—Libri sientifik publiked en ist idom potes estar lekted per omnihom in original.

It will be observed that the Volapük is unintelligible to a person of any nationality who has not studied it. The roots of the words are taken from English an Latin, but the system of forming them is so artificial that they are unrecognizable. Esperanto and "Idiom Neutral" can be easily understood by a Frenchman, Italian, or Spaniard without study, and present no great difficulty to an Englishman or German. The last version is manifestly the easiest.

There will never be a universal language. Schleyer's crude Volapük proved, however, that an international correspondence language is practicable, and Rosenberger has shown that it can be made vastly easier to learn than any natural language. The "Idiom Neutral" (Leipzig, 1902, 313 pages) is the latest and nearest to an ideal solution of the problem.

Freidenker
New York, Feb. 22, 1903

Published: February 28, 1903

* Idiom Neutral (publ. 1902): an international auxiliary language by Waldemar Rosenberger (St. Petersburg, Russia) and his *International Academy of the Universal Language* (previously the *Volapük Academy*).

In the Eternal City

Venice's New Campanile—Italy Uneasy About Albania—A Plea For Latin as a Universal Language

... No Italian editor, in reading the extensive reports of the International Latin Congress recently held in Rome, has seen that the general tendency of the speakers was in reality a plea for the revival of the Latin language as a modern tongue — and not only as a modern tongue, but as a universal language for diplomatic as well as for commercial usages. Signor Nasi, the Minister of Public Instruction, in the course of a remarkable address, predicted that, should a sincere effort be made to revive Latin, not only the so-called romance nations would be drawn into a closer artistic, literary, and even political accord, but also a great federation, at least for the advancement of culture, might be formed, which would also include America, Great Britain, Germany, and the Teutonic part of Austria. Prof.

di Gubernatis, who was the most distinguished polyglot present, spoke upon the insufficiency and futility of attempting to manufacture an artificial universal tongue, and condemned without stint the recently devised "Esperanto" and "Volapük." "Never," he said, "would the Latins have accepted an artificial language as an international tongue. There is no language better calculated than that of Cicero to play the rôle of an international medium of communication."...

Published: May 10, 1903

[Untitled]

"Esperanto," the new commercial language, made up compositely of French, English, and German, is having a great vogue. That is to say, London newspapers, following the lead of The Daily Chronicle, are printing many articles and letters about it. It is said that some business men are already putting it to use. So that Mr. J. C. O'Connor's "Complete Text Book" of "Esperanto," with grammar, exercises, and vocabularies, is assured a large circulation on the other side of the ocean. We have lately received a pamphlet describing another new commercial language, "Tutonish, or Anglo-German Union Tongue,*" the author of which is Elias Molee of Idaho. Mr. Molee has in mind a "future international Teutonic language conference" and believes that "some one must begin to agitate and advocate an international Teutonic language sooner or later." So he has taken time by the forelock. His tentative new language is made up of German, English, Scandinavian, and Dutch words, with ingenious modifications.

Published: May 30, 1903

---

* Tutonish (published first in 1902) is a language project by Elias Molee (US). He reformed it twice (1911 as Allteutonish; 1915 as Neuteutonish.) It was proposed as an "Anglo-German unifying language."

A New Universal Language.

"Esperanto" is the name of a new kind of Volapük that was invented by Dr. Zamenhof. Under that title J. C. O'Connor has issued a complete textbook for students, a 16mo of 170 pages, yet it contains full grammar, exercises, conversations, commercial letters, and two vocabularies. The originator of such a language has three principal difficulties to overcome—he must render the study of the language so easy as to be mere play for the learner; he must enable the learner to make direct use of his knowledge with persons of any tongue, whether the language be universally accepted or not; he must find some means of overcoming the vis inertia of mankind and disproving them, in the quickest manner possible and en masse, to learn and use Esperanto as a living language and not only in last extremities and with the key at hand. As to the first problem, Dr. Zamenhof says he has simplified his whole grammar to such a degree that it can be learned perfectly in an hour; his vocabulary has also been so constructed that, as he says, the student is enabled to create new words for himself, without the necessity of having previously to learn them. Problem 2 was solved, he says, by dismembering ideas into independent, unchangeable words. The final basis of Esperanto seems to be Latin; such words as are common to the languages of all civilized peoples, together with so-called "foreign" words and technical terms, were left unaltered; if such words are needed, and it is impossible to use an equivalent term, an ordinary dictionary must be used. By means of a tiny leaflet, a single sheet of paper that can be inclosed with any letter, a German is supposed to be able to write to a Spaniard, say, or an Englishman to an Italian in Esperanto, even though the recipient never heard of the language; the lilliputian lexicon will render the letter perfectly intelligible, it is claimed. The new language seems to have made some progress in France, since several books published in Paris are given in a list appended.

A New Universal Language

"Esperanto" is the name of a new kind of Volapük that was invented by Dr. Zamenhof. Under that title J. C. O'Connor has issued a complete textbook for students, a 16mo of 176 pages, yet it contains full grammar, exercises, conversations, commercial letters, and two vocabularies. The originator of such a language has three principal difficulties to overcome — he must render the study of the language so easy as to be mere play for the learner; he must enable the learner to make direct use of his knowledge with persons of any tongue, whether the language be universally accepted or not; he must find some means of overcoming the vis inertiae of mankind and disproving them, in the quickest manner possible and en masse, to learn and use Esperanto as a living language and not only in last extremities and with the key at hand. As to the first problem, Dr. Zamenhof says he has simplified his whole grammar to such a degree that it can be learned perfectly in an hour; his vocabulary has also been so constructed that, as he says, the student is enabled to create new words for himself, without the necessity of having previously to learn them. Problem 2 was solved, he says, by dismembering ideas into independent, unchangeable words. The final basis of Esperanto seems to be Latin: such words as are common to the languages of all civilized peoples, together with so-called "foreign" words and technical terms, were left unaltered; if such words are needed, and it is impossible to use an equivalent term, an ordinary dictionary must be used. By means of a tiny leaflet, a single sheet of paper that can be inclosed with any letter, a German is supposed to be able to write to a Spaniard, say, or an Englishman to an Italian in Esperanto, even though the recipient never heard of the language; the lilliputian lexicon will render the letter perfectly intelligible, it is claimed. The new language seems to have made some progress in France, since several books published in Paris are given in a list appended.

Published: July 4, 1903

Esperanto

The New York Times Saturday Review of Books:

Esperanto was first promulgated in the year 1887, only eight years after the very first appearance of Schleyer's Volapük, at the time that the latter was at the height of its ephemeral popularity. It was first known as "La Lingvo Internacia," and its author, Dr. Samenhof of Warsaw, concealed his identity for awhile under the pseudonym of "Esperanto," i. e., "the hopeful one," but later on that appellation was more or less appropriately transferred to the language itself, after its author had become better known.

Volapük failed to attract a sufficient number of adherents to justify for itself the title of an international language, chiefly because its use and advantages were not understood, and also on account of various dissensions among its chief supporters concerning the structure and amplification of the language, not because of any failure on its part to serve adequately as an international medium of communication. Its chief defects lay in the fact that its radicals, taken largely from existing languages, were often abbreviated and mutilated past recognition, while the elaborate system of arbitrary prefixes and suffixes rendered the whole quite illegible to those who had not learned the system, albeit the learning involved a very inconsiderable fraction of the time to master any one of the existing national tongues. This same defect exists, perhaps to a somewhat less degree, in Esperanto as well.

Esperanto, however, was the first step toward the utilization of those words and forms of expression, chiefly of Latin origin, which are common to nearly all civilized languages. A still further advance in this direction was made by Julius Lott of Vienna in 1889 in his "Mundolingue," which approached much more nearly to the form and spirit of modern methods of expression, and could be easily read by any educated man without previous study. The principle was still further and more forcibly set forth a year later by Dr. Liptay in his Lengua Catolica, a most interesting treatise of nearly 300 pages, which appeared successively in Spanish, French, and German editions, in which he disclaimed any intention of inventing a language, but tried to demonstrate that an international or "catholic" language already exists, there being in the neighborhood of ten thousand words in common use and practically identical in the English, French, German, Spanish, Italian, and Latin, from which last, of course, they chiefly have their origin.

Esperanto fails to utilize the greater portion of these international words, preferring, as did Volapük, arbitrary combinations of its own elements, ingenious indeed, but more or less of the nature of puzzles to be solved by readers equally ingenious. It has also the serious disadvantage of requiring the use of six letters not in the Roman alphabet, and consequently involving the use of special type. It has an unnecessary special form for the accusative case, an uncouth plural ending in j, and various other eccentricities quite as unacceptable as those which made Volapük the synonym of harsh and unmeaning jargon—to those who judged by sight rather than by hearing.

The nearest approach to a satisfactory international language, as was explained by one of your correspondents a few months ago, is the "Idiom Neutral," agreed upon by that international organization evolved from the old Volapük "Academy," under the direction of Woldemar Rosenberger of St. Petersburg. This is made up of words chosen from actual international forms of expression, rejects all arbitrary constructions and artificial combinations, and is certainly a most decided advance upon all preceding systems, even if it may not be destined actually to become the international neutral language of the future. We may boast of the supremacy of English, and rejoice at its ever-extending use in commerce and literature, but as long as other nations and languages exist there is need of an easily learned, simple, invariable, and precise international medium, such as would be afforded by an ideal—and necessarily artificial—neutral tongue.

E. D. F.
Saranac Lake, N. Y., July 7, 1903

Published: July 11, 1903

Mr. Alden's Views

Death of Farjeon—Popularity of the Elder Dumas—Esperanto—Literature and Free Trade

...

Esperanto seems to be looking up. Mr. W. T. Stead gives a good deal of space to it in the last number of his Review of Reviews, and the enthusiasts in behalf of the new language are advertising it largely in certain newspapers. From the specimens of the language that I have seen, it seems to be a sort of Italian gone wrong in company with some Slavonic tongue. It is certainly simple in its construction, but it must be extremely difficult to memorize its words. Of all crazes, the scheme of inventing a new universal language is the most preposterous. It recalls those amiable persons who from time to time find the divisions of Christianity intolerable, and so start a new sect and add another to the many divisions which they deplore. There are already too many languages in the world, and it would be far better if every one spoke the same language. How this undesirable state of things is to be cured by adding a new language to those already in existence is not clear. But newly invented languages have an unending charm for certain people, and Esperanto has succeeded to the place which Volapük held a few years ago., Conceive of English literature translated in Esperanto! How any one can face such a contingency and still labor for the spread of Esperanto is quite unintelligible.

...

Published: August 15, 1903

An International Language

To the Editor of The New York Times:

With reference to your remarks in your issue of Aug. 15 concerning Esperanto, it seems to me that you have overlooked the one point so strongly insisted upon by those who are promoting it. In these days of traveling and international postal and train arrangements an international language has become a necessity, not as replacing the mother tongue, but as promoting intercourse between various nationalities.

You in America have the great advantage of being able to use the Anglo-Saxon tongue universally, but Europeans are not so well situated, and for them this question is of great importance. At first sight it would seem that the Anglo-Saxon tongue would serve the purpose, but it must first be simplified and made phonetic. This would destroy its beautiful literature. Shakespeare phonetically written would certainly not impress the eye accustomed to our mother tongue, while Shakespeare in his Esperanto dress is better than Shakespeare in a French dress. It is for this, among other reasons, that Mr. Stead has advocated the adoption of Esperanto. If any European language could be as quickly acquired by unlearned people, such as porters, waiters, railway clerks, &c., who must learn this international language, he would accept that instead.

Esperanto must be heard to be fully appreciated. At a medical congress held a short time ago in Madrid, an English paper which was read was useless because scarcely understood, but at a political discussion at Havre lately, when French, Germans, and English were present, the discussion was warmly joined in by all, and it was held in Esperanto.

The difficulty is just this: French people will not consent to give up to English or Germans their proud position as using that language which for political purposes is the international one; but they would give it up to those using a neutral tongue, such as Latin or Esperanto. Now, we have to do with possibilities, not ideals as such. Esperanto, Latin, Italian, or Spanish might be accepted by the Anglo-American, French, and German speaking peoples, while neither would consent for many decades to accept the tongue of either of the others.

This is Mr. Stead's view as he gave it to me.

Annie Lawrence
Wimbledon, England, Aug. 21, 1903

Published: September 16, 1903

Letters to the Editor of The Times

Title of Inhabitant of Panama

To the Editor of The New York Times:

Referring to the recent introduction of the word "Panamanian" I would suggest that when circumstances or conditions call for additions to our language it might be well to compose them in accordance with the rules of the international language.

Thus: A native of the Isthmian district would be Panamo, plural Panamoj, (the "j" being sounded like the final letter of the English word "many.") A temporary resident would be Panamano. The chief executive of the nation or district would be Panamestro, while the name of the country itself, en lingvo Esperanto is Panamujo.

This language is so readily learned by any one with a liberal education that its use in this country should be encouraged, and is rapidly spreading in Europe.

H. G. P.
New York, Nov. 20, 1903

November 22, 1903

Mr. Alden's Views

There is no denying the fact that Esperanto is growing, and growing rapidly. A year or two ago there were probably not half a dozen persons in England who knew a word of the new language, but now the number of those who can speak and write Esperanto is estimated at 5,000. On the Continent it grows even more rapidly, and it is evident that it will at least outlast Volapük or any other of the so-called international languages. At a recent meeting of the National India Association, Sir George Birdwood, the Chairman, held up Esperanto as a new variety of terror, and prophesied that if it became popular it would mean that all the modern languages would speedily become as dead as Latin. Sir George did not conceal his dread that this might happen, and his speech will greatly encourage the Esperantists. Nobody was ever afraid of Volapük, but Esperanto is certainly a very great improvement on that ridiculous invention, and if it does come into anything like general use as an aid to commerce Sir George's gloomy prediction may be realized at no very distant day.

Published: February 6, 1904

Esperanto

The New York Times Saturday Review of Books:

The opponents of the idea of an artificial language, for lack of other argument, seem to fall back on the old objection that the common use of such an auxiliary would necessarily work harm to, if not destroy, existing national tongues, and your London correspondent quotes Sir George Birdwood as saying, the success of (e.g.) Esperanto "would mean that all the modern languages would speedily become as dead as Latin." We entertain no such fear for the future of English when our young men, at the cost of years of study, familiarize themselves with four or five European languages, and thereby multiply their capacity for both usefulness and enjoyment. Why, then, should we be apprehensive as to the result, if a single international language were authoritatively adopted, especially an artificial language which could be mastered in a small fraction of the time required for even a superficial knowledge of any existing national tongue? Were this international language adopted as such universally — only for intercourse with foreigners, be it understood — it would enable one to communicate with people of all nationalities, and would render unnecessary years of study under the present system. National languages and literatures would flourish as now, but in the matter of translations a single version in the neutral tongue would serve the purpose of a dozen.

As to translations, your London correspondent took occasion in a previous letter to shudder at the possibility of the gems of English literature being translated into Esperanto! I can assure him that such translations already exist, and preserve to a wonderful degree, as translations go, the charm of the originals. But why more cause for alarm in this than in the long-ago-accomplished fact of "Hamlet" rendered into French, or of the Divina Comedia translated into German? Because of varying idioms, in spite of his best intentions, the "translator" is always more or less a "traitor," but why should it be supposed that the "artificial" languages are less adequate in this particular than the "natural"?

The continued interest in the matter of an international language is evidenced by the recent publication by Hachette of Paris of a Histoire de la Langue Universelle, a large octavo of 600 pages, carefully compiled by MM. Couturat and Leau, giving exhaustive and impartial accounts of the structure and history of some seventy systems of artificial language, of which Volapük, Esperanto, and Idiom Neutral are the most important. While the authors are committed to the support of no one of these systems, they take occasion, nevertheless, to set forth the great advantages certain to result from the authoritative adoption of a neutral international idiom. It is not without interest to compare the critical opinion of authorities like MM. Couturat and Leau with the flippant utterances of certain newspaper writers on this subject.

FR.
New York, Feb. 6, 1904

Published: February 6, 1904

Mr. Alden's Views

The French Touring Club, which is the largest body of cyclists in the world, has adopted Esperanto as the means of communication between its members and cyclists from other countries. This would be an excellent plan, provided the other cyclists would also learn Esperanto. But of what use is even the very newest language when one who can speak it tries to converse with one who is ignorant of it? If the French club wishes its members to be able to converse with English cyclists, why does it not instruct them to learn English? Of course the club would never be so unpatriotic as to promote in any way the study of German. It is an extremely patriotic club, as it proved when it expelled Zola because he asked for justice for Dreyfus. The action of the club is of importance only as a fresh indication that Esperanto is growing rapidly in popularity. Not very long ago it was received in England with the ridicule which Volapük received when that ridiculous language first made its appearance, but there is no doubt that at the present time Esperanto has a large number of adherents here. It seems to be little more than a simplified and broken Italian. At least any one who knows Italian can read Esperanto with comparative ease. That it will ever become an international language is of course extremely improbable, not to say impossible. Languages are born, not made, and the coming international language will certainly be one of the languages that already exist, and not a language invented in the closet.

Published: May 28, 1904

From Readers

Esperanto

New York Times Book Review:

Mr. W. L. Alden in his London letter takes a little fling at Esperanto, the so-called universal language, with which apparently he has but the most cursory acquaintance, or he would hardly describe it as "no more than a simplified and broken Italian." As well describe English as "no more than a simplified and broken German," which is in a sense quite true. But Mr. Alden's quarrel is not with Esperanto, but with the folly of the French Touring Club in adopting it as a means of communication between its members and cyclists of other countries. "Why," he asks, "if the French club wishes its members to be able to converse with English cyclists, does it not instruct them to learn English?" Why not, indeed? With, say, five or six weeks' hard study any Frenchman having no special gift in languages could pick up a slight—a very slight—smattering of English; not so much as he could learn of Esperanto in five or six days, perhaps, for Count Tolstoy assures us he learned to read Esperanto with ease in two hours; but enough, perhaps, to allow him, with reasonable luck, to make known his more urgent needs to any Englishmen he met. Whereas, if he gave a single week to the study of Esperanto, he could communicate the same needs to the first intelligent stranger he met, whether English, German, Spanish, Russian, or of any other nationality. It is this element of the immediate availability which no doubt accounts for the interest aroused by this latest attempt to solve the problem of an international language. "Of what use," says Mr. Alden airily, "is even the very newest language when one who can speak it tries to converse with one who is ignorant of it?" No; clearly, Mr. Alden has not looked very deeply into the matter; precisely the most valuable characteristic of the new language is that the student of Esperanto can establish communication without difficulty with the intelligent foreigner who may never have so much as heard of the existence of Esperanto. The action of the French Touring Club is by no means so foolish as Mr. Alden would have us believe.

Edward W. Bryant
New York, June 2, 1904

Published: *June 4, 1904*

From Readers

A Consideration of the Merits of the Language called Esperanto

New York Times Book Review:

Every now and then a short article appears in THE TIMES BOOK REVIEW on Esperanto, the language made a number of years ago by Dr. Zamenhof of Russia. The question is usually asked in its discussion whether it will ever become the international language. The answer frequently given to this query is in substance: "Language is a growth and cannot be made." In reply to this it can be said: "So the horse is a growth; yet man makes the iron horse, and this marvelous creature of strength, speed, and endurance goes from New York City to Chicago in twenty hours, and takes along with it many a score of passengers."

It is preposterous for an age that can talk through a thousand miles of wire to say that it cannot speak any language that has never been used for centuries by savages and barbarians. Language has existed under countless forms, and there is no reason to suppose that it cannot exist under others. It is within the power of man to analyze the various languages and determine what are the essentials and what are the mill stones hung about their necks. It is within the power of the present generation, with its wealth of intelligence and power of execution, to construct a far better language than any that sprang up spontaneously in the untutored minds of savages ages ago, and that has been perverted ever since with inharmonious additions from dead languages — a plan never thought of by the uneducated barbarians.

It is true that Esperanto is not perfect. Nor is any other language perfect, or ever will be perfect. The vocabulary of Esperanto is far from being as complete as it ought to be; but this defect may in a great measure be remedied in the course of time. But, worse than this, Dr. Zamenhof gave case and number to the adjectives. He might have well profited by taking a lesson from the general tendency of the languages to throw off their useless inflections.

But notwithstanding all its faults, the Esperanto can be learned in far less time and with far less labor than any of the old tongues, and consequently is far better fitted and more likely to become international than any of them. Every linguist, scientist, and teacher should certainly have enough curiosity about himself to examine its wonderful regularity, whether he has any faith in its failure or not, and whether he cares to learn it or not, its casual consideration would give him a broader linguistic information.

Dr. Zamenhof and some of his followers have struggled with heroic perseverance in the propagation of his language, and it has slowly gained adherents, and will probably do so for some time yet. But, when it reaches that point where many will think that it stands a good show of succeeding, then a host of languages and schemes will be put forward in competition, and the people will have no confidence in any of them being adopted, and consequently the whole matter will end in confusion and failure, as in the case of Volapük, unless an international congress be called to discuss every phase of the great problem, and then to select or construct a language for common use among the nations. If such an assembly, after a full, free, and fair consideration of the subject, stamps a two-thirds vote upon a particular tongue, then that tongue will have a prestige that will go far to make it international.

If Esperanto arouses such a discussion as to lead to the formation of a great congress on international languages it will certainly perform a valuable service for humanity, though it will be defeated by a much better language. It seems clear that no language will become international without being backed by the decision of a great congress.

G. W. Wishard
Irvington, N. Y., June 4, 1904

Published: June 11, 1904

Esperanto

New York Times Book Review:

Mr. G. W. Wishard's temperate and judicial letter of June 4 on the subject of Esperanto afforded me much pleasure. Much of the stuff written against Esperanto is the product of an imperfect knowledge of the subject treated upon and is based on prejudices which, though they may be natural and spontaneous, are nevertheless unreasoning.

That Esperanto will not please every one is certain, but the strange part of it is that scarcely any two critics agree as to what are its defects. Mr. Wishard only mentions two, and one of them — the case and number of the adjective — is a device which helps to gain the adhesion of the Germans, Scandinavians, and Russians. The second, the incompleteness of the vocabulary, is more a surface objection than otherwise, vanishing almost to extinction with continued experience of Esperanto, oral and written. Personally, though I have only known Esperanto for less than two years, I find no lack of suitable words, except when requiring to use specially technical words, such as "picking strap," "feoffment," "heald." Even then the difficulty can generally be overcome by a flank movement after a little thought. But, department by department, any gaps there may be in technical words are gradually being filled up by devoted workers with a special knowledge of each branch.

True, Esperanto must be able to weather the storm and stress of competition. There have been, up to the present, more than 300 attempts to create an artificial language, and about fifty of the best of these have been summarized by MM. Coutourat and Leau in their new book, "Histoire de la Langue Universelle," and Esperanto has no need to fear the rivalry of any existing competitor. What the future may bring forth no one knows; but the prevailing idea among Esperantists is that if Esperanto once gets a fair hold in every-day usage any future improvement upon it will be so slight that it will not be worth while adopting in face of the dislocation caused by the innovation. Nor are the efforts of the International Association of Academies to be disregarded. This body has established a deputation whose sole purpose is to determine by impartial inquiry the relative merits of rival schemes. It is an open secret that the final vote of this deputation, which has been laboring since 1900, will be in favor of Esperanto. Mr. Wishard's idea that the decision of a congress on international language is requisite is thus in process of being effected.

Those of your readers who have the privilege of attending the St. Louis Exhibition have an opportunity of learning more of Esperanto by visiting the Esperanto exhibit in the French Section of Social Economy, Group 138, (General Progress of the Social Movement.) The exhibit is doubtless but an incomplete evidence of the strength of the Esperanto movement, as it was hurriedly put together by the Parisian Groupe of the French Esperanto Society, without any reward but that of serving and helping their fellow-men throughout the world. This broad humanitarian idea has been the sole motive of thousands of ardent Esperantists.

John Ellis
Keighley, England, June 24, 1904

Published: July 9, 1904

Mr. Alden's Views

There is a new universal lex called "Spokil*." This time it is a sort of broken French instead of broken Italian. A grammar and dictionary of the new language has been published, and any one who wants to learn it has now the opportunity. Judging from the single specimen of "Spokil" that I have seen, it seems to be much more maddening than either "Volapuk" or "Esperanto." The latter could be learned by almost any one without serious danger of becoming insane, but the man who masters "Spokil" is doomed. He will either commit suicide or go to a lunatic asylum and gibber in "Spokil" to the end of his days. Like the story of the diamond stolen from an Indian idol, the invention of new languages will go on forever. To invent a new language is even easier than to write a new "Moonstone." Any one with any capacity for invention can invent a new language in two hours by the clock. The wonder is that any one should feel proud of such a performance, and publish the fact of his guilt to the world.

Published: August 27, 1904

* Spokil (published in 1904) is a language project by the Frenchman Adolphe Nicolas.

Esperanto

New York Times Book Review:

I note that Mr. W. L. Alden speaks slightingly of Esperanto, and seriously doubt if he has given the subject any serious examination. The value of an international language will be conceded by all, and its dissemination will be in direct ratio with its ease of accomplishment and the philosophical basis on which it is founded.

At present there are probably more than 50,000 persons more or less familiar with the language. There are more than a dozen periodicals published in Esperanto, including one devoted to pure science, the Internacia Scienca Revuo. It also possesses a growing literature, partly original and partly translations. Of these I may mention Shakespeare's "Hamlet," Homer's "Iliad," the opening lines of which are readily comparable with the original Greek.

While the word roots are mainly traceable to Latin, a few are taken from English and German, and one, the conjunction "and," ("kaj") is apparently from the Greek.

The grammar is simplicity itself, as the parts of speech are recognized by the terminal letters, "o" for a noun, "a" for an adjective, "e" for an adverb. There is no grammatical gender as in French or German, and the feminine (sexual) gender is indicated by the letters "in" preceding the terminal letter, as "patro," father; "patrino," mother; "frato," brother; "fratino," sister. In French there are more than 2,000 verbal terminations. In Esperanto there are but twelve: "As," (present,) "is," (past,) "os," (future,) "us," (conditional,) "i," (infinitive,) and "u," (imperative.) "Anta, into, and onta" are the terminations of the participles of the active voice, and "ata, ita, and ota" of the passive.

Any one with a liberal education can acquire a good working knowledge of Esperanto in a few weeks. Should any of your readers desire further information concerning Esperanto you are at liberty to place my name and address at their service.

H.G.P.
New York, Aug. 30, 1904

Published: September 3, 1904

Mr. Alden's Views

Mr. Zangwill has joined in the discussion as to the value of Esperanto, which is now perpetually with us. He does not think it by any means a perfect language of the sort, and if one may be so bold as to speak lightly of Mr. Zangwill's views, what he has to say about it is not of very much interest or importance. But the fact remains that Esperanto is rapidly becoming a fashion. There was a time, not very long ago, when it was spoken by half a dozen people. Now it is spoken by hundreds of thousands, and there is actually growing up what the Esperantists call an Esperanto literature. The advocates of Esperanto seem especially anxious that it should be spoken by all persons who ride bicycles or rush about the country in motor cars. Their idea probably is that when the cyclist or the motor car driver runs down somebody and is charged with the offense he can pretend to speak nothing but Esperanto, and by that trick may tire out the constable who questions him, and the casual witnesses of cycle and motor accidents who may wish to express their views of his conduct in intelligible as well as strong language.

Published: November 5, 1904

The Eyes

On Becoming Blind. Advice for the Use of Persons Losing Their Sight. By Dr. Emile Javal. Translated by Carroll E. Edison. 12mo. Pp. xl, 191. New York: The Macmillan Co. $1.25.

There is a singularly sympathetic quality in this little book which gives it an appeal to a much larger class than that for which it is especially intended. Dr. Javal is a Parisian oculist, who, by an ironical trick of fate, became blind when he was sixty-two years old. For the benefit of the similarly afflicted he has given here some advice on matters of greater or less moment that he has derived from his own experience, backed by the intelligence and the scientific knowledge of a medical man. ...

... The reading and writing of Braille, the abbreviated system of raised letters, is shown to be a rather dishearteningly slow success, but it is indispensable, especially for the young, and for the more isolated. The cultivation of the memory is important for the blind, and Dr. Javal gives an interesting chapter to it. Of the international language, "Esperanto," as an aid to the blind, he seems to have great hopes, and thinks more highly of it than of Volapük.

Published: May 20, 1905.

Esperanto in Russia

Esperanto, the newly conceived and exploited universal language, is finding great favor in Russia. By means of it the revolutionists discover that they can manage to read political tracts printed in English, German, and even French and the other so-called Romance languages. The young woman singer, known as "the Russian Nightingale," who has been singing and reciting in Esperanto before Moscow audiences, has done not a little to spread a desire to acquire the language. In fact, her popularity has caused students of Esperanto among the political police to censor her songs and recitations.

Mlle. Tamara, the Russian "Nightingale" Who Sings and Recites in the New Language Esperanto.

Esperanto enthusiasts will be both pleased and pained at the latest evidence of the spread of their "universal language" in France. It is to be taught to the cadets at the military college of St. Cyr, and has actually been adopted by Anarchists. After the man Highboard, who narrowly escaped being blown to pieces by one of his own bombs, had been arrested the police searched his house and found a voluminous correspondence in an unknown tongue, which turned out to be Esperanto. Still, the natural feeling of pride and pleasure which Esperantists will feel on hearing of this discovery will be somewhat dulled by acquaintance with the surrounding circumstances. Esperanto was meant to be the language of peace, of mutual understanding, and goodwill, and it is being made use of in the cause of military education, murder, and wanton destruction. The prospect opened out is even more dreadful than the knowledge of what has happened. Esperanto may displace the old thieves' jargon, and may become a medium of communication between evildoers the world over.

Published: June 3, 1906

America's First Esperanto Journal.

OKLAHOMA CITY, Oklahoma, Sept. 8. — L'Amerika Esperantisto, the first Esperanto journal ever published in America, devoted to the new universal language, has commenced publication here. Over forty such journals are published in Europe, where the late Geneva Conference created widespread interest in the subject.

Published: September 9, 1906

Pages in Waiting

The first textbook on Esperanto, bearing the authority of the New York Esperanto Society, is being issued by the Universal Language Publishing Company of this city. The author is Dr. Max Talmey, President of the society. He is an American, and his book is said to be the first Esperanto textbook by an American author ever published in this country. It is entitled "Practical and Theoretical Esperanto," and is especially devised for beginners and advanced students desiring either self-instruction or the imparting of knowledge. The prospectus of the little volume states:

The student will find in this textbook numerous remarks and hints very instructive not only for the study of Esperanto, but also for the acquisition of the grammar of other languages. Attention is here especially directed to the chapters on "Pronunciation," "Adverb-Preposition," "Preposition," "Conjunction," "Participle," "Possessive Pronoun," and "Reflexive Pronoun," which, by their thoroughness and exactness, and yet clearness and conciseness, stamp the author as an excellent teacher of grammer in general and his book as the most perfect one for the student and teacher of Esperanto. Indeed, this is the view held by those who have had occasion to review the advance sheets of this handy manual.

Published: September 15, 1906

The "Code Roosevelt"

Plan for an International Language—Why Not "Spell" All Human Emotions, Thoughts and Actions in a Universal Alphabet Understood Around the World?

...

Mr. Cope Whitehouse, a scientist and scholar of recognized erudition, and an authority on Semitic history and languages, proposes the "Code Roosevelt." Compared with the new plan, the efforts to secure simplified spelling which have interested President Roosevelt are as nothing. Its originator suggests naming the universal system of communication the "Code Roosevelt," partly because of the President's declared interest in language reform and partly because were his name attached to such a plan the serious interest of foreign scholars would be at once aroused and held.

...

The plan proposed is, succinctly, as follows: That President Roosevelt issue a summons to the Orientalists and grammarians of all the nations and races of the earth to meet together. That this congress of scholars draw up a comprehensive list of all the basic needs, wishes, ideas, and thoughts of mankind. That then symbols, or ideagraphs, which shall represent these common sensations and ideas, be adopted and a method devised for their application. Then it will be the business of the teachers of the world to spread a knowledge of this system of universal communication. Thereafter, no man or woman of even the most ordinary intelligence and education, of any race, need be at a loss to communicate his or her wishes or thoughts to a man or woman of any other race. A Frenchman, for instance, who knew no English, but who did know the "Code Roosevelt," could express to a business man of New York who knew no French, but who also was acquainted with the "Code Roosevelt," whatever he wished to say; the New Yorker would think out his answer in English, but write or signal it to the Frenchman in the symbols of the "Code Roosevelt."

...

It rests with the President to say whether, at least, an attempt shall be made to make such a code a fact. Those interested in the plan have carried the matter to Secretary Wilson, who has asked the head of the Hydrographic Department to submit a report on the possibilities of the proposed plan, a report also embodying the advantages and disadvantages of the code systems now in use. Prof.

Brander Matthews, already busy with spelling reform, and Dr. Felix Adler of the Smithsonian Institution have also been asked to interest themselves in the idea. And it is thought that steps will soon be taken to lay the whole matter in an official manner before the President.

The idea of a universal language is one that strongly appeals to both commercial and scholarly men. There have been many attempts to break through the mists of confusion that have kept men of different tongues apart since the toppling of the Tower of Babel. There is Volapuk; there is the newer Esperanto. There is the international code of flag signals. There are the grips and signals of secret societies. When the Man Who Would Be King, in Kipling's story, penetrated the wilds of farthest Afghanistan, he communicated with the barbarians through Masonic symbols. There is the finger talk of the deaf-mutes. There is the telegraphic code. All these, however, are either inadequate to serve as a means of universal communication or are based on unscientific ideas. What is needed is a final and authoritative code built up from the root ideas of mankind.

...

Published: September 16, 1906

Advantages of Esperanto

From the London Graphic

Whatever may be the defects of Esperanto, if it comes to be a passport all over Europe, if it comes to aid the small merchant in establishing a foreign trade, if it comes to open a wealth of literature to all the nations—then it will be an accomplishment which none can afford to neglect.

Published: October 4, 1906

New Tongue at Hippodrome

They'll Talk in Esperanto and Pay $25 to Whoever Understands Them

English is no longer sufficiently up-to-date for the managers of the Hippodrome. Esperanto, the "universal language," will be used in a new scene, which is soon to be introduced into "A Society Circus" by Miss Rose La Harte and Miss Olive North.

The Esperanto scene has been written by Miss La Harte, who has coached her assistant in the dialogue. It will not take more time than three or four minutes, and the lines will be distinctly spoken. The managers announce that a prize of $25 will be awarded to any person in the audience who can tell what the two young women are talking about.

Published: October 17, 1906

E. D. French Dead

His Death Removes America's Foremost Engraver of Book Plates.

The death of Edwin Davis French of Saranac Lake in this city on Saturday removed a notable figure in American art. Originally an engraver on silver, he was led to the designing and engraving of bookplates, and he practically devoted his talent to that specialty. Among his few plates outside this field were the series of old New York views and the illustrations for Andrés journal, done for the Society of Iconophiles and the Bibliophile Society.

His work is characterized by a nobility of expression and a calm beauty of line in decorative effect, which caused a keen critic to say to the writer two days before Mr. French's death: "He is a classic figure in American art." The interest and artistic value of his work was shown by the publication in 1899, five years after he had begun to design ex-libres, of a "list of bookplates engraved on copper" by him, prepared by Paul Lemperly.

To this catalogue Mr. French himself added a supplement for the print department of the New York Public Library. To the bookplates by him in the S. P. Avery collection in that institution he added impressions from his more recent plates, so that students will find there a complete collection, over 200, of the work of one who was not only the most noted modern engraver of bookplates in America, but the equal of any in any land to-day. He employed the old art of copper plate engraving in a manner that brings him into comparison with the old French engravers who used similar means of decorative expression.

He was a student of the art of all countries and times, yet his education was American, for he studied drawing in the Art Students' League of this city. He was its President in 1889-91. And it was not until last Winter that his health allowed of his long-hoped-for trip to Europe, where he and Mrs. French, (née Mary Olivia Brainerd,) who survives him, spent several months.

Mr. French's hobby was universal language, for he was a facile linguist. He was Secretary of the Volapuk Society of America, and had a considerable library in that language. Esperante and Idiom Neutral similarly attracted him. He was a member of the American Fine Arts Society, the International Academy of Volapuk, Ex-Libres Society of London, Ex-Libres Verein of Berlin, the Grolier Club, National Arts Club, Club of Odd Volumes, and Bibliophile Society.

Published: December 10, 1906

House Bars Spelling in President's Style

No Public Funds for Printing "Simplified" Documents
Reform had Defenders
Won Preliminary Skirmish on Point of Order, but Final Vote Was 142 to 25 Against Them

Special to The New York Times.

WASHINGTON, Dec. 12 — President Roosevelt's reformed spelling received its death blow in the House to-day, in so far as concerns its chances of ever becoming the official spelling of the Public Printer, and its opponents are also congratulating themselves that the paragraph in the Legislative Appropriation bill which brings this about will also prevent the President himself from employing his hobby in any official document.

This paragraph in the section of the bill referring to the Government Printing Office follows directly upon a clause increasing the salary of the Public Printer from $4,500 to $6,000 a year, and reads:

"No money appropriated in this act shall be used in connection with printing documents authorized by law or ordered by Congress or either branch thereof unless the same shall conform to the orthography generally accepted in the dictionaries of the English language."

...

Mr. Lacey promptly rose to argue against the point.

"Suppose the President should order the use of Volapuk or Esperanto," said he, "would it be changing existing law to prohibit that? This is simply a declaration that the English language as she is spoke and spelled shall be preserved as she is. This is not the American language, it is the English language, and we have no more right to change it than they have in Australia or New Zealand." ...

Published: December 13, 1906

The Publishers

Essays and Historical Works—Features of January Magazines—Forthcoming Books

...

The Fleming H. Revell Company has in preparation a new edition of O'Connor's "Textbook of Esperanto." They are now, by the way, bringing out George W. Bullen's "Lessons in Esperanto."

...

Books and Magazines

Plans of Some of the Monthlies — Forthcoming Novels — Lawson's New Book

Some indications of the plans of magazines for the coming year were given in these columns last week. Of course, the character of certain periodicals is such as to preclude a look very far into the future, since their contents depend largely upon current events. In this category may be placed The North American Review. In the coming year the editor, George Harvey, will make special effort to have the world's thought in politics and other branches of science as well as art and literature "covered" every fortnight by authoritative expounders and critics. Special attention will incidentally be paid to the new international language, Esperanto, while Mark Twain and W. D. Howells will be among the more frequent contributors to the Review.

Published: January 12, 1907

Wants Esperanto Taught in Schools

PARIS, Feb. 28. — M. Cornet, Radical-Socialist, introduced a bill in the Chamber of Deputies to-day providing for a course of instruction in Esperanto, the proposed universal language, in the public schools.

Published: March 1, 1907

French Army Lectures in Esperanto

PARIS, Jan. 23. — War Minister Picquart has authorized the delivery of lectures at the Military Clubs in Esperanto, the proposed universal language.

Published: January 24, 1907

Shakespeare in Esperanto

Series of Plays to be Given When Esperanto Congress Meets

Special Cablegram.

LONDON, April 9. — A series of Shakespearean plays in Esperanto is promised for the edification of those who attend the annual Esperanto Congress at Cambridge in August.

Pretty nearly everybody in Cambridge will know some Esperanto by the time the congress assembles. Waiters, barmaids, cabmen, and policemen are being instructed in it so as to be able to understand and make themselves understood in the universal language.

Published: April 10, 1907

Latin the Language

Its Possibilities Overlooked by Those Seeking for a World Speech

To the Editor of The New York Times:

Your recent editorial on a "'Restored Latin" is somewhat suggestive. It has always seemed to the writer that if one-half of the energy and ingenuity displayed in the creation of Volapük, Esperanto, and kindred enterprises had been devoted to simplifying and regularizing Latin the dream of a universal language would have been nearer a fulfillment.

The scholars of the Renaissance were such extreme purists that they made a fetish of Latin and overlooked its possible utility for everyday use. The advantages of Latin are many; its adoption would excite no National prejudices, it is extensively studied even to-day, its vocabulary is copious and has yielded tribute to nearly every cultivated tongue. In fact, we have in Latin a ready-made language whose possibilities seem to have been overlooked by those striving for a world speech. Classical scholars sneered at monkishy and law Latin, but the monks and lawyers were making of Latin a working tool for thought and business; but because they coined words and did not always comply with grammatical rules and idioms of the Augustan age they were held up to scorn and criticism, and any departure from the standards of antiquity was regarded as sacrilege.

The growth of the language question in many countries, where it is considered as a badge of patriotism, would seem to postpone, at least, if not forbid, the adoption of any modern language as a master tongue, and until this spirit subsides no nation can hope to see its speech spread much beyond its borders.

The great difficulty with any speech, made, as you say, "ad hoc," is that the mother tongue of the builder plays, unconsciously perhaps, such a part in its construction; a glance at Esperanto reveals this. The utility and desirability of a world language are such that they prove themselves, but the question naturally arises, What shall it be? Each nation thinks its tongue is, or ought to be, the speech of Paradise, and to admit that there might be a better and simpler language would savor of treason.

It seems to the writer that Latin simplified and regularized would be more readily accepted by the world than any purely artificial language, however ideal and scientific in its construction.

X.
Norwalk, Conn., April 17, 1907

Published: April 20, 1907

And Now the Exposition at Jamestown

Preparations to Celebrate Virginia's 300th Anniversary Practically Complete—On Friday President Roosevelt Will Start the Machinery

Americans will turn next Friday from thoughts of peace to the most splendid international war spectacle this country and probably the world has ever seen. At noon on that day President Roosevelt will press an electric button that will unfurl the flags and start the machinery of the Jamestown Ter-Centennial Exposition. The newest world's fair will be "a military, naval, marine, and historic exhibition," according to the official statements. Historically it commemorates the day in April, 1607, when the first English settlers in America moored their frail ships in the neighboring harbor. History will be given its due at the Exposition as well as the arts of peace, but the distinctive feature will be the sight of Hampton Roads—already a famous naval arena—alive with the fighting craft of many nations, the shores glittering with soldiers in friendly rendezvous.

...

Two hundred conventions and special events fill the Exposition calendar from May 6 to the middle of November. July 4 will be Jefferson Day. Virginia Home-Coming Week begins on June 10. The Colonial Dames meet on June 5 and the Sons of the Revolution on Oct. 11. There will also be the first congress of students in Esperanto—the new universal language.

...

Published: April 21, 1907

Esperanto

Familiarity with the new universal language which is obtaining so formidable a support, will be helped by an excellent little Esperanto grammar published by Messrs. A. S. Barnes & Co., and written by C. S. Griffith, editor of "Our Times." This book is entitled "Esperanto in Twenty Lessons," and so attractive and easy are its lessons that we believe it could be done. For the roots from the component languages, French, Spanish and Italian, besides English, that can be guessed at when not known, and the rules for uniform and regular endings make the learning distinctly easier than the ordinary learning of a new language and easy, even, as it is its intent to be, for one who does not know any foreign language at all. The printed page is puzzling in appearance, for the use of many ks, js, and signs of accent and elision presents the appearance of a cross between Russian and Scandinavian. The biggest matter is, doubtless, the vocabulary to be learned, and it seems surprising that the vocabulary given at the back of the present book covers but twenty-three pages. The book is a thin 12mo, price 50 cents net.

Published: April 27, 1907

Foreign Words abhorred

German Society Working Against the Use of All Alien Expressions

Special Cablegram.

BERLIN, May 11. — The German Language Association, which aims to remove and avoid foreign terms, has held a meeting to protest against American signs containing foreign words displayed in the streets of Berlin.

The association sent a delegation to the manager of the new Rapid Messenger Company and urged that he change the name of the company to German. The manager refused on the ground that it was not his business to purify the German language.

Next, the association secretly petitioned the German Automobile Club, of which the Kaiser is protector, to eradicate all foreign sporting expressions. The club promised its co-operation.

The second International Esperanto Congress met in Dresden on Thursday. Prof. Ostwald of Leipsic, who has lectured at Harvard under the auspices of the Committee on Professorial Interchange, was the chief speaker. He declared that Esperantists were practical idealists who daily made sacrifices for the accomplishment of their purpose.

Published: May 12, 1907

Esperanto

The North American Review is publishing two new Esperanto books, and promises a third for a later date — a complete Esperanto dictionary. The first of the books on hand is a primer, made up from the lessons in Esperanto that have been running serially in The Review, with selections of Esperanto prose and verse and with the vocabulary constructed by Dr. L. L. Zamenhof, the founder of this new universal language. The primer will be sold for 25 cents.

The second book is a textbook, the most complete one to date, and a thorough and elaborate piece of work. It is compiled by Major Gen. George Cox, and was brought out in England last Fall by the British Esperanto Association. It will probably be sold for 75 cents.

Such work is undertaken by The North American Review under the auspices of the General Esperanto Society, organized by The Review some four months ago, for the purpose of interesting its readers in the study of Esperanto and of diffusing what knowledge about it might be desired. It may not be amiss to add here what news we have from the society. Its membership is now about 1,200, and has enrolled, through correspondence, many from South and Central American countries, and even some people in Portugal. These widely separated members are looking forward to the general meeting of Esperantists to be held in Cambridge, England, Aug. 10 to 17. The latest incident that indicates the interest of established educational institutions in this study is the extending of an invitation to Henry James Forman, the Esperantist of The North American Review, to lecture during the coming Summer at Chautauqua.

Secretary Root, speaking in the light of his recent trip through the Portuguese and Spanish-speaking countries of South America, has expressed himself regarding Esperanto in a way that has delighted Esperantists and that has suggested a definite use of the language at a time not so far off. For he thinks that it could be of great value in our work toward Pan-Americanism, and he is interested in the possibility of it for the Consular Service.

Published: May 18, 1907

Universal Languages

Col. George Harvey, President of Harper Brothers, has been chosen as American delegate to the meeting called for next month of the body known as the "Délégation pour l'Adoption d'Une Langue Auxiliare Internationale." Col. Harvey is sent out by the Philadelphia Commercial Museum.

The work of the delegation is to study the question of an international language, and decide upon the best of those suggested. This Summer one of the new languages will be definitely chosen. The four that will probably receive the most attention are Nummerlingve, a language based on numerals; Parla, with a principle similar to that of Esperanto; Neutra, also with a principle similar to that of Esperanto, but said to be not so complete and finished a product; and Esperanto, of which much has been said. Esperanto will probably be chosen.

The whole work of the delegation was started and promoted by Prof. L. Couturat, Doctor of Letters, of Paris. He has succeeded in enlisting the active co-operation of some 300 associations, in all countries, of educators, scientists, merchants, &c., the list of whose delegates presents a remarkable galaxy of names.

Published: June 15, 1907

Esperantists to Meet

Congress Will Open in Cambridge, England, Next Week

LONDON, Aug. 4. — "La Tria Kongreso," which means "The Third Congress," of the Esperantists, will begin at Cambridge on Monday, Aug. 12, and will continue for several days. Hundreds of Esperantists from Europe and America have promised to attend, and there will be many novel features.

The programme for the opening session includes speeches and singing in the Esperanto language, and a play consisting of scenes from "She Stoops to Conquer," with eleven performers, each from a different country. It will conclude with the singing of "God Save the King" in Esperanto.

The Vice Chancellor of the University and the Mayor will receive the delegates on Monday, but most of them will have arrived before then, and on Sunday services will be held in St. Mary's Church and the Catholic and Congregational churches, where sermons will be preached and hymns sung in Esperanto and the Esperanto version of the Scriptures will be used.

Tuesday and Thursday will be theatre evenings, and "Bardwell versus Pickwick" and "Box and Cox" are to be presented by international companies. On Tuesday the Dean of Ely will receive the delegates, on Wednesday there will be an open-air fête and police sports, on Friday there will be a ball which the delegates will attend in the native costume of their countries, and on Saturday many of the delegates will come to London, where arrangements have been made to entertain them for several days.

Services are to be held in St. Clement Dane's, in the Strand, on Sunday, Aug. 18; there will be visits to many places of public interest, a reception by the President of the London Club, Felix Moscheles; dinners, dances, conversaziones, and excursions.

Nine hundred delegates have promised to attend, and many more are expected. This is the third congress of the Esperantists. The first assembled in Boulogne in 1905, and was attended by delegates from eighteen countries. At Geneva in 1906 the town buildings and the university were opened for the second congress. Eighteen countries were represented, the delegates including ninety from England and five from the United States.

The committee in charge of the arrangements for the third congress fully expects that, in point of representation and enthusiasm, it will surpass either of the others. The London County Council and other municipal bodies have promised to send representatives to listen to the proceedings, and Scotland Yard proposes to have some one on hand to see whether Esperanto might not be useful in its foreign work.

Published: August 5, 1907

[Untitled]

CAMBRIDGE England, Aug. 15.—An American delegate to the Esperanto Congress read a letter at the session to-day from Col. George Harvey of New York, inviting the Congress to hold its meeting in 1908 in New York City. The delegates generally were enthusiastic over the invitation, but the Germans strongly pressed the claims of Frankfort.

Published: August 16, 1907

New Dances Devised

"Esperanto" Waltz and the "Motor" Polka for This Winter

LONDON, Aug. 7.—What is known as the Imperial Society of Dance Teachers has just been holding solemn conclave in the Hotel Cecil. Dutch, German, French, Spanish, and American were spoken; also English with the afore-mentioned accents.
...

Three wonderful new dances are expected to electrify ballrooms next Winter, two of which are the invention of a Dutch master, Mr. Koopman. One is the "Apollo" waltz, a figure dance with sinuous gliding movements; the other is a "Motor" polka, which goes above the regulation speed, and into which are introduced the brightened effects of heel-and-toe episodes. There were also demonstrated before the society the "Esperanto" waltz. All three were unanimously adopted, while much curiosity was shown for R. M. Crompton's invention, the "Cecilian" waltz, the mysterious details of which, however, were not revealed on account of the illness of the demonstrator. ...

Published: August 18, 1907

A Service in Esperanto

Held in St. Clement's Dances Church— Cosmopolitan Congregation

Special Cablegram.

LONDON, Aug. 18.—St. Clement's Danes Church in the Strand, familiar to American tourists as the place of worship frequented by Dr. Johnson, was filled with a cosmopolitan congregation this morning, when the entire service was conducted in Esperanto. Among the hymns sung in the new language were "Lord of Our Life" and "Onward, Christian Soldiers."

Many of those present were delegates to the Esperanto Congress, which has just concluded its sessions at Cambridge.

Published: August 19, 1907

Socialists and Esperantists

Two international congresses, both of peculiar interest to the student of psychical phenomena, have just been brought to a close, one at Stuttgart and the other at Cambridge, England. The first was made up of those who labor to overthrow the existing social order, by fettering individual genius, capacity for toil, and the lucky chance of environment, and by diverting the residue of fortune's favors to the benefit of those who lack genius, the inspiration for work, and elevating, stimulating surroundings. The second represented an attempt to obliterate the literature of the world and the beauties of national speech, by the universal substitution of an artificial language, which, in a similar manner, would fetter individual capacity for the benefit of the unfit. And the curious thing about both Socialism and Esperantism is that each owes its popularity to those very attributes which these cults condemn in others, if exercised along lines other than those set by themselves.

There is no question of the genius of Bebel, Jaurès, and Vandervelde; none whatever of Dr. Zamenhof, the inventor of Esperanto. But all ignore the simple scientific fact that humanity cannot be grouped under a single head of mechanically-operated Individualities, and that climate, custom, tradition, and environment shape minds as well as mouths differently. Although the tents of political and social economy may differ in widely separated communities, their differences, if traced deep enough, will be found to be due to individuals whose genius is the outcome of particular gifts. There can be no commonly accepted idea of the universal brotherhood of man. The tenets of philology and phonetics bring one to the same point in regard to language. The genius of a Dante might make the Tuscan dialect acceptable as the language of Italy, but the genius of neither a Dante nor a Dr. Zamenhof can invent a language and expect all tongues to articulate it.

All humanity, whether politically or linguistically considered, move along the lines of least resistance, and the fittest, which inevitably survives, is the result of evolution. The political institutions which experience will prove the most worthy as offering the best opportunities to individual gifts and ability will survive in those places where they may reach their fullest development and expression. It is the same with languages. In neither category is there room for an artificial social system or a language that lacks a history.

Published: August 27, 1907

"Socialists and Esperantists"

To the Editor of The New York Times:

In your editorial of yesterday, "Socialists and Esperantists," you place both these classes of people on the same footing as to the universality of their intentions, and lose sight of the fact that while Socialists would, if they could, apply their principles to the whole world to the exclusion of all other forms of government, this is not the idea either of the inventor of Esperanto or of those persons who are so enthusiastic over its introduction. Esperanto is not meant "to obliterate the literature of the world and the beauties of National speech by the universal substitution of an artificial language." Its object is not substitution at all, it is merely intended to be, in addition to their respective National tongues, the common property of future generations of all nations, in order to overcome the present difficulty in conversation between people of two nations, neither understanding the language of the other, and having no common speech.

In the Diplomatic Service, French is used at present, but as this is a difficult language for many people to learn, there are many objections to its use as a common tongue. As regards Dr. Zamenhof's expecting "all tongues to articulate it," in view of the fact that Esperanto is based on the initial principles and common root-words of practically all civilized tongues, this expectation is not so monumental as might at first appear. A perusal of the principles of Esperanto and the expectations of its founder, might simplify matters somewhat.

Student
New York, Aug. 28, 1907

Published: September 1, 1907

Fall Books From Many Publishers

... Fleming H. Revell & Co. announce for Fall publication "The Rhodes Esperanto English Dictionary," together with a translation of "Pilgrim's Progress" into Esperanto. The forthcoming dictionary is a large and comprehensive one, the smaller one at present in use being inadequate to meet the demands of those interested in the new language. ...

Published: September 7, 1907

Personal and Otherwise

An amusing notice published abroad concerning Dr. Ludwig Lazare Zamenhof, the inventor of Esperanto, the so-called universal language, states that last year, at the Esperanto Congress at Geneva, he was not only treated as a popular hero, but had several offers of marriage made him. Dr. Zamenhof has the degree of M. D. and is an oculist practicing at Warsaw. He is a Russian by birth, having been born at Byalistock in 1859. Owing to the racial hatred between the mixed population of his native town, he became interested in the question of a universal language. Esperanto is his second attempt at it, as he previously practically completed another which was not at all successful.

Published: September 22, 1907

Esperanto's New York Home

To the Editor of The New York Times:

Perhaps your readers who are interested in Esperanto may like to know that the New York Esperanto Society now has a meeting hall of its own at 80 East 116th Street. The meetings take place every Friday evening at 8:30. The first one happened last Friday, and was enthusiastically attended.

Instruction is free to all, and a cordial welcome is extended to your readers to visit us in our new quarters.

Andrew Kangas
Acting Secretary
New York, Oct. 23, 1907

Published: October 26, 1907

Esperanto's New York Home.

To the Editor of The New York Times:

Perhaps your readers who are interested in Esperanto may like to know that the New York Esperanto Society now has a meeting hall of its own at 80 East 116th Street. The meetings take place every Friday evening at 8:30. The first one happened last Friday, and was enthusiastically attended.

Instruction is free to all, and a cordial welcome is extended to your readers to visit us in our new quarters. ANDREW KANGAS,
                                      Acting Secretary.

New York, Oct. 23, 1907.

Esperanto Tried at Normal College

It's Easy to Learn if It Does Look Queer, and Maybe Some Day the World Will—

M. Privat Believes in it

And the Girls Are Singing "Walk with Me in the Moonlight" in Words That Are Strange

Liberland' de l' bravul' kaj de ni.
Kolombio, la perlo de l' maro.

The Normal College girls began to sing this yesterday afternoon, and have been humming it to themselves ever since, only stopping occasionally, when a number of them get together, to shout in unison:

"Vivu la Ruĝ-blank-kaj-blu'!"

This is not Latin, as some parents thought, or Hindustani or Chinese, as others who knew Latin said it must be, but "Columbia" in

Esperanto, in which the girls had a lesson yesterday afternoon, and which they say is to be the upper class language of the future.

The lesson came in the form of a lecture on Esperanto at the college by a good-looking young apostle of a universal language, M. Edmond Privat, who has come over from Geneva, his home, at his own expense, to help build the Esperanto bridge which he believes is sure to bring about a loving understanding between nations. It is also, he thinks, going to do away with unpleasant irregular French verbs and yard-long sentences in German in the schools. This appealed to the Normal girls.

Mr. Privat's English is only four months old, and although it was excellent, he would not undertake to give a public lesson in Esperanto grammar in it. This was done by J. Charles Walker, Professor of French at the college, who illustrated the construction of Esperanto on the blackboard.

"You know," he said, in beginning, "that the French verb is rather difficult."

A ripple of laughter through the room seemed to indicate assent.

"Well," he continued, "the Esperanto verbs can be learned in two minutes."

Then with a crayon he gave illustrations of the construction of the words, and in about two minutes the girls had learned "belulo" to be a handsome man, "belulino" to be a handsome woman, and rattled off the words signifying, in Esperanto, "a bevy of pretty little girls" with a pure Esperanto accent.

"I'd like to teach French as easily as that," said Prof. Walker with a sigh, and the girls laughed again.

At the close of the lecture at which Miss Marie Caglieris, one of the Normal girls, sang songs in Esperanto, fifty names were given of girls who will take lessons in a class which M. Privat will start this week. Some of the Washington Irving High School girls, who attended the lecture, made an appointment for M. Privat to give them an idea of Esperanto at their school next week. The language is to be taught in twelve lessons, three a week.

Young Mr. Privat is enthusiastic about the value of the universal language. He is quite young, though he has edited a magazine in the new language and been a delegate to different congresses. Living is expensive in this country, he says, so he pays his expenses by writing for the French journals and what pay classes he can get. The school class is free. He came to New York with introductions to Fleming H. Revell, who introduced Esperanto into this country some three years ago at the instance of his friend William Stead. It was then received only with amusement

The Normal College girls say they are going to talk nothing but Esperanto among themselves. The sentimental ones who are not singing "Columbia, Gem of the Ocean," have learned the words of a song sung yesterday, "Ho venu, promenu sub luno, Ho venu, promenu kun mi," "Oh, come walk with me in the moonlight."

Published: December 3, 1907

There are Flaws in Esperanto

Dr. Talmey, the President, Says So, and Gets Out Pending a Pledge to Mend Them

Some Danger to the Jaw

Involved in Saying "Ĉu ŝi scias ĉiam ĉion," and He Would Have This Remedied

There is trouble in the rank of the local Esperantians, and the trouble is all about things like "Ĉu ŝi scias ĉiam ĉion." Esperanto, of course, is and should be the coming international language—in the opinion of all Esperantians.

This trouble is between the progressive branch of the New York Esperanto Society, composed largely of Dr. Max Talmey of 62 West 126th Street, the President, and the conservative branch, consist-

THERE ARE FLAWS IN ESPERANTO

Dr. Talmey, the President, Says So, and Gets Out Pending a Pledge to Mend Them.

SOME DANGER TO THE JAW

Involved In Saying " Cu si scias ciamo cion," and He Would Have This Remedied.

ing of the rest of the society. So keenly does the author of the first Esperanto grammar to be published in this country feel about such small matters as "Ŝi ŝanceliĝis ĉar ŝi ne sciis ĉu ĉiuj gastoj ĉeestos ĉe la festoĉambro ĉirkaŭ la sesa" — which means in English "She hesitated, for she did not know whether all of the guests would be present in the festival hall when it was 6 o'clock" — that yesterday he wrote a letter to the society (afterward carefully translating it into Esperanto) in which he resigned the Presidency.

Dr. Talmey fears that the society which he helped to form has not adhered to the spirit of its constitution provided in a clause that the society should work for the improvement of Esperanto. He believes, in fact, that there are imperfections in the universal language which can and should be remedied. The other members think not.

But the doctor has left a way of escape open. The Presidency he has resigned and his membership, too, but he says in his letter that if the society will adopt at once a resolution pledging itself anew to work for reforms in Esperanto he will reconsider severing his membership relation.

"But they believe that the language is perfect," he said last night, "and they will not vote. A way to get rid of the imperfections in the language was pointed out by an European scholar of international repute, but the Esperanto lovers vilified him, and even attacked his private character. Some of the devotees to Esperanto are childish. I think that the language, which is made up of words whose stems are in all languages, or at least several of them, will, in the end, be the language of the universe, but I do not think, as they do, that it will tend to peace in the world. They paint a picture of the Japanese falling on the neck of the Russians when both can speak Esperanto. But will they? Does the Irishman love the Englishman? He does not, yet they both speak English.

"It is quite certain, however, that no national language will ever become the universal language. The moment, for instance, that German was chosen, the French would refuse to learn the language, and would even forget what German they knew. English is spoken by many people of many nations, but other nations would refuse to adopt it as the universal language, contending that a mistake had been made when their own language had been ignored."

Dr. Talmey, who is a slight man, bearded and spectacled, was asked what imperfections he found in Esperanto to cause his difference of opinion with his society.

"The first objection," he said, "is that THE NEW YORK TIMES could not appear in Esperanto because they haven't the characters. No newspaper could. For example, there is the C with the grave accent over it, and the G with the grave accent, and the S. likewise with the grave accent. No newspaper has these characters. They should be changed. And there are such sentences as this—"

Here a succession of hissing sibilant sounds came from the doctor's bearded lips as his teeth were set very near together. These sounds he wrote down afterward as "Ĉu ŝi scias ĉiam ĉion?" with a liberal supply of grave accents over all of the c's and one of the s's.

"That is really a very important sentence," he said. "I myself have occasion to say it much. It means, 'Does she know everything all of the time?' You can see how it goes. I myself have practiced it so that it does not harm my jaws, but it would split yours. There are too many silibants in it. Yet it would be easy to change it so that it would make the students of Esperanto feel easier. The spellings of the words could be changed so that they would be much pleasanter."

"What are some other specimens?" asked the reporter.

The doctor unlocked a drawer and took out a number of sheets of typewriting. He said:

"Ŝi ŝanceliĝis ĉar ŝi ne sciis ĉu ĉiuj gastoj ĉeestos ĉe la festoĉambro ĉirkaŭ la sesa."

"That is even troublesome for me to say," he admitted, "and yet it is the lady of the house sensing her fear that all of the guests will not arrive in time. 'She hesitated, for she did not know whether all of the guests would be present in the festive hall around 6 o'clock.'"

"That last sentence about the lady of the house you do not have occasion to use very often, but it would completely tear out your jaws if you were to try it. It shows you, as does the other specimens, that Esperanto, as at present composed, is not a musical language. But all that can be remedied."

Dr. Talmey was asked whether, if the society continued recalcitrant, he would drop Esperanto. His eyes gleamed as he walked back and forth.

"I would never give it up," he said. "If I am compelled to work alone I shall do so for the sake of a more melodious and a modulated Esperanto."

Published: December 29, 1907

New European State

Prof. Roy's Plans for Moresnet—Only for Esperantists

PARIS, Feb. 14.—Prof. Gustave Roy, the enthusiastic inventor of the "universal language," Esperanto*, has explained his project for a "universal nation." He intends to found a State in Europe where only Esperanto will be spoken and where Esperantists from all over the world will stop on their way to the different resorts.

Prof. Roy has chosen Moresnet, a small commune on the outskirts of Belgium and the Prussian Rhine province, neutral territory claimed by the adjoining countries. It is seventy acres square and contains about 3,000 inhabitants. It is near the transcontinental railway lines from Constantinople to Ostend and London and from Madrid to St. Petersburg.

The professor will not buy the State, but will turn it into an Esperantist community. Every one in Moresnet will learn the universal language, so that travelers who will stop there may be understood. Prof. Roy hopes that from this little nation the whole world will be "Esperantized." He has been taken rather seriously until now, even by those who do not believe in him. But now that he has stated that it would take only six months to turn Moresnet into an Esperanto country even his most enthusiastic disciples have begun to doubt.

Published: February 23, 1908

* One of the many factual errors in the newspaper. Gustave Roy was a teacher of German and Spanish. The inventor of Esperanto was L. L. Zamenhof.

Esperantist Sees President

Tries to Interest Him in the New Universal Language

WASHINGTON, March 2.—An effort was made to-day to interest President Roosevelt in Esperanto, the new universal language.

The matter was brought to his attention by Edmond Privat, who represents the Esperanto Congress and the Universal Congress of Peace, which met in Munich in September. He was presented by Leo Vogel, Minister of Switzerland.

The President said he would look over the papers submitted to him, which point out the advantages of the universal language and of the campaign which is to be started to have Esperanto talked in the public schools of the United States.

Published: March 3, 1908

The Growth of Esperanto

There is in this country just at present a young Esperanto enthusiast. Edmond Privat, he is called, and his title is Secretary of the International Esperanto Congress. He is still a youth in his teens, but his lack of years is amply atoned for by the energy and enthusiasm with which he lectures and writes for the cause he has so much at heart. He reports an amazing degree of progress in Europe of this language, which he hopes to see adopted universally as a result of the campaign in which he is so indefatigable a laborer. The United States also, he declares, is taking up the new idea and gives promise of joining the Esperanto column with other nations. In addition to his lectures Mr. Privat has now written a book he calls "Esperanto, the International Language, Its History, Grammar, and Vocabulary," which will be published early this month by the Fleming H. Revell Company.

Published: March 7, 1908

Is the Good Old-Fashioned Melodrama Really Doomed?

Villains Have Been Too Villainous and Heroines Have Been Too Rudely Annoyed—A New School of Writers Supplies Polite and Courteous Scoundrels

...

For years you have doubtless considered melodrama a small body of femininity entirely surrounded by Near-Death. Well, you ought to see the rough outlines of H. Percy Swivelbrain's new one. It is called "The Discomforts and Dangers of Having Two Men After You," or "Why, Girls, Leave Home?" The author has aimed to produce a genuine melodrama absolutely devoid of the sensational features of the past. Honestly, you ought to read that rough outline. Here it is:

ACT I.

Discovered, a dear old farmhouse, full of rural atmosphere trained to the minute. Enter Sophonisba, the Pallid Metaphysician, left centre. Prance out her mother, right centre. Slink in Despard Fletchmere, also right centre. Despard comes of a very old Esperanto family and has the great advantage of being able to wear a dress suit at breakfast without looking as if he hadn't had time to change before the bell rang, but Sophonisba simply will not marry him.

...

Published: March 15, 1908

German Plays in Esperanto

To be a Feature of the Next Universal Language Congress in Berlin

By Marconi Transatlantic Wireless Telegraph to The New York Times

BERLIN, April 11, (by telegraph to Clifden, Ireland; thence by wireless.)—Following the example set by Charles Frohman when he produced "The Morals of Marcus" before the Esperanto Congress in London, the German Esperantists plan to give some classic German dramas in Esperanto on the occasion of the German Esperantist Congress at Dresden next August.

Manuel Riecher, the well-known dramatist and manager, has undertaken to carry the project through.

Published: April 12, 1908

"The Witching Hour" in Esperanto

The latest idea of John Mason—or his press agent—is to give a performance of "The Witching Hour" in Esperanto, the new "universal language." A translation of the play into Esperanto is now being made.

Published: April 16, 1908

Announcments of New York Books

...

"Esperanto at a Glance" is the title of a book by Edmond Privat, published this week by the Fleming H. Revell Company. It contains the history, grammar, and vocabulary of the "International Language." It will be followed next month by "Esperanto in Fifty Lessons," by the same author, who is a native of Switzerland and is at present in this country, where he is actively engaged in an Esperanto campaign.

...

Published: April 25, 1908

Carnegie an Esperantist?

His Educational Representative at Pittsburg Addresses Their Meeting

Special to The New York Times.

PITTSBURG, PENN., April 29—There was an enthusiastic meeting of exponents of the Esperanto language here this evening, at which the principal guest and most important speaker was Prof. A. A. Hamerschlag, personal educational representative of Andrew Carnegie and Director in the Carnegie Technical Schools.

His presence was taken as an indication that Mr. Carnegie had interested himself in the new language. Director Hamerschlag said he hoped great things for it. Prof. John A. Brashear, the noted scientist, closely identified with Mr. Carnegie, acted as Chairman of the meeting.

Published: April 30, 1908

New York to See English Comedies

...

The London season of Marie Doro, who will appear in portions of "The Morals of Marcus" in Esperanto in May, Mr. Frohman tells me, has to be postponed or transferred to another theatre on account of the unexpected success of "The Admirable Crichton" at the Duke York's. Miss Doro was to have appeared in this theatre, where a revival of Barrie's play was expected to run fifty nights. It has already run 100 nights and is still doing good business, so Mr. Frohman will allow it to continue for the present.

...

Published: May 10, 1908

Esperantists Invited Here

Col. George Harvey Wants Them to Meet Next Year in America

Col. George Harvey, who for some time has been interested in the adoption of Esperanto as an auxiliary international language, has decided to invite the Esperantists of the world to come to America in 1909.

Last year at the congress held in Cambridge, England, where thirty-one nationalities were represented by the 2,000 delegates, Col. Harvey extended his invitation to them, but Germany had put in a prior bid. Accordingly the 1908 congress will be held at Dresden next August, but Dr. L. L. Zamenhof, the inventor of the language, as well as most Esperantists, is anxious to bring Esperanto home to Americans. Col. Harvey will therefore again send a representative to the congress to offer the hospitality of America, as well as his personal aid, to make a 1909 congress in America a success.

The Chautauqua Institution in this State has offered its co-operation, and this year, on July 21, an Esperanto conference of American students of the language will be held there. Addresses will be made by Prof. D. O. S. Lowell of Boston, Henry J. Forman of The North American Review, Edmond Privat, and others.

Published: June 29, 1908

Views of Readers

A World Language

[The following note and its answer have been forwarded to THE NEW YORK TIMES SATURDAY REVIEW OF BOOKS by Dr. Charles L. Dana. Mr. Avellanus, Dr. Dana's correspondent, is a Latin scholar and has published various Latin books.]

New York, June 8, 1908.

Mr. Arcadius Avellanus.
Dear Sir: Why do you not turn your activities into promoting Latin instead of Esperanto as a world language?

Yours truly,
C. L. Dana

Philadelphia, June 9th, 1908.
Dr. Charles L. Dana.
New York City, N. Y.

My Dear Doctor: As to the Esperantists, I have neither the means of reaching them nor do I consider them a class of people with which one could argue or reason. No man of thinking nature will concede that mutilating, Germanizing, and barbarizing Latin word-stems will make a "language." That process has already been utilized by the Italic, Gallic, Iberic, and other barbarians, creating, in the course of centuries by popular and everyday use, the respective idioms now spoken in Italy, France, Spain, and other countries; and those idioms are nothing else than as many "Esperantos." But while those barbarians had no other tongues and could not help developing their respective "Esperantos," the present asininity has no chances nor right to exist.

Neither has that idiotic product the stamp of scholarship on it; quite the contrary. It is the work of a Russian, whose vernacular is German, educated in the Bismarck epoch of spite-spelling reform in Germany, which is still raging, substituting k's in Latin words in the place of c's, &c., entirely ignorant of the principles upon which all that rests. Wherefore, anybody professing Esperantism and the German spite reform spelling, in my eyes is an ignorant man.

Arcadius Avellanus
Philadelphia, June 29, 1908

Published: July 4, 1908

Views of Readers

Simplified Spellers and Esperantists

New York Times Saturday Review of Books:

One reads with much interest the letter of Mr. Arcadius Avellanus in to-day's NEW YORK TIMES SATURDAY REVIEW OF BOOKS, in which he quaintly calls Esperantists idiotic and ignorant. He condemns Esperanto as barbarizing Latin word stems, just as do the idioms of Italy, France, and Spain, idioms that he does not consider languages. Esperanto is indeed a Romance language, with an added charm over French, Spanish, or Italian in that it is more highly inflected. Mr. Avellanus also deprecates the substitution of "k's" for "c's" in Latin words. When "c" and "k" are sounded alike, any one objecting to such a substitution seems to me a shriveled pedant. What would he say to us simplified spellers, who substitute "t" for "ed" and leave out the "b" in "doubt," the "n" in "Autumn," "column," or "solemn" altogether?

Frank H. Rathbun
New York, July 4

Published: July 11, 1908

Views of Readers

New York Times Saturday Review of Books:

I was much interested in your July 4 issue to read the tirade against Esperanto by Arcadius Avellanus. It is a pity this Latin scholar cannot study the "helpa lingvo" with an unbiased mind. It takes time and study to appreciate such simplicity as is shown in the construction of Esperanto; it is a far cry from the complicated conjugations and declensions of the Latin words, and the still more complicated arrangement of words in sentences, to the marvelous and almost childlike simplicity of everything grammatical in Esperanto. Naturally, one who has spent a lifetime trying to find the real meaning of Latin sentences would be inclined at first to look down with scorn upon a language that any one of ordinary intelligence can read and understand without scientific study. But let him study it again, and yet again, bearing in mind that Esperanto was never intended to be a "world language," a language to take the place of any other, to be spoken to the exclusion of any mother tongue, but that it is to be what its author calls it, a "helping language," a language of commerce, of science of literature if you wish, a universal go-between of all nations, doing away with the absolute necessity of learning more than one language other than one's own. National distrust and national inborn hatred of other languages will prevent any present national language from becoming international, except by force of circumstances sometimes; but Esperanto, while partaking largely of the roots of the Latin and Germanic languages, is not a national language, and hence will arouse the jealousy of no nation. I do not consider myself competent to judge whether Esperanto has upon it the "stamp of scholarship" or not, but I do know that professors, school teachers, doctors, lawyers, ministers, literary people in general, scientists — the so-called learned people of the world — thousands of them, are studying Esperanto and are ardent supporters of it in all that it claims. Esperanto is not another Volapük. The latter was a really, truly, scientific language like Latin, in fact it was so scientific that no ordinary mortal could master it. Esperanto is "so easy that even a child can learn it," and yet so marvelously expressive that the best of literature can be translated into it without losing its value. The vocabulary is as yet too limited, especially in technical terms, which can and will be remedied; but the means of using the vocabulary is perfected, and a wonderful instrument it is. I have been studying the language for over two years, and am continually surprised at its wealth of expression and its adaptability to all circumstances. I would suggest to Arcadius Avellanus that he try it again.

William A. Lewis
New York, July 8

Published: July 11, 1908

Views of Readers
Esperanto and Latin

New York Times Saturday Review of Books:

It is rather remarkable in this progressive age to find a man of intelligence and education burying himself so deeply in ancient literature that he becomes an academic fossil. The letter of Mr. Avellanus in your issue of July 4 might not have been so startling had it come from a person of lesser erudition, but it is rather incomprehensible how a man of his culture can condemn others as ignorant because they "profess Esperantism." Even the most enthusiastic Esperantist will admit that his kara lingvo has not that "stamp of scholarship" dreamed of by our learned friend, who can see in the poesy of Petrarch, the romances of Cervantes, and the fables of La Fontaine merely the uncouth speech of barbarians, but they do insist that it has abundant reasons for existing. Esperanto is not intended to displace any natural language in everyday use, nor yet to supplant Mr. Avellanus's worshipped Latin classics, but as a means of communication between the various races it is of greater utility than any natural language, ancient or modern. Although practically in its infancy, Esperanto is capable of expressing almost every shade of meaning in a concise manner, and is splendidly adapted for commercial purposes. One great merit is its simplicity. It can be learned in a few weeks, while Latin will cost the student years of study before he can read it easily. "The world do move," Mr. Avellanus, and while you are entombed among the musty ideas of ancient Rome, a million of "ignorant men," among whom happen to be some very good Latin scholars, too, are exchanging thoughts with their fellows in every country under the sun, and through the medium of that "asininity," Esperanto. Back to your catacomb, dear Mr. Avellanus, until some philological Gabriel toots his bugle and opens your eyes to the fact that Latin is a "dead one" and you have been sleeping.

Myles Murphy
Weehawken, N. J., July 6

Published: July 11, 1908

Views of Readers

New York Times Saturday Review of Books:

The letters that have appeared in the last two issues of THE SATURDAY REVIEW OF BOOKS indicate rather clearly that the followers of Esperanto do not keep abreast of the times in the literature on their subject. At all events these letters contain so many errors that it seems worth while once more to correct certain statements that are constantly made and just as frequently shown by competent critics to be erroneous.

The letter of Mr. Avellanus is undoubtedly wrong in one important particular. He condemns the modern Romance languages, one and all, on the ground that they are but barbarized Latin. This bears upon the one fundamental question, linguistically speaking, that concerns the creation of Esperanto or any other artificial language. One may admire a machine that runs smoothly; so do I admire Esperanto. But a language that grows up naturally and acquires the spirit of the people using it has a kind of personality that is utterly lacking in the artificial language. It is the spirit that inheres in a natural language that gives it its charm and that seizes upon the affection of the student.

But Mr. Rathbun's statement that Esperanto possesses "an added charm over French, Spanish, or Italian, in that it is more highly inflected," is delightfully naïve. Why do people continue to make such preposterous offhand remarks when everybody knows that the French and Italian verbs are a bugbear to the average schoolboy and college student on account of their seeming complexity and irregularity? This remark is interesting from another standpoint. The author of Esperanto, Dr. Zamenhof, states that the chief merit of Esperanto is that it omits every unnecessary inflection. He says, "The whole grammar of my language can very readily be learned in the course of one hour." So, too, Prof. Jespersen, one of the very few students of the science of language who have espoused the cause of Esperanto, claims in one of his earlier books that the fewer inflections a language has the closer it approaches to being a perfect language.

And yet Mr. Rathbun is not so far from the truth. Esperanto

is not so simple as it is often represented. The sixteen rules of Dr. Zamenhof can readily be learned in the course of one hour, but that does not finish the study of Esperanto. To say that it is "so easy that even a child can learn it" is nonsensical. The best grammar of Esperanto written in English (that of Cox) requires 357 pages to explain its inflection and syntax. On this point it will suffice to give the experience of Prof. Leskien, the gifted linguist of Leipsic: "I have attempted to learn to speak Esperanto, and have found to my astonishment that this artificial language was difficult for me, although it is probable that I possess as good a knowledge of Latin, French, and Italian as the majority of Esperantists, and so have as much relief from the burden of acquiring the vocabulary as they. As to a thorough mastery of Esperanto in a few months, to say nothing of weeks, that is for me quite out of the question."

Mr. Lewis says that Esperanto is "so marvelously expressive that the best of literature can be translated into it without losing its value." This is a strange expression, in view of the well-known fact that translation is universally regarded as one of the most difficult of linguistic feats. The very fact that a language has a peculiar native characteristic differing from that of every other language renders an adequate translation almost impossible. But examples constitute the best test, and surely it cannot be maintained that Kofman's translation of "The Iliad" into Esperanto retains the quality of the Greek. The same will apply to Zamenhof's translation of "Hamlet," to Grabowski's translation of the "Arrow and the Song," and to others. But some translations have a real charm, such as Kipling's "La Miraklo de Purun Bhagat" and Longfellow's "La Pluva Tago." Here the Esperanto machine runs beautifully.

These are only a few statements relative to the recent letters in THE TIMES. They have nothing to do with the main issue of the lasting service of Esperanto. That might provoke long discussion. Here I may say only that in the last two centuries about 150 artificial languages have been created, and not one of them has outlived its creator. The same fate probably awaits Esperanto.

R. Wellington Husband
Hanover, N. H., July 13

Published: July 18, 1908

Views of Readers

The Problem of Grammar in Esperanto and the Plea of Mr. Avellanus to Make Latin a World Language—Webster on Simple Spelling—Were the Homeric Poems Given in Writing? —Various Commentaries

New York Times Saturday Review of Books:

Having noticed several communications in your issue of July 11 about Esperanto, I wish to say that I have made a more or less thorough study of that language since the time when The North American Review published a series of very good lessons in the idiom. To me it seems that the average Esperantist is too prone to unwarranted boastfulness, and is not always careful to tell the truth — at least the whole truth. The public, or that portion of it which has read the various articles in the newspapers about Esperanto, probably is completely unaware of the fact that there is at present a determined, extensive effort being made to "reform" the language of Dr. Zamenhof, in the line of making it more simple, more scientific, and more complete. Dr. Zamenhof tried to reform the language himself back in 1894, at which time he published in his journal a series of articles outlining the desired improvements, and then submitted the matter to a vote of his subscribers for a decision as to whether these changes should be made. The subscribers, however, turned down the proposals, and the language continued to be used in its primitive form. Then in 1905, at the Universal Congress of Esperantists at Boulogne, a "declaration" was adopted, to the effect that Dr. Zamenhof's book known as the "Fundamento" should be accepted as the unchangeable basis of the language; that no one had any authority to make any change whatever in the language. In spite of this, however, many new words have been added, formed according to individual tastes, and without any governing rules, resulting in irregular forms and unwarranted meanings. For instance, Dr. Zamenhof adopted the root-word "luli," meaning "lull to sleep." Now, the termination "ilo" means a tool or implement. Therefore, "lulilo" is a cradle, an implement for lulling to sleep. But a cradle is rocked, and in this way the word "lull" came to be used in the sense of "to rock," although it means nothing of the kind. Some months ago a writer in The American Esperanto Journal, describing the Jamaica earthquake, said the island "luliĝis," (he meant "was rocked," but really said was "lulled to sleep" by the earthquake.) "Manki" means to lack, to be missing; but it has come to be used by some persons not understanding its derivation to mean to miss. They say "Mi mankis la vagonaron," meaning "I missed the train," but really saying "I lacked the train." I remember one letter in which the writer, evidently finding in his dictionary that "ĉambro" meant "room," said he had no "ĉambro" to write more. In this way the language is getting full of absurdities, and of the total number of professed Esperantists the proportion using the language with anything like correctness is very small. The average "English speaking" seems to be unable to use the accusative case properly, or to get the adjectives right. In Esperanto the adjective agrees in number and case with its noun. For example, "Bona homo" is "A good man." "Good men" is "Bonaj homoj," ("j" is pronounced as "y.") When the noun is in the accusative, ("Mi vidis bonan homan—I saw a good man,") the adjective must agree with it.

> Li estas bona homo—He is a good man.
> Ili estas bonaj homoj—They are good men.
> Mi vidis la bonan homon—I saw the good man.
> Mi vidis la bonajn homojn—I saw the good men.

Although this seems quite simple, the average man utterly fails to use the adjective and the accusative correctly.

The attempt at reform is being conducted by a committee elected by the "Delegation for the Adoption of an Auxiliary International Language," which was founded in 1901, consisting of over 300 societies, (scientific, trade, educational, &c., in all countries,) and has received the approval of some 1,200 members of academies and universities. The committee elected by this body in 1907, consisting of eminent scientists and linguists, examined the various proposals for an international language, of which there are a number, and approved Esperanto, subject to certain changes being made in it in accordance with a scheme submitted under the pseudonym "Ido*." This scheme does away with the accusative in all cases except those in which clearness requires its use—that is, if the object precedes the subject, then the accusative is used. It also dispenses with the plural and accusative in the adjective, and corrects the badly chosen root forms. It also establishes regular rules for the derivation and formation of the words, so that when one has the root, he can form all the derived words in a regular manner.

When this scheme was submitted to the Lingvo Komitato, the committee supposed to have charge of the language of Dr. Zamenhof, they refused to make the changes. Then the secretaries of the "delegation," Messrs. Couturat and Leau, under the direction of a "Konstanta Komisio," went ahead in the effort to introduce the changes in spite of the Lingvo Komitato. They have already gotten out dictionaries in various languages, lernolibri (text books,) and have established an aggressive monthly magazine, Progreso. The old Esperanto "Chefi" (chiefs) seem to be making every effort to conceal from the body of Esperantists and from the general public all knowledge of this condition of affairs, but signs of the collapse of this effort are beginning to appear.

No doubt we will some day have an efficient artificial language, but it will not be the "primitive" form of Esperanto.

W. J. P.
Brooklyn, July 13
...

Published: July 18, 1908

* Ido (first published in 1907) was an attempt at reforming Esperanto. It retains a small following today.

Esperantists Raise Flag

Are Called Dynamic Dreamers—Col. Harvey Is Interested

Special to The New York Times.

CHAUTAUQUA, N. Y., July 20.—With solemn ceremony to-day the first Esperanto flag to float over American soil was raised at the Chautauqua Assembly grounds. While the choir was singing the Esperanto hymn, the green and white ensign with a green star on the white field was hauled to the masthead and hundreds of Esperanto enthusiasts cheered. To-day was the official opening of the Esperanto Convention, the first in this country.

Prof. Vincent, acting head of the Chautauqua institution, bade the Esperantists welcome. "This language," he said, "seems to be superior to volapuk or to any other previous attempt at a universal language." Henceforth, he added, it would be a feature at Chautauqua.

In the afternoon W. E. Sterrett of Pennsylvania made an address in Esperanto, saying that soon millions would be speaking and using Esperanto, and after him Henry James Norman of The North American Review, speaking in English, said:

"At present we are but a few dreamers of dreams. Only let us not forget that all great projects were made real by men who were dreamers, indeed, but dynamic dreamers—from Copernicus to Graham Bell, from Galileo to Morse. Col. Harvey is such a dynamic dreamer, for, not only is he interested in the success of Esperanto, but he has authorized me to figure with steamship companies and railway companies on rates so that we may invite the next universal Esperanto Congress to come here, a project very near his heart."

The convention will continue to the end of the week.

Published: July 21, 1908

Views of Readers

Arcadius Avellanus Elaborates His Reasons for Considering Latin Eminently Fitted to be Used As a Universal Language—More Light on the Miller Quotation—Various Communications

New York Times Saturday Review of Books:

As I am gazing upon the beautiful harbor close by under our windows, with the tide just rolling in with its deep murmur, I behold the heavy mist rising from the waters and swept toward the mainland by a gentle breeze, sooner or later to descend again in the form of rain, irrigating and fertilizing far-distant fields. The tides, rolling back and forth, evenly distributing the salt of the sea, preserve the waters from stagnation, and the evaporation provides purified waters for fertilizing food-bearing farms and gardens.

This same process is going on in our intellectual life. Books and periodicals are the tides that carry thoughts, some with salt, some without, the net result of which is carried and distributed far and wide, creating, sometimes clashing, public opinions. Such has been the case with my letter, published in your columns on July 4, and the answers of three Esperantists published in your issue of July 11. In this correspondence, then, two layers of public opinion, Romanism and Latinism, clash with barbarism and Esperantism. With the kind permission of the editor I shall uphold the former and answer the latter in the following:

1. One of your correspondents regards a defender of Romanism and Latinism an "academic fossil." By "fossil," from Latin fissile (fodio, I dig,) we mean ancient things dug up from the ground, but he uses the term as a reproach, implying undue veneration for ancient things and institutions. I do not know whether any mosquitos, flies, and other vermin had ever been dug up, but I know of ichthyosauri, dinosauri, mammoths, &c., dug up, which, with the giant trees, ferns, coal, gold, &c., are less ridiculous and contemptible than some would make us believe.

2. The same correspondent refers to Roman ideas as "musty," and sends me back to the catacombs. In answer I ask: Has our modern civilization anything that has not come down to us directly from Rome? Have the Teutonic, Celtic, Sarmatian, or other barbarians contributed anything to it from their forests, swamps, and huts? While I readily admit that we have a larger world to-day; that we can travel faster to reach out for the other man's dollar; that we hang brighter lights for the nightly prowlers; that we can send word and written messages ahead of elopers, thieves, and burglars; that we do have many material advantages over the peoples of 3,000 years ago, I deny that intellectually we are superior and that Roman ideas can justly be called "musty." It was Rome which forced the barbarians to settle down; gave them national existence, taught them agriculture, trades, commerce, alphabet, letters, law, medicine, philosophy, theology, a highly developed language for intercourse; she gave a language to Italy, one to Spain, another to France, still another to Portugal, some 40 per cent. to Germany, and some 60 per cent. to the English-speaking peoples. She digested the doctrines of Socrates, Plato, Aristotle, Zeno, Democritus, Epicurus, and, welding it with Jewish thought, gave the world Christianity. She gave us models in jurisprudence, in statesmanship, in strategy, in generalship, in patriotism, in rigid honesty, in self-devotion, in oratory, in poetry, in grammar, in arts, never to be surpassed, forever to be admired and emulated by the best talents of the human race, inspiring our race during 2,000 years, educating the greatest men the Aryan nations have ever produced. Is all this "musty"?

The ancient barbarians have not added to this grand treasury a penny's worth, but, be it said to their credit, they have proved faithful and honest pupils; they have imbibed the immortal institutions and their vehicle, the Latin language, using it for centuries in their intellectual existence, some up to the Reformation and after, others until the French Revolution, Hungary until our own age, while the Roman Church is still using it as a living speech. Neither is there a civilized nation that has as yet discarded Latin as the central subject in its secondary schools. I, myself, have never met a man who had not valued his knowledge of Latin higher than any other of his accomplishments; neither have I met a person who despised Latin, or who did not esteem a Latinist higher than the possessors of other erudition or profession.

3. The so-called "modern languages," meaning the Neo-Latin idioms, are not, as generally supposed, a development of the language of the Roman people, as those speaking them are not the descendants of the Romans, but a mixture of the native tongues of the barbarians, and the language of the Vulgata (the Latin Bible) spread by the Roman clergy in their missionary work in Church and school. Each set of barbarians, according to its instincts, has mutilated the language of the Roman Church, itself much changed by Hellenic and Hebraic words, phraseology, and ideas.

4. Latin being split by the barbarians into so many different idioms, not understood by each other, differing both from the Church Latin and this from the Roman mother-stock, and other non-Latin races having settled in Europe, while Latin proper, particularly in Germany, gradually was changed into a useless philological speculation, and a childish bickering about Cicero and Classicism, the ever-expanding intercourse among the nations gave birth to a natural desire for a medium of communication among the nations through the agency of a language common among the cultured of all. One would naturally think of Latin as the one so employed for 2,000 years and taught in the schools of all nations. Strangely enough, but for natural reasons, those who were shipwrecked in their Latin studies, unable to master the endings, have rebelled, and have hatched out spite "languages," stitched together from the tatters and rags of third-fourth-hand Latin, in the method of the ancient barbarians, chipping off the formidable endings which they so hate, patching the leaky parts of their scanty supply of Latin from their barbarous sources at command. Among these monsters is Esperanto, or Desperanto.

The victims of this crazy-quilt reproach me for calling their hobby "asinine." Here I give some of my reasons for so doing:

(a) Because, while they want to interest all the world, they forget that the barbarous fragments of Latin material they stitch together are only known to the smaller portion of the human family—that is, to those born in the Neo-Latin idioms, and to the English. The middle classes in Germany are already using a special dictionary of foreign words. Hundreds of millions of Germans, Slavs, Chinese, Touranians, Hindus, Japanese, &c., would have to learn honest Latin, or a Neo-Latin idiom, and then learn to corrupt the same in order to become infected with Desperantism, just as if they insisted on wearing patched garments, when they could have the real thing at less cost.

(b) In all great or petty movements it is one man who starts the thought, few men push the manœuvre, the unthinking crowds follow and shout. What I have seen of Esperanto convinces me that neither the master mind nor the promoters have a sufficiently clear idea of the subject matter they handle, and they show an utter disregard for the genius of Roman Latin as well as of the Vulgata Latin, their proper material, of history, of philological principles, and they go blindly, aimlessly raking up anything they consider a "language." Of course, they will say, "We are no philologists, we do not care what each word may originally mean, we take them in their present form and meaning." Words, consequently, like "company," "conversation," "battery," "to mount," &c., are just delightful material for them, as they may be for any unthinking and ignorant man, and as no man of classical education and good taste will ever swallow such a vocabulary for a new language, the system (?) must be meant for ignorant people.

(c) One of the most flagrantly "asinine" practices of Esperantism is the insistence of obtruding and defending "k" in the place of "c," ordered by Prince Bismarck after Sedan, and which is so dear even to-day to German hearts. Now, one would expect that linguistic reformers, using the Roman alphabet, would know the principles of that alphabet, long since set down by the highest authorities, the Roman grammarians themselves. According to them there are three signs to express "k" sounds: "c," "k," and "q"; "c" (ké) to stand before "e," "i," and "o"; "k" before "a," but only in a few words, and "q" before "u," followed by another vowel, hence their names, "cé," "ká," "qú." If the Esperantists still insist upon ignoring this 2,000-year-old principle they must acquiesce in the adjective their ignorance elicits and their insistence justifies.

5. The Esperantists say, with a deplorable amount of complacency, that Latin is dead. No man is more familiar with the true state of this question than am I. Since 1893 and up to 1902 I have been editing and publishing first one, then another Latin periodical, the only ones in the world. I have published manuals to learn and to teach Latin speech in a practical way for practical as well as for literary purposes, embodying a vocabulary of more than 3,000 words, gleaned from Roman authors on all subjects of daily life. For, while there are still several hundreds of thousands of people in the world who can speak Latin fluently, much of this speaking is done by the Roman clergy on theological and philosophical subjects, and in the schools it is restricted to the narrow channels of Ciceronian orations, military histories, a little poetry, mostly in the light of German philology, parsing, analyzing, spelling; the general impression has spread that that was the sum total of Latin, therefore Latin was not adapted to practical purposes, it had no vocabulary, it was not a speech. Besides, a fanaticism grew up in Italy in the seventeenth century, known as "Ciceronianism," which would banish every word and phrase not found in Cicero. This was renewed in a small measure in Germany in our days, spread thence to the schools in all the world, and it is still affected by people who are not beyond spelling, parsing, and translating. Hence the justification of Volapükism, Nov Latinism, Lang Bleuism, Esperantism.

All these people never reflected on the facts that Rome was the centre of the greatest industry, commerce, navigation, architecture, trades of all kinds the world has ever beheld. They have never considered that the teeming millions in the mines, metal shops, shipbuilding, fortifications, roadbuilding, at the looms, at the potter's wheel, building, decorating, farming, cattle raising, &c., were not all Ciceros; that the term "classical" was unknown in Rome, and that fetich is a later device; that Cicero was but one man among the many millions of Italy, Spain, Gaul, Africa, &c., in the whole history of Rome; that Roman language and literature have only developed during the early empire, when writers arose in all branches of knowledge down to the fourth and fifth centuries, when also law came to culmination under the auspices of Emperor Justinianus.

6. But Roman civilization is of a too distant age, therefore its language cannot supply the terms for the variety of modern ideas. This is the objection most frequently urged against Latin by modernists. And it is quite justified if by Latin is meant that senseless and aimless drudgery in which the schools are engaged. The schools are looking upon Rome through a one-inch iron pipe, made for them in Germany, and they see at the other end nothing else than Cicero, Cæsar, Virgilius, Horatius, Ovidius, and Livius. For people of common sense Petronius, Apuleius, Lucretius Carus, Seneca, Varro, Cato, Palladius, Columella, Vegelius, Vitravius, Pomponius Mela, Plinius Major, Quintilianus, Gellius, Macrobius, Donatus, Charisius, Priscianus, Celsus, Apicius, Caius, Ulpianus, Justinianus, &c., are as much classics in their own respective fields as are the above in theirs. They offer us a vocabulary which must be stunning to a one-inch dumb Ciceronianist, and open the eyes of the miseducated world, which can only laugh in the face of the hypocritical "Classicists." Do not all modern inventors have recourse to Latin (or Greek) for a supply of new words and terms? Do the Esperantists not do the same? Have modern Latinists not the same right to form new Latin words from old roots and stems on approved principles? When editing my Latin magazine I was compelled to form words, like "cistrum," for ignorant "locomotive"; "digo," for ignorant "automobile," and hundreds of others to express modern inventions.

7. Granting all this, the misguided college-bred people will say, Latin is too difficult a language for the average student to learn. Quite so, I say, if the high school and college methods, made in Germany, handled by teachers without professional Latin training, without ability to speak, gnawing away at spelling, parsing, translating during eight years are the standards by which to measure this difficulty. I should sooner forget my Latin three times, and study it anew, than to undertake to master German from books. The Latin grammar has fewer irregularities than almost any language, and even these follow certain systems, while the general mechanism, by its simplicity, precision, and consistency is the recognized model and regulator of all European languages, indispens-

able for every cultured person, even for regulating his own native speech. The difficulties are artificial, made by German philologists, who could rake up similar difficulties for any language, just give them a chance; but the essentials of Latin speech can be mastered in some 125 hours, as tried and demonstrated by my own experience. We do not mean to be Shakespeares, Voltaires, Göthes when we study English, French, and German; why should we be supposed to become Ciceros when studying Latin? When a student is able to express his thoughts in speech and writing he can pursue the work of polishing himself, or with little outside aid. Those wishing to see my statement demonstrated may write me now, and I shall be glad to convince them by a public demonstration in New York next October.

Arcadius Avellanus
Bar Harbor, July 27

Published: August 1, 1908

Views of Readers

New York Times Saturday Review of Books:

Arcadius Avellanus, in his discourse of last Saturday, makes two points in favor of Latin as a universal language. It would be possible, by the lawful formation of new words, to adapt it to the complexities of modern life. It is not so difficult to learn, if properly taught, as it is when taught improperly. Both these statements we may grant, without feeling that its superiority to Esperanto is thereby demonstrated. In a controversy of this kind it is well to remember that all superiority is purely relative, depending solely on the purpose to be served. Which is more useful, one might ask, a pair of scissors, or a fountain pen? The query remains meaningless until the question, useful for what? is satisfactorily answered. So in the present controversy. Much of what Mr. A. A. says, though learned and interesting, is wholly irrelevant to the point at issue. It is not necessary to seek reasons for the inadequacy of Latin. Latin has had its chance, and failed. And, even admitting that its grammar is simple, (an admission in which very few who have struggled with it will concur,) its word order is so totally foreign to the modern habit of mind that it would require years of laborious and incessant practice ever to learn to think in Latin naturally. And unless one can think in a language he cannot be said to know it in any true sense of the word. The whole structure of the sentence has radically changed since the days of Macrobius, Columella, et ceteri. A universal language, to serve its purpose, must be "understanded of the people," rather than by its subtleties, and strict adherence to classical tradition, remain merely a toy of the erudite. It must be easily learnable, and it must be capable of expressing accurately and copiously the world's thought. That Esperanto fulfills brilliantly these two conditions no one who has ever looked into the matter will for a moment question.

We have the word of no less an authority than François Gouin (who in the circumstances would be under no temptation to exaggerate) that thoroughly to assimilate a new language requires between eight and nine hundred hours. Mr. A. A. asserts that "the essentials of Latin speech can be mastered in some hundred and twenty-five hours." Now, Tolstoy said of Esperanto, "It is so easy to understand that when I received a grammar, a dictionary, and some articles in this language, I was able in two short hours if not to write, at least to read the language fluently." So much for the relative ease of acquisition of Esperanto and Latin.

As to their relative value for literature, "much might be said on both sides." But that question is extraneous to the subject in hand. The National literatures will flourish unhampered by the parallel development of the international tongue, and this latter will be used for communications between persons of different languages, where the form is less important than the substance.

Not that we for a moment admit the unavailability of Esperanto for literature. We merely assert that not by this criterion does it stand or fall. In this connection might one suggest to Mr. A. A. that he read Dr. Zamenhof's wonderful translation of "The Tragedy of Hamlet, Prince of Denmark," and then try to imagine himself or any other Neo-Latinist making a Latin version which will so nicely render the subtle shadings of the original, while it at the same time follows so closely the order and the rhythm of the words. Let him read it carefully, with that openness of mind, that suspension of judgment which is the characteristic of all ripe scholarship, and before he has reached the end he will be as ardent an Esperantist as any one of us!

W. P. Bonbright
New York, Aug. 4

Published: August 8, 1908

Views of Readers

New York Times Saturday Review of Books:

With your kind permission I will again take up the discussion of Esperanto in the endeavor to answer some of the objections as set forth in a recent issue of the BOOK REVIEW.

Referring to Mr. Husband's letter, no one denies the charm to a student in any national or natural language which is not present in Esperanto. But in this age of commercialism in everything, including literature, few have the time or the inclination to learn many languages for the purpose of merely getting at their charm, when more likely they "need them in their business" — whether commerce, science, or general information. Let us compare the natural languages with the natural products of the earth used in commerce, many of which at one time or another have been made a basis of exchange, and Esperanto with coined money, which now is the basis of exchange for everything; there certainly is not the "natural charm" to coin that there is to wheat or corn, meat or vegetables, wool or silk, products of the earth beautiful in their growth, but the members of the family of nations need one basis of exchange now when dealing with each other, not a dozen or more. The time is past when men meet and barter their products with each other direct, however charming and picturesque that may be, they now use one basis—money. This place Esperanto will fill in the meeting of the nations in business, science, literature.

The same gentleman seems to question my statement that "even a child can learn it." Does he mean to say that a child, whose mind is naturally logical, cannot learn the logical language Esperanto, when he can and does learn a language as illogical in its construction as the "grammatical genders" or the involved sentences of the German or the intricate uses of verbs and propositions in English? Children somehow must have learned Latin and Greek and Hebrew, with their multitudinous inflections, surely they can learn the almost uninflected Esperanto with its lack of "exceptions to the above rules." If Mr. Husband has studied Cox's Grammar he will find that only a small part of the 357 pages are given up to grammar, the greater part being what Cox calls "Commentaries," or explanations of the grammatical rules, with numerous examples, idiomatic phrases, &c. An Esperantist can easily make himself understood without this book, but he will secure a "better style" by referring to its contents frequently. Prof. Leskien's idea of a "thorough mastery" of Esperanto is probably far in advance of that of the average man who studies it, just as his knowledge of his own language probably is in advance of that of his countrymen. The average man cannot speak and write English like our best littérateurs; but he knows it for all practical purposes.

I might say also, in this connection, that the faults of translating mentioned by W. J. P. are largely due to the imperfect dictionaries so far published, which make few distinctions in word meanings and leave much to the language faculty of the translator; and secondarily they are due to a lack of this language faculty, the ability to choose the right word, which faculty is absolutely necessary for a good translator. This lack of the language faculty shows up even worse in translating into a natural language, and is not the fault of Esperanto. "Ido" will not make it any easier for one who is not gifted with the language faculty than does the present form of Esperanto. If, however, makers of dictionaries, English into Esperanto, will take the trouble to give the proper equivalent in Esperanto for every meaning of each English word—just as Webster's Unabridged does for the English language alone—much of this difficulty of translating will disappear. As I said in my former letter, Esperanto is not a finished language, it is growing, and growing very rapidly—in fact, it outgrows its dictionaries as a boy outgrows his clothes.

Let me give some of the directions of growth, chosen from an article which recently appeared in the Amerika Esperantisto. The Red Cross Society will send a delegate to the fourth congress at Dresden this year and expects to make Esperanto its official international language. The United Societies of Christian Endeavor publish their official organ in Esperanto, making it available for members all over the world. The Good Templars have an international password in Esperanto, and at their last international convention they recommended Esperanto as their convention language. Many Masonic publications are urging the use of Esperanto in the same way and for other international purposes. The international organization police and detectives in Europe has taken up Esperanto as a means of intercommunication. In Europe there is much advertising matter sent out printed partly or entirely in Esperanto, (some of which I have seen.) A large body of scientists, with headquarters at Geneva, is pushing Esperanto as a means of disseminating scientific information and are collaborating a scientific dictionary in Esperanto. The London office of the Swedenborgians is issuing pamphlets in Esperanto. The last international congress of European Socialists considered favorably the adoption of Esperanto as an auxiliary language for meetings. Books and pamphlets for Catholics have been issued in Esperanto, and the Pope has given the language his apostolic benediction.

This certainly shows life and growth—evidently the time is far off when Esperanto will be added to the other "dead languages."

William A. Lewis
New York, Aug. 3

Published: August 8, 1908

Views of Readers

The Problem of a Universal Language

New York Times Saturday Review of Books:

Mr. Husband, in a recent issue of THE REVIEW, finds my remark that Esperanto has an added charm over French, Italian, and Spanish, in that it is more highly inflected, "delightfully naïve." "Why do people," he goes on to say, "continue to make such preposterous offhand remarks?" and cites the difficulty schoolboys and college students have with French and Italian verbs; the statement of Dr. Zamenhof that Esperanto omits every unnecessary inflection, and that its whole grammar can be learned in an hour; and the remark of Prof. Jespersen that the fewer inflections a language has the more nearly perfect it is. "And yet Mr. Rathbun is not so far from the truth," he continues, citing the facts that Cox's grammar contains 357 pages and that Prof. Leskien has found difficulty in mastering Esperanto in weeks and even months.

Esperanto is less inflected than the Romance languages in the following respects:

1. The definite article, as in English, is invariable.
2. The comparison of adjectives and adverbs is made by means of auxiliary words.
3. The verbs have no forms to indicate person and number, these being made clear by the accompanying nouns or pronouns. The imperfect and subjunctive, as direct inflected forms of the stem, are lacking.
4. There are no forms to indicate gender.

Esperanto is more highly inflected than the Romance languages in the following:

1. In its relative pronouns and many interrogative pronouns.
2. In its verbs, as regards the participles, the six participles including a future active and a future passive. These are all inflected to

show not only singular and plural, but also the accusative case of these numbers. By further inflection each participle may become a noun or adverb, and the noun in turn may be inflected.

3. Nouns and adjectives have an accusative form for both singular and plural. This is of the highest importance, and as the object is rarely lacking in a sentence, the accusative contributes more than anything else to give the impression of a highly inflected language. To take an example from W. J. P.'s letter "Mi vidis la bonajn homojn" can be written, without an absolute sacrifice of the sense, "La bonajn homojn mi vidis," or "Mi la bonajn homojn vivis"; the accusative fixes the meaning unmistakably, and thus Esperanto has within its scope the old freedom of position of the Latin or Greek.

4. Viewing inflection in a larger aspect, as a development of roots, one may mention the principle whereby the addition of "o" to a stem produces a noun; of "a" an adjective, or "e" an adverb. Add to this the great number of prefixes and suffixes in use in Esperanto, the numerous inflections from a single root become surprising.

In its essentials, therefore, it seems to me that Esperanto is more highly inflected than French, Spanish, or Italian, and Dr. Zamenhof's remark that he omitted every unnecessary inflection must be considered with reference to a high conception of language, which requires this added inflection for the sake of adequate expression. Than Esperanto I believe there is no language, excepting Greek, more delightful.

Frank H. Rathbun
New York, Aug. 2

Published: August 8, 1908

Announcment of New York Books

...

A 600-page "English-Esperanto Dictionary," prepared by Joseph Rhodes, will be published shortly by the Fleming H. Revell Company. In addition to this two books are in preparation by Edmond Privat, one "Esperanto at a Glance," and the other "Esperanto in Fifty Lessons." Mr. Privat is the Swiss representative of the International Esperanto Society, and is now in this country as ambassador of the new tongue. He has succeeded in organizing an American Esperanto Association here, which has invited the next international conference to meet at Chautauqua next year.

...

Published: August 8, 1908

Queries from the Curious and Answers to Them

C. M. Murphy. — Please tell me about Esperanto, the proposed international language.

The New York Esperanto Society has issued a statement regarding it which is in part as follows: "Esperanto is an artificial language invented by the Russian Doctor L. L. Zamenhof, Warsaw, Poland. It has only one object in view, namely, to serve as an international auxiliary language; it is not in the least intended to replace the national languages. The first book in the new language was published in 1887. The Esperanto words are mostly of Latin, but to some extent also of Anglo-German origin, so that at the first glance Esperanto has the appearance of a Roman language. The great success of Esperanto, which is now known and studied all over the world, is chiefly due to the facility with which it may be mastered. The pronunciation is strictly phonetic, making the study of spelling unnecessary. The grammar does not admit of any exceptions to the rules, and it is so logical and simple that it may be learned completely in a few hours by any person who is familiar with the grammar of his mother tongue. The vocabulary consists of about 2,500 root words, a large majority of which is known to any one whose language contains a great number of Latin roots, for instance, English. In spite of this small number of root words Esperanto has been made rich in words and expressions by the adoption of certain affixes and certain methods of word combination. By these simple and easy means a considerable vocabulary may be obtained. Esperanto is a well-sounding language when spoken. While in Canada, Mexico, and South America Esperanto has been zealously studied, for many years it was almost unknown in the United States, until 1905. In the beginning of that year the first society for the study and propagation of Esperanto was formed in Boston, and the following July the New York Esperanto Society was founded. The meetings of the New York society take place every Friday evening at 80 East 116th Street. Andrew Kangas, 1,061 Prospect Avenue, New York, is Secretary."

Published: August 9, 1908

OPERA IN ESPERANTO.

Also Sir Purdon Clarke Is in Berlin and Doctors There Are Ill Paid.

Special Cable to THE NEW YORK TIMES.

BERLIN, Aug. 15.—Several Americans will attend the congress opening on Aug. 22, at which the Dresden Royal Opera will perform Goethe's " Iphigenie in Tauris " in Esperanto. The cast includes Miss Reicher of New York.

Opera in Esperanto

Special Cable to THE NEW YORK TIMES

BERLIN, Aug. 15.—Several Americans will attend the congress opening on Aug. 22, at which the Dresden Royal Opera will perform Goethe's "Iphigenie in Tauris" in Esperanto. The cast includes Miss Reicher of New York. ...

Published: August 16, 1908

Esperanto Congress Meets

1,800 Persons in Dresden Join in Singing Esperanto Hymn

DRESDEN, Aug. 17—The fourth International Esperanto Congress was formally opened here to-day, with 1,800 persons in attendance singing the Esperanto Hymn. The delegates were welcomed by representatives of King Frederick August of Saxony and of the municipality.

Dr. Zamenhof, the inventor of the Esperanto language, made an address on the ideals of Esperanto. The United States is represented at the congress by Major Paul H. Straub of the army Medical Corps.

Published: August 18, 1908

Tolstoy to Esperantists

Sends Letter to Congress—
New Language Making Great Progress in Japan

DRESDEN, Aug. 18.—A greeting from Count Leo Tolstoy was read to-day to the members of the fourth International Congress

TOLSTOY TO ESPERANTISTS.

Sends Letter to Congress—New Language Making Great Progress in Japan.

DRESDEN, Aug. 18.—A greeting from Count Leo Tolstoy was read to-day to the members of the fourth International Congress of Esperantists, who are now in session in this city. Invitations to hold next year's meeting in Japan and the United States have been received by the congress.

Of the 175 new societies reported to the congress, ten are in the United States and five in the Philippine Islands. The total of esperantist societies in the United States, old and new, is sixty-six.

The Japanese delegates declared to-day that extraordinary progress had been made with Esperanto in Japan, where Count Hayashi, former Foreign Minister, had accepted the honorary Presidency of the local association. In a letter to his countrymen the Count had called Esperanto the "gospel of the world."

Twenty-four members of the Dresden police force learned the Esperanto language in order to be of assistance to the delegates to the congress.

---

of Esperantists, who are now in session in this city. Invitations to hold next year's meeting in Japan and the United States have been received by the congress.

Of the 175 new societies reported to the congress, ten are in the United States and five in the Philippine Islands. The total of esperantist societies in the United States, old and new, is sixty-six.

The Japanese delegates declared to-day that extraordinary progress had been made with Esperanto in Japan, where Count Hayashi, former Foreign Minister, had accepted the honorary Presidency of the local association. In a letter to his countrymen the Count had called Esperanto the "gospel of the world."

Twenty-four members of the Dresden police force learned the Esperanto language in order to be of assistance to the delegates to the congress.

Published: August 19, 1908

Books in Esperanto for the Blind

DRESDEN, Aug. 19.—The Esperantists, who are holding their fourth international congress here, have decided to publish books in Esperanto for the blind and to prepare proper exhibits to give information relative to Esperanto.

Published: August 20, 1908

Views of Readers

Esperanto

New York Times Saturday Review of Books:

I have noted with great pleasure and interest the remarks of several of your readers on reforms in Esperanto in your issues of July 11th and 18th, and beg to extend to you my sincere thanks for opening your columns to the discussion of this question at such a very opportune moment. I was particularly pleased with the frank statements of W. J. P. on the general situation, which describes the state of affairs exactly.

Ever since the resignation of Dr. Talmey from the Presidency of the New York Esperanto Society, some eight months ago, Esperanto papers have been lauding this group as an example of fidelity to that most holy of books, the Fundamento, pointing to the action of Dr. Talmey as an awful warning to all those traitors, rebels, conspirators, and archenemies of the International Language, who so much as dared to think for themselves, but being careful to maintain a strict silence on the question of reforms or to explain what those proposed reforms were. Strangely enough, they have utterly ignored the fact that the writer, Dr. Talmey's successor, shared the identical views regarding reforms which he started unequivocally when elected to the Presidency, and that he has ever openly insisted on the necessity of changes and additions in Esperanto to make it a more effective and accurate instrument of intercomprehension for scientists, diplomats, travelers, and merchants having foreign relations, instead of a mere "bungle-tongue" for the use of a few amateur collectors of postal cards, which is the only practical use to which it has hitherto been put. Moreover, the society in one of its recent meetings frankly and unanimously approved of the tolerant and liberal declaration of Michaux, the founder of the first International Esperanto Congress, which concedes to all the right to examine other competing universal language projects and to discuss them and urges the immediate institution of a "reprezentantaro," or representative body, to be elected by the Esperantists of the world, which in turn will elect from the membership and from among eminent philologists, scientists, and authors of other international languages an "Esperanto Akademio," to which all projects of reforms can be submitted and which alone will have the authority to recommend (never to force upon any one) such reforms as it deems of utility. Moreover, the society stated that it has never been opposed to reforms per se, but to those introduced by private individuals. The New York group formally denied the authority of the present "Lingva Komitato," (Linguistic Committee) or any other body claiming to represent the Esperantists; neither did it recognize the right of any congress to force reforms upon any one or demand allegiance to some established standard, as those present at such conventions did not substitute a body properly elected and representative, but solely represented those having the time and funds to attend.

In spite of these facts, conservative papers continued to cite our society as an example of "either submit or get out," using this occurrence as a cudgel with which to thump the more timid members of the various groups into subscribing to oaths of allegiance to a book which, mistakes and all, was arbitrarily fixed upon as a standard by a few commercial interests, deviation from which meant an injury to the sale of their publications. Ever since the Congress of Boulogne the Author of Esperanto, Dr. Zamenhof who, while admittedly a very lovable character, is of apparently weak and yielding nature, has been in the hands of a few "Pontiffs," who have used him as a mouth piece for issuing various ukases enjoining faithfulness to established traditions and branding all who dared to criticize the present "bungle-tongue" as "conspirators," "traitors," "rebels," and urging them to ignore the reformers. In fact, nothing has been left undone to make the international language ridiculous in the eyes of the public. An international religion has been established, a fictitious monetary system instituted, various Esperanto republics have been projected and the audacious statement made that the Esperantists of the world already constitute a real nation, with "nia kara majstro" Zamenhof as quasi king and the green flag as our standard. Beautiful promises have been made that a common tongue would make all pugnacious peoples throw away their weapons and join in a brotherly embrace, realizing at least the prophecy of the old Hebrew prophet whereby the lion and the cow would be satisfied with a vegetarian dinner of hay and the wolf and the lamb no more quarrel about drinking water. What a pity that the beautiful Spanish tongue has not yet succeeded in pacifying the scrappy little Central American republics, in spite of its being the common language of them all!

I want to warn the conservatives that the reformers are after them. Our textbooks and official organ are already on sale by one of the largest bookdealers in New York, and new books are constantly coming out. The Marquis de Beaufront, their greatest leader, turns out to be Ido, the chief reformer; their best men are constantly joining our ranks. They threaten to force all who refuse to take the oath of allegiance to the Fundamento to resign. That's good! Pluck out your eyes! Throw away your brains! We want them! You may try to maintain "a united front" for a short while longer, but you are rotten at the core and a comparison by the disinterested public of the merits of the two systems, Primitive and Simplified Esperanto, will infallibly result in a decision in favor of a language which contains an unpronounceable sound, variable adjective, perplexing accusative, or accented letters which render the printing of the language in any ordinary paper impossible. The new Esperanto boasts of a regular system of derivation and a much richer vocabulary, the latter based not as in Primitive Esperanto on the personal caprice of an author, but on the fixed rule of the minimum of internationality, thus making it readily understandable by any educated person without previous study. Thanks to the help of the scientists in the delegation and on the committee, Simplified Esperanto is the only international idiom likely to be some day adopted by all Governments and introduced into the schools of all civilized countries.

Andrew Kangas
President of the N. Y. Esperanto Society
New York, Aug. 15

Published: August 22, 1908

Views of Readers

New York Times Saturday Review of Books:

Let me make a suggestion in regard to a "universal language." Esperanto is an absurdity; it only adds one more to the present Babel. As for Latin, its complicated inflections render it entirely unfit for the purpose. Few college graduates after seven or eight years' study can speak it.

There is only one language that can ever become universal; that is English. It is understood now to some extent by about half the people in the civilized world: that saves half the trouble in the first place. Except for the matter of spelling it is the easiest language to learn. It is almost entirely free from grammatic inflections. Now I suggest that for the purpose of a world language those few be dropped and the spelling made phonetic. This would be, of course, very much like the "Pidgin English" of the Orient, easy to learn and generally understood. It would probably simplify the matter if the Continental sounds of the vowels were to be adopted. If the Universal Language Society were to issue some primers of instruction in this modified and simplified English it would meet the problem in the most practical way. This does not imply a modification of the language for home consumption; only for informational use.

Rummede
Wallingford, Penn., Aug. 18

Published: August 22, 1908

Esperanto Congress Here

One of Next Year's Sessions Is to be Held at Chautaqua, N. Y.

DRESDEN, Aug. 22.—The fourth Esperanto Congress, which has been in session in this city for a week past, came to an end to-day. Before adjournment it was decided to hold two congresses in 1909, one at Chautaqua, N. Y., and the other at Barcelona, Spain. It is presumed that the leading spirit in this movement for the adoption of a new language will visit both conferences.

Hundreds of the delegates from Europe, who might not be able to go to America, will be able to attend and derive advantage from meeting at Barcelona.

Published: August 23, 1908

Simplified Esperanto

New York Times Saturday Review of Books:

The communication from Mr. Kangas, President of the New York Esperanto Society, which you printed in your issue of the 22d, is very interesting reading.

As he says, it would seem that Dr. Zamenhof has allowed his better judgment to be overruled by the ring of "pontiffs" which absolutely controls the "regular" or "orthodox" Esperantists, does their thinking for them, and only permits them to know what it (the ring) considers promotive of its own interests—wholly commercial. Dr. Zamenhof has made repeated efforts to reform his language, but in each instance has yielded to the pressure of this ring and its commercial interests in the sale of the existing stock of textbooks, translations, &c., the aggregate of which is quite formidable. In the last number of the reformist organ, "Progreso," Prof. Otto Jespersen, probably one of the first linguists of our times, who is a member of the "Konstanta Komisitaro" of the "Delegation," says (in Simplified Esperanto):

We are convinced that if we could imagine the impossible situation, that Dr. Zamenhof could now commence the labor of his youth, enriched by the experiences which he now possesses and free from all that which ties him now to the old form of his language, then he would create undoubtedly (a) language very much resembling that which we recommend. It suffices, in order to become convinced of that, to consider the proposals of changes which he himself made in 1894, in 1896, and in the commencement of 1908, proposals which his adherents did everything to suppress, not discussing them even, and which show in the manner the most honorable that he does not think that his "primitive" language can not or must not be improved.

In the limited amount of misinformation about the reform project, which the "pontiffs" allow the "fideli" (faithful) to receive, the claim is constantly made that the new words are much longer than the corresponding ones in the old language. Now the English is one of the shortest, if not the very shortest, of the natural languages; but the above citation shows that simplified Esperanto is shorter than the English, and we also claim that it is shorter than Primitive Esperanto. Some of the words, of course, are longer, but so many others are shorter that the net balance is considerably in favor of the reformed tongue.

W. J. P.
Brooklyn, Aug. 26

Published: August 29, 1908

Views of Readers

Scientific Technology

New York Times Saturday Review of Books:

English, Latin, and Esperanto, simplified or regular, have all been proposed by your correspondents as suitable for a world language. Yet no one of them can be used in such a way as to simplify the polysyllabic terms of scientific nomenclature, although the progress of civilization is constantly increasing the number of words in our dictionaries. It is certainly not the deliberate intention of scientists to inscribe "Procul, O procul este" over the portals of their temple;

but any language built on wornout root-words must remain as inadequate a vehicle of thought as a wheelbarrow would be if used to transplant the wheat crops of Kansas to the Eastern markets.

E. P. Foster
Cincinnati, Sept. 1

Published: September 5, 1908

Views of Readers

Wants Esperanto Unchanged

New York Times Saturday Review of Books:

Of the many communications relative to Esperanto, which have appeared in your valued paper, many have been interesting and instructive, some quite amusing, and others so framed as to cause false impressions on the mind of your readers. We are amused when "Veritas" emphatically insists that Latin should be the universal language, and we are led to conclude that either he knows nothing about that language or else thinks, dreams, and lives in Latin to the exclusion of everything else.

Replying to those who favor English as the universal language, we are certainly in accord with that view if there were any possibility of simplifying it and having it universally adopted. A radical way of simplifying English would be for the Governments of the different English-speaking countries to appoint and employ suitable persons who would meet in conference and change the spelling of all necessary words so that our language would be absolutely phonetic, simple, and clear, and then print and sell at a low price dictionaries comparing the simplified language with our present tongue. By vigorous work, such a plan might be carried out, but what would happen in the transition period between its introduction and complete adoption almost baffles the mind to imagine. The gradual simplifying of English may be accomplished, but from present appearances a great many years will be required to do this. Even if English is simplified and rendered phonetic, the very many vowel signs required will still make the language complex and difficult for foreigners to master. To those recommending the adoption of English as a universal language, we will ask what would be the reply of prominent representatives of France, Germany, Italy, and Spain if asked whether English is not best adapted for a world language. We are sure that each country would have strong reasons for showing that English is not the best suited language for international communication. The question of national jealousy would of itself prevent the adoption of any modern language for universal purposes.

All the points above mentioned have been freely discussed at different times, but the one communication above all which should be answered promptly by Esperantists is that of Mr. Andrew Kangas, which appeared in the issue of Aug. 22. If Mr. Kangas actually believes what he has said he is no longer an Esperantist because he is not following the instructions of the many different Esperanto books now published. He is not an Esperantist any more than a person who has devised a language consisting of partly English and partly French and who speaks the same could be considered an English-speaking person.

If the members of Mr. Kangas's society are Esperantists, he has no right to sign himself President of the "New York Esperanto Society," because such would indicate that he is voicing the opinion of its members. If the members of his society are not Esperantists, he certainly should not have used the word "Esperanto" at all, but "Ido," or that word best expressing his particular hybrid language.

In this world there is always someone ready and anxious to detract from the beauty and glory of some great achievement. Such a person is the Marquis de Beaufront, who gave up his own international language, learned Esperanto, and then making certain changes that he thought would appeal to French linguists, made a language which he called "Ido." Next year someone will probably change "Ido." Any sensible person can see that no international language can be a success under such rapidly changing conditions. The followers of Ido can go on as they please and remodel their language as often as they please, but they have no right to represent themselves as Esperantists or interfere in any way with Esperanto, which is rapidly growing throughout the world. Within a short time, it has been adopted as a means of international communication by the Good Templars, Red Cross Societies, Christian Endeavor, and some large business firms.

If the world thought that Esperanto was continually being changed in accordance with the whims of language cranks, the great faith which individuals and societies have in it would soon be shattered.

The vital principles of Esperanto do not change, and so Europe believes in it, Japan believes in it, Chautauqua believes in it, and gladly extends a welcome hand to the Fifth International Congress, which will be held there in 1909.

With such a bright future it is perhaps no wonder that the disappointed followers of Ido are trying to assert themselves on all occasions with the vain hope of being heard, and they are the ones who are doing practically all the talking; and such talking, quoting from Mr. Kangas: "Pluck out your eyes, throw away your brains," shows the frenzied condition of their minds.

Many of the wide departures from Esperanto which are found in the so-called "Ido" are unimportant; some positively disfigure the language, and while the inflection changes would be acceptable to the English and French, yet they would not be to the Germans and others. A change, therefore, would stir up strife, which Esperantists will not do.

Esperantists are every ready to have their language discussed, and we are grateful to THE TIMES for giving so much space to this subject, because we know that when your readers become sufficiently interested to look over Esperanto instruction books they cannot help being impressed with the merits and beauty of the language.

Henry W. Fisher
President of the Pittsburg Esperanto Society
Pittsburg, Sept. 1

Published: September 5, 1908

Views of Our Readers

The Esperanto Oligarchy

New York Times Saturday Review of Books:

It is encouraging to see that at least one of the faithful is willing to enter the arena in defense of the cause of Esperanto netuŝebla. The writer remembers seeing somewhere something about doing unto others that which we would have them do unto us; but Mr. Fisher does not seem to believe in this. He is willing to change the English, but wants Esperanto let alone. Pro quo? Or, as he would say, with Dr. Zamenhoff, "Kial"? Is not "primitive" Esperanto in need of simplification? Does not our own language show that a special ending for the accusative is needed in but very few cases? Does one need a plural or an accusative form for the adjective? We say "good dogs," but Esperanto says, in substance, "goods dogs." We say, "I have a black dog"; Esperanto says, "I have a blackn dogn." For "I have two black dogs," their equivalent is "I have two blaksn dogsn." Pro quo? "Kial"? Because (Pro ke - "ĉar") the present Esperanto literature, dictionaries, and textbooks contain these forms, and those books are for sale.

Mr. Fisher says Mr. Kangas has no right to call himself an Esperantist. The "Declaration of Boulogne," which established the doctrine of the "untouchable Fundamento," defines "Esperantismo" as "the effort to spread in the whole world the use of a neutral human language ... which would give to the men of different nations the possibility of intercomprehension." According to that declaration, any one trying to spread a neutral human language is an Esperantist — whether his hobby is the language of Zamenhof, Ro*, or any of the others. Cannot one advocate changes in the Constitution of the United States and still retain his citizenship? An Esperantist, in the language of the Declaration, is "one who hopes" that we will some time have an auxiliary universal language. But that language has not yet been developed, and Dr. Zamenhof's proposal will have to compete with its rivals.

Dr. Zamenhof "discovered" the principle upon which the coming international "artificial" language must be constructed—the maximum of internationality. In other words, such a language is not to be created, à priore, but already exists, at least rudimentarily, in our modern languages. By selecting words having the greatest internationality, and applying the principles which the evolution of our languages justifies and establishes, we hope finally to produce an idiom containing all possible difficulties and irregularities. Simplified Esperanto is certainly a long step forward in that direction.

The present "orthodox" Esperanto movement is not so much a language movement as an oath-bound international society, ruled, unfortunately, by an oligarchy, with Dr. Zamenhof as a figurehead. They call him, sacrilegiously, the Master, have their sacred book, the "Fundamento"; their creed of "netuŝebleco," their Sanhedrin, "The Central Office." Excommunication is the lot of all heretics, and if they could re-establish the Inquisition they would "jump at the chance." Such a movement will never become universal, and those who expect to see the language which it advocates adopted by the Governments and taught in the schools and colleges will, before long, I think, see the futility of their efforts.

W. J. P.
Brooklyn, N. Y., Sept. 10

Published: September 12, 1908

* Ro is a language project by Edward Powell Foster published in 1906.

Views of the Readers

Irish a Possible World Language

New York Times Saturday Review of Books:

I have been reading with much interest the letters in THE NEW YORK TIMES SATURDAY REVIEW OF BOOKS on the subject of a universal language. The advocates of Esperanto, (both reformed and unregenerate,) of Ido, French, German, and Latin, have all urged cogent reasons in behalf of their favorite tongues, but not one of them has advanced any claims such as may be made for Irish as a universal speech. ...

... Irish is not as simple as Esperanto, but it is no less logical, and it is far more concise, clear, and expressive. For these reasons I advocate the claims of Irish as a universal language.

John E. O'Malley
2,341 Birney Avenue, Scranton, Penn., Sept. 8

Published: September 12, 1908

Theatrical Notes

Augusta Reusch, who arrived yesterday on the Deutschland, acted in Esperanto the role of Iphegenia in Dresden on Aug. 19. She comes to this country to fill an engagement at the German Theatre, Madison Avenue and Fifty-ninth Street. ...

Published: September 18, 1908

Drift of London Literary Gossip

Esperanto Dictionary

...
Esperanto seems to be getting on. We now have "The English-Esperanto Dictionary," published by The Fleming H. Revell Company, an octavo volume of over 600 pages, prepared by Joseph Rhodes, a Fellow of the British Esperanto Association. This work is based

upon the "Fundamento," the Esperanto literature of which there is now a very considerable volume, and the several National Esperanto dictionaries that bear the "aprobo" of Dr Zamenhof. Appended to the dictionary is a vocabulary of geographical names, and another of personal namers.

...

Published: September 19, 1908

Views of Readers

The Irish Language

New York Times Saturday Review of Books:

Perhaps all the objections to Irish as an international language are embraced in the fact that Irish is a national language. The qualities which an Irishman most admires in it may be the very qualities which a foreigner would find most unnatural. As to the order of words, for instance, Mr. O'Malley writes: "The verb, the soul of the sentence, impatiently assumes the first place, its logical position. In fact, Irish is the most logical of languages." In answer to this claim it is only necessary to say, as did M. Michel Bréal with reference to the French phrase: "Every nation is tempted to think that it alone places its words in their true position. One can easily, without being wanting in logic, conceive a different order." One may employ almost any order in Esperanto and still be understood.

John Ed. Hearn
New York, Sept. 14

Published: September 19, 1908

Views of Readers

An Orthodox Esperantist

New York Times Saturday Review of Books:

The death blow to Volapük was the internal dissensions among its adherents. They attempted so many improvements upon the language that their quarrels brought about its downfall.

Unconsciously and unintentionally, perhaps, this is just what the reformers and simplifiers are striving to do with Esperanto. Esperanto can be killed in only one way, and that is by lack of unity among its followers.

We will grant, for the moment, that the reforms advocated are good and valuable ones, but, however good they may be, they are unimportant when compared with the value of unity among our ranks.

"W. J. P." cites the apparent absurdity of the plural adjective and the accusative case. He knows this will appear as a popular contention among English-speaking people, but he can take almost any of the national languages and prepare an equally popular argument against it. Esperanto is not for the English-speaking people alone, but for a universal instrument, and it has shown itself well fitted for the office. These features of which "W. J. P." complains are the very secret of the immense spread of Esperanto among nations foreign to us. Further he complains that excommunication is meted out to all heretics. He is indeed right. A heretic ceases to be an Esperantist, and, come to think of it, I know of a religious organization that has followed this policy of excommunication for several hundred years, and the stability and strength of that organization to-day certainly speaks well for the policy pursued.

Harry H. Pratley
New York, Sept. 15

Published: September 19, 1908

Electronic Wonders Show at Garden

Cows Are Milked and Chickens Hatched by Electricity at the Commemorative Exhibit

Speeches by Phonograph

Gov. Hughes Opens the Exhibition with a Machine as His Mouthpiece — Thomas A. Edison Also Heard

They are milking cows and hatching out chickens now down at Madison Square Garden, where the second annual Electrical Show began last night for a run of ten days. They are doing simple and complicated, old and new things with electricity. Gov. Hughes opened the show last night with a speech by way of an electrically driven phonograph.

The Esperanto Association of North America is holding forth at Madison Square Garden, too, and will be there every night the show goes on, if any sort of interest is shown in the new language of all men. Just what connection Esperanto has with electricity was explained by the man at the door of the concert hall in the Garden last night in this way:

"Electricity is the quickest and most modern force of its kind. Esperanto is the quickest and most modern language. You see why we are here. Whenever there is an airship convention we shall be there. We must be at the front.

"Quick? Esperanto is lightning quick. You hear that man in there making a speech? He is Arthur Baker of Chicago. The audience is enjoying itself, thinking it's getting a fine humorous lecture. When that audience comes out of there he will have slipped into their heads so that they can't forget them more Esperanto words and phrases than they could pick up in two years studying French. That's how quick it is."

Mrs. S. Rhodes even sang in Esperanto.

To come back to the Electrical Show, the programme says that it commemorates the first fifty years of transatlantic communication by cable, and also the passage of the first twenty-five years of electrical service in New York ...

Published: October 4, 1908

Universal Tongue Needed, Says Mr. Wu

Chinese Minister Makes This the Keynote of Speech at the King's Birthday Dinner

The annual King's birthday dinner of the British Schools and Universities Club was held last night in the large banqueting hall of Delmonico's. It was artistically decorated with American and British flags, palms, and chrysanthemums. The dais was covered with scarlet cloth, and at the back of the President's chair the American and British flags were draped with the imperial Chinese dragon in honor of the presence of Wu Ting-fang, the Chinese Minister to Washington. ...

... After the toasts of the President of the United States and King Edward VII. had been drunk standing with the singing of the National anthems, "The Star-Spangled Banner" and "God Save the King," Wu Ting-Fang responded to the toast, "China."

"I was very fortunate," said Mr. Wu, "in having had an English education, which I received in Hongkong and completed in London, where I studied law and was admitted to the bar of Lincoln's Inn the same day as the present Prime Minister of Great Britain. ...

... Life is too short with all the new inventions for us to learn five or six languages besides our own. We should have a universal language which could be agreed upon by all nations and that would be a splendid medium for doing away with all friction, domestic or foreign, that might arise in the future.

"I would like to see the Chinese language made universal, but as that is impossible, and the nations cannot agree on Esperanto, I think that the English language would meet the exigencies of the case very well.

"English is a sound language, but it needs a little improving in spelling and pronunciation.

"Language is the best medium for friendly relations, and I feel sure that a universal tongue would result in an intercommercial and intellectual alliance among all the great nations of the world."

...

Published: November 10, 1908

Topics of the Times

Language and Interests

Minister Wu, after his humorous fashion, exaggerated the benefit to be expected of a universal language when he said that "it would be a splendid medium for doing away with all friction between nations that might arise in the future," but he was undoubtedly right in calling it a convenience in that it would obviate the necessity for anybody to learn more than one language in addition to his own.

Everybody admits that, but somehow the universal language idea really appeals only to a rather small group of enthusiasts and other people remain content with the ability to wag their tongues as their mothers taught them. The Chinese diplomat evidently has no great hope for the general adoption of Esperanto, and half hinted—being in an English-speaking country—that English would or might spread all over the world in time. That is a pleasant dream—for us, but it is not very popular in other lands with languages of their own, and its realization will not be for many a day after days cease to interest anybody now alive.

Diversity of speech is probably less of a bar to international friendship and understanding than the theorizers assume. It separates human beings much less than does diversity of interest, and no universal language would put an end to that.

Published: November 11, 1908

More Than a Million People Are Using Esperanto

Some Interesting Facts Brought Out at the Dresden Congress Show Growth of an Artificial Language

The fourth International Congress of Esperantists assembled this year at Dresden. Those who composed the congress are the adherents of the new universal language, which they call Esperanto.

In the Dresden gathering, which held its sessions from Aug. 16 to Aug. 22, there was no evidence of any diminution in the enthusiasm of those enrolled among the Esperantists, or in the rapidity with which the new medium of communication is spreading throughout the world. The press of Germany notes a vitality in this artificial language which leads to a general recognition of its practical value and of its adaptation to meet the logical demands as an auxiliary to the current tongues of mankind.

There was, in fact, much enthusiasm in the gathering of delegates, 1,200 in number, from all parts of the world. The gathering elicited an unusual amount of sympathetic interest in the city where it met and throughout Germany. The Emperor sent a special greeting. The King of Saxony accepted the position of its protector, and placed at its service the Royal Opera House for the production of a drama in Esperanto, and in other directions evidenced his appreciation of the purpose of the gathering. The City of Dresden showed an exceptional degree of cordiality and hospitality in welcoming the guests. A score of policemen had been drilled in advance to a fluent use of the language, and with distinctive badges were constantly at the service of the delegates.

In the congress itself as high a degree of differentiation was reached as is ordinarily found in the gatherings of great scientific bodies. A few general sessions were held, but the bulk of the work was done by the various sections devoted to some particular phase of the multiple interests now connected with the growth and usefulness of Esperanto.

The following briefly summarizes the results of the congress and portrays the position occupied in the world to-day by Esperanto, as shown by the reports from the various countries represented.

The number of those using the language is now a million or more. Of organized societies and groups there are about 1,000, an increase of 30 per cent. since the close of 1907. The countries leading in the movement are: France, with 193 groups; the United Kingdom, 145; Spain, 84; Germany, 72; the United States, 66; Switzerland, 40; Austria, 46; Sweden, 39. There are now ninety special and professional Esperanto societies, including six women's clubs, artisans' unions, policemen's societies, temperance organizations, &c.

In July the number of periodicals published in Esperanto numbered fifty-five. This is an increase of eleven during the preceding six months. Most of these journals are monthlies. The majority are for the purpose of propaganda. Some are for the international use of specialists, physicians, chemists, police, religious and secret organizations, &c.

Public recognition of the language is steadily advancing. The Postmaster General of the United Kingdom has admitted Esperanto on the same footing as modern European languages for use in telegraphing; the committee of the Jubilee Exhibition at Prague issues its circulars in Esperanto, as in other languages; Count Hayashi, the Japanese Minister of Foreign Affairs, has accepted the Presidency of the Japanese Esperanto Association and has advised his countrymen in a public letter to master the language. In Germany general attention is awakened to its value in connection with international trade. Various firms issue price lists and catalogues in Esperanto.

Much attention is being devoted to the standard translation of the Bible, intending particularly for missionary work. The section in charge of this feature reports that the Psalms are now in print, and that most of the New Testament is ready for the press. Short portions of the Old Testament have been published, but the greater portion of the translation is still to be accomplished and is in the hands of scholars.

Numerous delegates from Red Cross societies were united in a section which advocates strongly the value of Esperanto for ambulance service and in general connection with the activities of this preeminently international organization. An equal degree of importance was given to the usefulness of the language in police service.

The medical and legal sections are engaged actively in perfecting the nomenclature of their professions. The stenographers have formulated schemes for the official shorthand system of Esperanto, which will be laid before the next international stenographic congress at Rouen.

Great weight was laid upon the value of Esperanto for the blind. Books in raised letters are exceedingly costly, largely on account of the limited demand. It is hoped that by the general introduction of Esperanto for use by the blind the number of publications available for their use can be notably increased and the cost incident to publication in the several languages be correspondingly lessened.

The sentiment of the great majority of the congress was opposed to any innovation or alteration in the accepted standards at present, and opinion was decided that Esperanto, as now constituted, must be left to the natural play of the laws of evolution, as they will make themselves felt in course of time.

Much interest centered about the production of Goethe's classic drama, "Iphigenie," in the Royal Opera House. The translation of the latter had ben made by Dr. Zamenhof, the inventor of Esperanto, and the play was presented by some of Germany's best actors. It awakened much enthusiasm among the representatives of over a score of nations, able to enjoy a masterpiece of German poetic thought in a linguistic garb common to them all. Critics of the production state that, while the words have much of musical value, on account of the prevalence of vowel terminations, still there is manifest difficulty in approaching the harmonious flow and rhythm of Goethe's verse.

Published: November 15, 1908

Give Up Esperanto, Will Now Speak Elo *

Members of New York Society Decide That Esperanto is an Impossible Language

Say It is Full of Defects

They Vote to Take Up Elo in its Place — Col. Harvey Defends the One They Abandon

Although Esperanto has been hailed as the coming world-tongue for several years on both sides of the Atlantic, with the Young Men's Christian Association conducting classes in it, and Col. George B. Harvey giving much space to its promulgation in his North American Review, the officers of the New York Esperanto Society have decided that Esperanto is as faulty as Volapuk, its predecessor, was found to be twenty years ago.

At the last meeting of the society on Nov. 19 the members, who have dwindled down from several hundred to fifteen, voted unanimously that Esperanto was too full of logical defects to be worth wasting any more time on. They decided to take up in its place the study of Elo, another international language brought forward by the Marquis L. de Beaufront at the meeting of the Committee of the International Language Delegation in Paris in October, 1907.

Officers of the New York Esperanto Society pointed out yesterday that the discredit into which the international language has fallen was not local, but worldwide. They showed recent depreciating articles written about the language by such former enthusiasts as L. de Guesnet, formerly editor of the Paris Esperanto organ, Tra La Mondo; Henry J. Strutton, formerly Secretary of The London Progresso; the Marquis L. de Beaufront, Dr. L. Couturat, P. L. Meyer of Dresden, R. Auerbach of Dresden, O. H. Meyer of Chicago, and Dr. J. R. Harger of Seattle, all of whom were leaders in the Esperanto movement in Europe five years ago, and the movement three years ago here.

Among the leading New York City Esperantists who think the language is not practical are A. Kangas of 920 Longwood Avenue, the Bronx, the present President of the New York Esperanto Society, and Dr. Max Talmey of 55 West 126th Street, who was the original organizer of the New York Esperanto Society and was its President up to a year ago.

President Kangas himself introduced the resolution at the society's meeting last Thursday to give up Esperanto and take up Elo.

Dr. Talmey, the original New York City Esperantist, who resigned from the society last year because he became disgusted with Esperanto, said yesterday that it was so illogically constructed that, in his experience, "students of Esperanto were unable to write even a few lines or speak a few words of it correctly after several years' study." He added that the Esperanto fad, in his judgment, was doing considerable harm in inducing young men to study it instead of German, Spanish, or other practical present-day languages.

"Esperanto contains sounds unpronounceable by many nations," he said. "It has no logical system of derivation. Instead, many words, like everything, for example, are formed arbitrarily. It is extremely poor in root words. But its greatest defect is that it lacks facility for study.

"The accusative case and declension of adjectives makes it much too difficult for persons of average education, and especially of English nationality. The Esperantists of this country are unable even to write a few lines correctly, and can only stammer a few phrases."

When Col. Harvey, President of the National Esperanto Society, was told last night about the schism of the New York Society, he said:

"I know nothing about the local society. But the National Esperanto movement is constantly growing. The National Society has 2,000 members, and the North American Review's Society has 2,000 more. I should judge there were about 6,000 other Esperantists scattered through the country. The North American will certainly continue to advocate Esperanto. The International Esperanto Congress will be held here next year."

Published: November 27, 1908

* Elo seems to be Ido (cf. the second paragraph of the article: During the meeting of the Committee of the International Language Delegation, 1907, Beaufront presented Ido).

Talk Elo? Absurd!

Real, True Blue Esperantists Scorn the Secessionists

Esperantists of New York said yesterday that they were surprised at the statements made by individuals who professed that they have found a substitute for Esperanto, as recorded in yesterday's TIMES. They said it in just that way.

One of the editors of The North American Review, who has made a study of Esperanto, further remarked:

"Elo, or whatever they call their alleged substitute, is a sort of telegraphic code rather than a language. Marquis de Beaufront, the originator, was jealous of Dr. Zamendorf, the author of Esperanto, and is therefore promulgating a new, half-baked idea of very small intrinsic value. The New York followers of Beaufront are malcontents who, as officers of the New York Esperanto Society, were deemed failures by the promoters of Esperanto. So, naturally, they turned 'agin the government.' They are not people of great importance. The New York Esperanto Society, which is a flourishing institution, would have nothing to do with them.

"There are now perhaps half a million persons speaking Esperanto in the world. So simple is it that at the last congress in Dresden many of the 2,000 delegates were Esperantists of only a few weeks' standing, and yet they spoke the language fluently and easily participated in the proceedings.

"Among the delegates at Dresden were Gen. Sebert and Prof. Boirac, Rector of the University of Dijon; Felix Moscheles, the artist and peace apostle; Prof. Geillon of Philadelphia, Prof. D. O. S. Lowell of Boston, Col. John Pollen, C. B., of London, and many others. Elo has very few followers *if importance."

Published: November 28, 1908

A Few Points for Aspiring Rhymesters

There are Several Knotty Problems in English Rhyme, but Some Simple Rules Conquer Them

...

Returning to the statistics, it is worth while to observe how suffixes and inflections affect the availability of an English word for rhyming purposes. Verbs which end in -ate, like agitate and educate, are the most pliant, for their roots suffer the least change as the inflections alter. The various forms of educate, for instance, are rhymable in this order: (educatee,) education, educates, educatest, educate, educated, educating, educator, educative, educateth.

And as to the word rhyme itself, though it has not more than thirty actual rhymes, including "I'm," it is misspelled. It should be "rime," a correction which has nothing whatever to do with the efforts of the Simplified Spelling Board to make it so, for the mistake arose at its birth from confusion with the word rhythm. Rhymes first came into existence in English about the time of the troubadours, but the Chinese, the Hindus, and the Arabs have used them for many ages. Rhymes please the eye as well as the ear, though less frequently, and will doubtless continue to be popular so long as words exist. Esperanto, the international auxiliary language, is rich in them, and its rhymed literature, both translation and original, contains some attractive lilts.

Published: December 6, 1908

Esperantists All Aroused

They Rally to the Defense of Their Pet Universal Language

Aroused by the recent charges of Ex-President Max Talmey of the New York Esperanto Society that Esperanto is a philological joke, and that it is rapidly becoming as dead as Volapük, Esperantists throughout the United States are rallying to the support of their pet universal language.

"The aim of Esperanto is to furnish a practical international auxiliary language suitable for general correspondence and conversation between people of different nationalities," said Councilor Henry D. King of the New York Division of the Esperanto Association of North America yesterday. "Its grammar can be learned in an hour.

"A month's study should give the average English-speaking person a fair grasp of the language. Two hundred books have been printed in it. It is already known to over 500,000 people. An Esperanto grammar and root vocabulary is so small that it can be carried in the waistcoat pocket."

The Esperanto Bulletin for January will quote a statement from Secretary Edwin C. Reed of the North American Esperanto Association to the effect that in the last three months the membership of the association has multiplied six times.

"These are merely some more of the absurd and exaggerated claims which the panic-stricken Esperantists are making," was the comment of Dr. Talmey, now Treasurer of the New York Ilo* Society. "Five hundred thousand people may know of Esperanto, but I defy any one to tell me the whereabouts of 500,000 people who can speak or write the language. Its grammar is so difficult that, far from being conquerable in an hour, officers of the society write me ungrammatical letters in it after years of study."

Dr. Talmey's attacks on Esperanto are, he says, due to the conviction that a great number of young men are wasting a great deal of time studying it when they might better be learning Italian, Spanish, or some practical modern language. He has written, he said yesterday, a complete criticism of the language's philological defects, which will soon appear in a Western magazine.

Published: December 28, 1908

* Cf. the note on page 121. Both Elo and Ilo seem to refer to Ido.

He Condemns Esperanto

Prof. Hunt of Princeton Says None of the Universal Tongues Can Succeed

Special to The New York Times.

PRINCETON, N. J., Dec. 30.—The Modern Language Association of America closed its twenty-sixth annual convention here to-day with the reading of several papers and the adoption of three resolutions, one petitioning Congress in the proposed revision of tariff laws to remove the duties on books printed in foreign countries, works of art, and scientific instruments intended for the private use of investigators.

Prof. Theodore W. Hunt of Princeton University declared that the mechanical artificial or purely conventional character of preferred universal tongues, such as Esperanto and Volapuk, prevents them from representing the most vital and essential relation of thought and language. He said:

"Whatever purely commercial or utilitarian purpose they may subserve, they can never rise to the plane of language as the expression of thought for the highest ends, the outward revelation of man's innermost mental and spiritual self. For this reason, if for no other such language codes and schemes can never compass the area of universal speech and meet the deepest needs of man as a thinker."

Published: December 31, 1908

New York Book Announcments

It is also reported that four of the stories in Mr. Charles Battell Loomis's "Cheerful Americans," which is in its ninth American edition, have been translated into Italian and are published in the magazine La Rassegna Nazionale. His "Mother of Little Maude and Little Maude" has also been translated into Esperanto and published this month in the American Esperanto of Chicago.

Published: January 9, 1909

Views of Readers

Esperanto and Ilo

New York Times Saturday Review of Books:

There recently appeared in this REVIEW an admirable account, by Mr. Edward Cary, of Prof. Curtis H. Page's translation of Molière's plays. Having just read Prof. Emile Boirac's Esperanto version of "Don Juan," this passage in Mr. Cary's article caught my attention: "One of the most successful pieces of work in translation is the rendering of the present dialect in the second act of 'Don Juan,' in which Prof. Page says he has 'followed closely' the translation of 1732 and 1748, where the peasant dialect of England is boldly used."

Is there peasant dialect in the Esperanto version? I had not noted any. So I compared the renderings of the charming paragraph in which Pierrot describes the discovery of Don Juan and his valet in the water. The result seems to show that Esperanto is out of its sphere in attempting to reproduce homely dialect.

The first sentence of Pierrot's speech in the original is: "Aga, quien, Charlotte, je m'en vas te conter tout fin drait comme cela est venu; car, comme dit l'autre, je les ai le premier avisés, avisés le premier je les ai."

Prof. Page's version is: "Aye, marry, Charlotte, I'se tell this autright haw it fell out; for, as the saying is, I spy'd 'um aut first, first I spy'd 'um aut."

"Peĉjo" (Pierrot) says in primitive Esperanto: "Nu do, Ĉarlino, mi tuj rakontos al ci tute rekte, kiamaniere tio okazis; ĉar, kiel diris la alia, mi ilin ekvidis unua, unua mi ekvidis ilin."

This is a literal English rendering of the Esperanto text: "Well, then, Charlotte, I at once shall relate to thee quite straightforwardly in what manner that occurred; for, as said the other, I them perceived first, first I perceived them."

Can one wonder that authors are incredulous toward the claims of Esperanto as a language for all purposes? It is not surprising that they are beginning to look with more favor on the modest programme of Ilo as a purely auxiliary language; for it is certainly not within the scope of an international medium of communication to make itself ridiculous by trying to rival the barbarous but fascinating homeliness of the various regional tongues.

"Don Juan" in Ilo, however, would be more pleasant reading than the Esperanto "Ŝtona Festeno," because Ilo avoids the cacophony of the earlier effort.

John Ed. Hearn
New York, Jan. 4, 1909

Published: January 9, 1909

In the Real Estate Field

Buyer for $250,000 Apartments

F. R. Wood & Co. have sold for Lorenz Weiher to an investor 223 to 227 West 105th Street, a six-story elevator apartment house known as the Esperanto, on plot 100 by 100.11. The building was completed last November, and has been held at $250,000.

Published: February 12, 1909

Socialist for Eserpanto

J. H. Work Wants It Adopted for the Party's Correspondence

Socialists in this and other cities were notified yesterday by John H. Work, an Iowa member of the National Committee of the Socialist Party, that he had made a request of the National Committee to order that Esperanto be made the universal correspondence language of the party. The National Committee is now voting on the subject.

Work holds that it is necessary to have a universal correspondence language because the Socialists are found in so many nations. Those opposed to this idea say that to make this plan effective it would be necessary to be able to bring pressure on the Socialist groups of all other countries to make Esperanto the universal correspondence language, and they do not believe this can be done.

The proposition to make Esperanto the official universal language of Socialism at international congresses was voted down a week ago by the National Committee.

Published: February 14, 1909

Hedwig Reicher, Who Turns to a Play in English

Like Nazimova and Kalich, She Abandons Her Mother Tongue on the Stage—To Interpret Martha Morton's Adaptation of "On the Eve"

She has a soft, smooth, rich voice, and the harsh Teutonic gutterals do not obtrude unpleasantly. Probably she has a gift for language. At any rate, the mere mastery of a modern English part ought to be comparatively easy after one experience she tells about.

Last Summer, toward the end of her engagement with the German company in Irving Place, she received a cablegram from her

father, Emanuel Reicher, the director of the famous Deutsches Theatre in Berlin, asking her if she would come to Dresden to play "Iphigenia" in Esperanto, the occasion being an International Congress of Esperantists, at which the representatives of forty-two nationalities were present.

"I did not know the least little thing about Esperanto," averred Miss Reicher, as she laughingly told of her experience, "and as I had never played the rôle in any tongue it looked to me like an impossible attempt. But father was anxious for me to do it, so I took passage, and after arriving in Germany had two weeks in which to prepare. My fears were entirely justified. It was a tremendous strain. But I got through with it, and, really, it was worth while. The King of Saxony was present, and the enthusiasm was wonderful. My father said that he could recall only one occasion which was equally impressive—the opening night with Wagner in Baireuth."

Published: February 28, 1909

To Make English a World Language

Andrew D. White Tells Simple Spellers Their Plans Would Make It So

Other Lands Would Follow

Chinese, Japanese, Germans, and French Would Surely Take It Up, Says the ex-Ambassador

The Simplified Spelling Board held its third annual dinner at the Waldorf-Astoria last night. Not even the enforced absence of Andrew Carnegie, one of the founders of the body, could altogether dampen the ardor of the reformers in the face of the "reports of progress" which came from both sides of the Atlantic.

Mr. Carnegie was expected to be present and act as toastmaster, but was said to be ill with a cold, his physician advising him to stay in the house. Ex-Ambassador Andrew D. White took his place, declaring that he thought he knew as much about the problem of simple spelling as Mr. Carnegie did, though unequal to Mr. Carnegie in other directions. Dr. White predicted that if the spelling of the English language was simplified, English would certainly become the "universal language." Dr. White declared that with the spelling simplified English was the easiest of all languages, and would be adopted by the Chinese, the Japanese, the Germans, and even the French. He thought this would be far more likely than the adoption of a "universal" language such as Esperanto or the Volapuk....

Published: April 7, 1909

How Modern Civilization Pushes Into Far-Off Lands

Novel Movements in Foreign Countries Change Old Customs

...

The propagation of Esperanto in Spain is the work of two associations, the first of which, La Hispana Societo por la Propagando de Esperanto, devotes its attention to the Spanish-speaking provinces of the Peninsula, while the activity of the Espero Kataluna is confined to those provinces in which the Catalan language predominates.

The Espero Kataluna has some twenty-five affiliated societies throughout Catalonia, all of which teach Esperanto free of charge, several of them maintaining public courses. In Barcelona alone are held forty-eight distinct courses of instruction in Esperanto, and a monthly review, Tutmonda Espero, is published.

Published: April 18, 1909

On the Atlantic Highway

Col. John Pollen, a Leading Esperantist, Met by Followers Here

The transatlantic steamships arriving yesterday and some of those on them were:

... Col. John Pollen, British philologist and prominently identified with the world movement for the adoption of Esperanto as a universal language, arrived yesterday on the Cunard Line steamship Campania. Col. Pollen was President of the British Esperanto Association in 1904 and President of the Third International Congress of Esperantists at Cambridge, England, in 1907. He will be the guest here of well-known American Esperantists.

Col. Pollen was met by a number of friends, who greeted him in Esperanto. He carried a green flag bearing a single white star, which is the emblem of the Esperanto Association, and symbolizes "Brotherhood and Justice Between the Nations."

Published: August 8, 1909

Delegates to Esperanto Congress

WASHINGTON, Aug. 17.—The Secretary of State has designated Herbert Harris of Maine and Edwin C. Reed of New York as delegates on the part of the United States to the Fifth International Esperanto Congress to be held at Barcelona, Spain, Sept. 5 to 11.

Published: August 18, 1909

[Untitled]

BARCELONA, Sept. 6.—The International Esperanto Congress was opened here to-day. Among the American delegates are Herbert Harris of Portland, Me., who represents the Government, and Arthur Baker of Chicago, editor of The American Esperanto Magazine.

Published: September 7, 1909

Esperanto Congress Ends

Thirty-three Nations Were Represented by 1,300 Delegates

BARCELONA, Sept. 13.—The International Esperanto Congress, which has been in session here for some days, came to an end today. The next congress will be held at Washington in August of 1910.

This year's gathering has been most successful and was attended by 1,300 delegates representing 33 nationalities.

Published: September 14, 1909

ESPERANTIST ASKS FOR FUNDS

Archdeacon Appeals to Carnegie for Financial Support.

PARIS, Sept. 15.—Ernest Archdeacon, a member of the Chamber of Deputies, who has just returned from the International Esperanto Congress at Barcelona, says he was amazed at the facility with which persons of different nationalities communicated in Esperanto.

He has issued an appeal to Andrew Carnegie to investigate the Esperanto movement and give it his financial support.

Esperantist Asks for Funds

Archdeacon Appeals to Carnegie for Financial Support

PARIS, Sept. 15.—Ernest Archdeacon, a member of the Chamber of Deputies, who has just returned from the International Esperanto Congress at Barcelona, says he was amazed at the facility with which persons of different nationalities communicated in Esperanto.

He has issued an appeal to Andrew Carnegie to investigate the Esperanto movement and give it his financial support.

Published: September 16, 1909

Taft Tribute to Cannon

Follows Speaker's Reference to His Own "Meanness" at Dartmouth Dinner

WASHINGTON, Jan. 24—President Taft, in an address to-night before the Dartmouth College alumni in the presence of their new President, Ernest Fox Nichols, praised the value of the small college and paid a tribute to Speaker Joseph G. Cannon, who had spoken before him.

Mr. Cannon had said that he bowed to the President, a son of Yale; Mr. Roosevelt, a son of Harvard; Andrew Jackson, and to Abraham Lincoln, who had not had the advantage of a college education, and that he himself might be a little jealous because he had not had such an advantage, for culture might have eradicated "some of the meanness in me which both my enemies and my friends say I have."

The President referred to the Speaker as "my friend, Uncle Joe," called attention to his tribute to Abraham Lincoln, and said:

"When we hear that mellifluous voice, sometimes full of English and sometimes full of Esperanto, we are carried back to the magnificent days of Daniel Webster. Great must be the country that can produce a man without a college education who can deliver such a tribute as has been paid here to-night to Andrew Jackson and Abraham Lincoln."

The President declared the small college was one of the bulwarks of the Nation and pleaded for more of the spirit of fraternity throughout the lifetime of college men.

Among the other speakers were the French Ambassador, the British Ambassador, and Congressman McCall of Massachusetts.

Published: January 25, 1910

ESPERANTO, BLACK HANDER.

District Attorney Trying to Identify Him with B. C. Silver, Merchant.

An attempt to identify Bennett C. Silver, a merchant of 358 East Fifty-seventh Street, as the man who signed various extortionate letters with the words, "Esperanto, Chief of the Black Hand," was started by Assistant District Attorney Buckner yesterday before Judge Malone in General Sessions. The letters were addressed to Mrs. Rebecca Cohen of 212 West 137th Street, the wife of a produce merchant and the mother of four girls.

On Jan. 17 the Cohen family was noti-

Esperanto, Black Hander

District Attorney Trying to Identify Him with B. C. Silver, Merchant

An attempt to identify Bennett C. Silver, a merchant of 358 East Fifty-seventh Street, as the man who signed various extortionate letters with the words, "Esperanto, Chief of the Black Hand," was started by Assistant District Attorney Buckner yesterday before Judge Malone in General Sessions. The letters were addressed to Mrs. Rebecca Cohen of 212 West 137th Street, the wife of a produce merchant and the mother of four girls.

On Jan. 17 the Cohen family was notified that they were next on the list of the Black Hand, that $2,000 was wanted immediately, and that failure to meet the demands of the band was always followed by death, or else by the kidnapping and ruin of the daughters.

After consultation with detectives a bogus package was given to the driver of the taxicab that called for the money. The pursuit finally led to Silver's arrest. He was indicted for attempted extortion.

Mrs. Cohen and her daughter testified yesterday that they had known Silver for a number of years and in proof produced a number of gay postal cards said to have been sent them by him from Africa. They were admitted as evidence over a storm of protests from Abe Levy of counsel for the defense.

The most interesting witness was Joseph Devlin of 264 West Twenty-fourth Street, the chauffeur, who identified Silver as the man who had instructed him to call at the Cohens' for the package. This was to be surrendered later at a rendezvous, which the stranger failed to keep. It was not until several days later that Devlin pointed him out to the detectives in a drugstore.

The jury to-day will hear the testimony of handwriting experts.

Published: March 23, 1910

Esperanto Church Services

Delegates to International Congress in Washington Will Attend

WASHINGTON, Aug. 4. — Church services in Esperanto, the international language, will be conducted in this city on Sunday, Aug. 14. Two services have been arranged for, and most of the 1,000 or more delegates to the congress will probably attend one or the other. In St. Paul's Episcopal Church the Eucharistic service will be conducted in Esperanto by the Rev. Paul Hoffman of Baltimore and the Rev. James L. Smiley of Annapolis. Father Bianchini, a delegate to the congress from Italy, and Father Solas of France will officiate in the services at St. Patrick's Cathedral.

Twenty-two nationalities will be represented at the congress. Official delegates ill be sent by the Governments of Mexico, Spain, Ecuador, Honduras, Italy, France, Panama, and Guatemala.

John Barrett, Director of the Bureau of American Republics, is President of the congress.

Published: August 5, 1910

In With Record Ship Load

1,908 Passengers on the George Washington— Esperantists Aboard

The North German Lloyd steamship George Washington arrived last evening, bringing the greatest number of passengers to New York that have arrived so far this season on a single steamship. The ship had 1,908 passengers, of whom 426 were in the first cabin, and there were fifteen Esperantists, who are on their way to the Esperanto Congress which will begin in Washington next Monday.

Though the delegates represent a number of countries, they could speak the one language, and this, as Dr. L. L. Zamenhof, the creator of the language, said, proved not only the need of a common medium of intercommunication but the advantages of being able to command such a medium. The delegates were very enthusiastic, and all the way across they did missionary work on board.

The Esperantists are: Dr. J. Arnhold, Dresden; Miss Henrietta Martin, France; Dr. and Mrs. L. L. Zamenhoff of Warsaw, Richard Sharpe of England, Mrs. Marcelle Tiard, France; Sergius Winkelmann, Dresden; Miss M. Hutchinson, and Miss F. Schaeffer of England; William Mann, assistant editor of The British Esperantist, and Col. John Pollen, President of the British Esperanto Association.

Dr. Zamenhoff pointed out that there are now published monthly eighty-five Esperanto gazettes and magazines, representative of every country of importance. This, he said, was double the number issued a year ago.

Published: August 11, 1910

"Kiel Vi Sanas?"

This is How Esperantists, Gathering in Washington, Greet Each Other

WASHINGTON, Aug. 12. — Esperantists from all parts of the world are arriving in Washington to attend the Esperanto Congress, and when Greek meets Russian, or German meets American in hotel corridor or avenue the mother tongues are overwhelmed by the language of hope.

"Kiel vi sanas?"

"Tre bone, mi dankas vin."

Or, translated from the Esperanto, "How are you?" "I am very well, thank you."

Edwin C. Reed, secretary of the Congress, was notified by the State Department to-day that Ali Kuli Kahn had been designated to attend the Congress as the official representative of Persia, making the ninth nation to send an official representative. Representatives from at least thirty-seven countries will be in attendance.

Dr. Albert Hale was to-day appointed as official representative of the International Bureau of American Republics. The State Department also will have an official representative.

An informal reception will be given tomorrow night to Dr. L. L. Zamenhof of Warsaw, Poland, inventor of Esperanto. The first gathering of the Congress takes place on Monday.

Published: August 13, 1910

"KIEL VI SANAS?"

This Is How Esperantists, Gathering in Washington, Greet Each Other.

WASHINGTON, Aug. 12.—Esperantists from all parts of the world are arriving in Washington to attend the Esperanto Congress, and when Greek meets Russian, or German meets American in hotel corridor or avenue the mother tongues are overwhelmed by the language of hope.

" Kiel Vi Sanas?"

" Tre bone, mi dankas vin."

Or, translated from the Esperanto, "How are you?" "I am very well, thank you."

Edwin C. Reed, secretary of the Congress, was notified by the State Department to-day that Ali Kuli Kahn had been

Esperanto Congress Opens

"Bonan Vesperon" The Greeting on All Sides in Washington

WASHINGTON, Aug. 13.—With a reception, at which Dr. Zamenhof of Poland, author of Esperanto, the language of hope for international peace, was the central figure, the sixth international congress of Esperanto opened informally here to-night. Delegates from nations all over the world were mingling the smooth-flowing, liquid Esperanto with an occasional phrase or sentence in English, French, German, Russian, or Japanese.

Standing at the doors were four blue-coated Washington policemen, who, when asked a question, surprised many of the delegates by answering in perfectly good Esperanto. To-day they received a greeting from brothers across the sea, the Esperantist Police Club of Paris.

"Bonan vesperon" was the evening greeting which to-night was heard in the National capital oftener than any other. It fell from the lips of people from more than a score of nations. All understood its welcome tone and felt "at home."

Church services in Esperanto will be conducted to-morrow in St. Paul's Episcopal and St. Patrick's Catholic Church, the latter being in charge of Father Bianchini, delegate to the congress from Italy, and Father Solas of France. On the following morning the congress will formally open and continue in session throughout the week.

Published: August 14, 1910

Esperantists at Church

Also Attend a Concert Where Songs Are Sung in Esperanto

WASHINGTON, Aug. 14. — Delegates to the International Esperanto Congress, which will open here to-morrow morning, attended services conducted in Esperanto at St. Paul's Episcopal Church to-day. The whole service, hymns, ritual, and sermon, was in the universal language. The ritual was read by the Rev. Paul F. Hoffman of Baltimore, and the Rev. James L. Smiley of Annapolis preached the sermon, using for his text: "Go ye into all the world and preach the Gospel to every creature."

In the afternoon several hundred delegates were escorted about the city, and to-night a concert was given, at which soloists sang in Esperanto, and a chorus rendered "La Espero," the Esperanto anthem.

The formal proceedings of the congress will begin to-morrow morning, when an address will be delivered by Dr. Ludwig L. Zamenhof, inventor of the language. H. W. Yemans of Detroit, Vice President of the American Esperanto Association, will preside, in the absence of President John Barrett, who is ill in New York.

Nothing but Esperanto is used by the delegates in conversation, and four Washington policemen, who were taught the language in a few weeks by Dr. Edwin Reed, are stationed at the congress headquarters to answer questions.

Published: August 15, 1910

First Lieut. H. W. Yemans, Medical Reserves, is designated as the representative of the War Department at the International Esperanto Congress.

The United Service

Special to The New York Times.

...
The Army.

First Lieut. H. W. Yemans, Medical Reserves, is designated as the representative of the War Department at the International Esperanto Congress.

Published: August 17, 1910

PRIZES FOR ESPERANTO.

Two Americans Among Winners of Awards for Literary Productions.

WASHINGTON, Aug. 17.—Suggestions for the building up of a world-wide organization for the promotion of Esperanto were made and discussed before the Esperanto International Congress to-day. Although no definite plan was reached for the enlargement of the international organizations, many delegates expressed their determination to stimulate interest in the new language in their own localities in every way possible.

Prizes were awarded to-day for the best literary productions in Esperanto in both prose and poetry as follows:

Poetry, Universal Brotherhood, Joao Baptista Mello Souza of Brazil, silver medal.

Prose, Universal Brotherhood, Miss Esther Higgs of England, silver medal.

Short story, "How Bill Became an Esperantist," Herschel S. Hall, Cleveland, Ohio, first, and "Fate," Raymond T. Bye, Germantown, Penn., second, silver medal.

Essay, "The Use of Esperanto for Commerce," W. A. Vogler, Germany, prize $10.

For an essay on the Bible and for one on the similarity between Zamenhof and Lincoln, W. L. Church of Boston and James Robbie of Edinburgh, Scotland, were respectively awarded sets of Zamenhof's works.

On account of the death of President Pedro Montt of Chile invitations for a reception to-night by John Barrett, Director of the Bureau of American Republics, were recalled.

Prizes for Esperanto

Two Americans Among Winners of Awards for Literary Productions

WASHINGTON, Aug. 17—Suggestions for the building up of a world-wide organization for the promotion of Esperanto were made and discussed before the Esperanto International Congress to-day. Although no definite plan was reached for the enlargement of the international organizations, many delegates expressed their determination to stimulate interest in the new language in their own localities in every way possible.

Prizes were awarded to-day for the best literary productions in Esperanto in both prose and poetry as follows:

Poetry, Universal Brotherhood, Joao Baptista Mello Souza of Brazil, silver medal.

Prose, Universal Brotherhood, Miss Esther Higgs of England, silver medal.

Short story, "How Bill Became an Esperantist," Herschel S. Hall, Cleveland, Ohio, first, and "Fate," Raymond T. Bye, Germantown, Penn., second, silver medal.

Essay, "The Use of Esperanto for Commerce," W. A. Vogler, Germany, prize $10.

For an essay on the Bible and for one on the similarity between Zamenhof and Lincoln, W. L. Church of Boston and James Robbie of Edinburgh, Scotland, were respectively awarded sets of Zamenhof's works.

On account of the death of President Pedro Montt of Chile invitations for a reception to-night by John Barrett, Director of the Bureau of American Republics, were recalled.

Published: August 18, 1910

Umpires Speak Esperanto

Delegates to Congress of Neutral Tongue See Ball Game in Washington

WASHINGTON, Aug. 18.—Group meetings of Esperanto Societies from various sections of the country led the programme for today, the fourth of the session of the sixth international congress of Esperanto. John Barrett, Director of the International Bureau of American Republics, was re-elected President of the North American Esperanto Association. Dr. H. Yemans of Detroit, Mich., was elected Vice President, and Dr. E. C. Reid of Columbus, Ohio, Secretary and Treasurer.

At the session of the international body the aims of the congress were discussed by the Rev. Paul Homan of Baltimore, Dr. B. F. Schubert of Washington, and Georges Warnier of Paris.

In the afternoon the delegates to the congress, representing about thirty-five nations, attended the ball game and saw the Washington and Cleveland teams play. Umpires' decisions were given in Esperanto, and books of baseball rules, printed in the international language, were distributed among the delegates.

Published: August 19, 1910

Esperanto

The Esperanto Congress in Washington last week was largely attended and excited a great deal of public interest. The interest is natural. When a body of intelligent men get together for the purpose of promoting a project which is easily comprehended but must seem, to most of their fellow-beings, unpractical and visionary, they are bound to attract a great deal of attention. The comments on Esperanto are generally humorous, but the promoters of the new world language, as it is called, are not humorists, and they are very much in earnest.

They believe that the advancement of civilization would be greatly helped by the use, especially in trade, of a new, universal language, which could be easily learned. But enough of any language can be easily learned, for trade purposes, by one who will apply himself to the task sedulously, and Esperanto cannot be learned without serious application. Of course it is no answer to the arguments of the Esperantists that languages have never been made deliberately, but have been of natural growth. The fact that there is no precedent for Esperanto does not detract from its possible merits.

But time is valuable and the time employed by an English-speaking person in learning Esperanto might be better employed in learning French or German or both. With command of one of those two languages in addition to English he could make his way with little trouble in all civilized countries; with both he would be in touch with the whole world. Then new avenues of culture would be open to him and the world's literature would be at his command. In time the whole world may have one language, but it will never be Esperanto. The more fervent advocates of the new and agreeable jargon claim too much for it. Its moderate upholders do not convince us of its utility.

Published: August 23, 1910

A Universal Tongue

Is Not Sure It Will Be Esperanto, but It Will Come

To the Editor of The New York Times:

A universal language is imperatively needed. What shall it be? Can one of the existing languages be adopted for this purpose? German is out of the question on account of its difficulty. Mark Twain said that it ought to be called a dead language, for only the dead had time to learn it. French is easier in some respects. Still it takes a long time to acquire the art of writing correct French, and the pronunciation presents almost insuperable obstacles. English is grammatically the simplest of the three. But the antiquated and misleading spelling of English makes it difficult for foreigners. If English were spelled phonetically or even with the moderate simplification advocated by Mr. Carnegie and others, it would be better fitted to become a universal language.

What is required is a language copious enough for practical purposes, freed from irregularities, simple enough in its grammar to be learned in a short time. Perhaps the new artificial language called Esperanto meets these requirements. If not, something better can be devised. At all events it seems safe to predict that a universal language is coming and that when it comes it will be a great instrument of civilization.

Herbert Morrison Clarke
Milton, Vt., Aug. 19, 1910

Published: August 23, 1910.

Esperanto and Culture

To the Editor of The New York Times:

Why create a new, artificial language like Esperanto when we have at our elbows English, French, German, Spanish, each of which can be acquired for commercial purposes within three months at the very most? Acquiring a trade smattering of some of them may lead many a one to delve eventually deeper, thereby unlocking new paths of knowledge with their attendant delights. For mercantile purposes, therefore, we need no new, easy, "penny-in-the-slot" language; and as for culture, we do not want a language so simple in structure as not to admit of flexibility. In time it would simply mean being reduced to a state of mental apathy with reference to language study, the supreme instrument in education.

Leo Freedman
Brooklyn, Aug. 23, 1910

Published: August 25, 1910

Esperanto and Business

To the Editor of The New York Times:

Will you kindly allow one who has just returned from the Sixth International Esperanto Congress to say a few words in reference to some strictures that appeared in your issue of the 23d in regard to that language?

In an age where "time is money," where none but the specialist in any calling can hope for a reasonable success, and especially in an age where commerce is reaching out in the remotest corners of the earth, to advise Americans to go through the long and tedious ordeal of studying both French and German in preference to Esperanto, which can be learned in one-tenth of the time, and which has already penetrated into thirty-three nationalities, because "new avenues of culture" would then be opened to them, "must seem to most of their fellow-beings unpracticable and visionary," and hardly calculated to help them in the struggle for ascendancy in the world's market.

Joseph Silbernik
New York, Aug. 24, 1910

Published: August 26, 1910

Spanish a World Language

To the Editor of The New York Times:

If there were no such language as Spanish, Esperanto, or something like it, would be a necessity to a world of intelligent beings who could perceive the absurdity of being stricken deaf and dumb the moment they crossed an imaginary boundary line. But I think the chief merit of Esperanto lies in its being so like Spanish in its simple, musical sounds and in its regularity; and I wonder whether the greater simplicity which is undeniably in favor of the former could ever balance the advantages possessed by Spanish in being alive and full grown, and accessible for practical uses here and now.

A language which embodies in such delightful form so great a part of the common lingual inheritance of nearly all the countries of Europe, which will be the mother tongue of undreamed-of millions in the vast continent to the south of us, deserves to be, if not a world language, then the Western World language; and it would not be unfitting that the language of the European country which opened up the New World should serve as a bond to unite both hemispheres.

An Irish Woman
Hartford, Conn., Aug. 25, 1910

Published: August 27, 1910

Esperanto Gaining Ground

Tristan Bernard's Next Play to be Written in "Universal Language"

Special Cable to THE NEW YORK TIMES.

PARIS, Nov. 20. — Esperanto is steadily gaining results in France, and, what is more significant, many of these recruits are men of letters.

Tristan Bernard, the playwright, says that his next piece will first be written in Esperanto, although, of course, it will have to be translated into French for the common public.

"The day is coming," he says, "when French will be merely the language of luxury, while Esperanto will be on everybody's tongue."

Published: November 27, 1910

Views of Readers

Need of a Universal Language

New York Times Saturday Review of Books:

Last Summer I sat at the board of a bright Swiss lady in Lucerne and noted how easily she chatted with her guests in German, French, Italian, and English. It appeared to make no difference to her what we spoke. Presently she exclaimed, "I wish we had a universal language. I can talk with you, but you can't talk with each other. I learned Volapük, but it is dead. I have tried Esperanto, but it can never make headway. These made-up things seem to have no life in them."

Later in the season, as my way led through Basel, Strasburg, Luxembourg, the language changing at almost every stop, the need of a real world-speech was brought home to me. Of course I could get on at hotels and shops, but only in a poor, stumbling way, with my small French and German.

Here and there in Belgium I noticed signs or directions posted in four languages—Dutch, German, French, and English. Street signs in Brussels are written in Dutch, which is translated into French. Naturally I fell to comparing the terms employed. In many cases one of the words for a given meaning was shorter and simpler than the rest. It occurred to me that if the labor spent on made-up languages were applied to selecting the best words now in current use a language could be compiled with the seeds of life in it.

Most of the words chosen will come from Indo-European sources, but there need be no restriction. The Turkish "dibs" may taste better than our rather sickish "molasses" or the French "mélasse." False spelling should condemn a word. Our "one," absurdly sounded "won," will give place perhaps to una. Quips of pronunciation should exclude certain words. Thus dog will drive out chien. A term may be trimmed and then admitted. At Brussels I observed on a sign "Waiting Room, Wachtzaal, Wartesal, Salle d'Attente." Let the German drop out an "e," and we may adopt his "wartsal." Short, straight words will win their way, such as "man," "bed," "kammer," "cat," (spelled cet,) "buffet," "rue," "sleep," "ora," "exit."

The fact that in essentials there is a common syntax will help. Already declensions and conjugations happily are dying out. We need not be too particular about arrangement or construction. I understand Carl perfectly when he says, "I will the big dog out of your garden quickly drive." We understand at once "What name has he?" or "How calls he himself?"

The words of this world-speech or "Franca" will be living words. They say that laboratory foods, though chemically correct, do not nourish. A food, or a word, which has grown possesses life. Again, the terms of our new language will be already familiar to thousands. The student of Franca is encouraged by meeting old friends along the way. He can read many passages at sight, especially if, like many dwellers in central Europe, he is bilingual.

Let a band of scholars take up the task of building this much needed language out of living material. Let them first select the most common, and therefore important, words for immediate use. Simple rules of syntax may follow. Then they may build up the new speech gradually, holding everything subject to modifications taught by experience. Especially let them publish specimens of their product and invite suggestions. This will furnish a drill ground where the elements may be tried out. What gives a good account of itself will go into the new and possibly may be invited to strengthen some of the old languages. Five years of this should give us a foundation, and twenty-five something of living, permanent value.

Wayland Spaulding
New York, Jan. 2

Published: January 7, 1911

Views of Readers

A Word for "Esperanto"

The New York Times Review of Books:

The desire for Mr. Wayland Spaulding to create a hodge-podge language for international purposes evinces a realization of the need of a suitable medium for international communication but a total lack of acquaintance with the actual essence and function of Esperanto, whose claims he dismisses so airily. Esperanto is the flower of 200 years of experiment and of actual testing of some 150 distinct propositions for a universal language. It is succeeding, and spreading with rapidity over the earth, simply because it has scaled the rocks which Volapük and its other predecessors met shipwreck, because it is not a mere example of philological legerdemain, but practically adapted to the actual needs of the average person. It is no longer a theory, but a living fact. So far has its actual use been developed that one large organization, numbering several thousands of members, and growing with immense rapidity, especially throughout Europe, has entirely abandoned the domain of propaganda to other Esperanto bodies, and confines itself exclusively to facilitating the interchange of numberless international services by means of the wonderful instrument at its disposal. Hundreds of thousands of men and women, of every degree of education and in every walk of life, are not merely talking about Esperanto, but actually using it every day, and constantly finding new uses for it. Already a complete Esperanto library, including translations from all tongues and a huge amount of original Esperanto literature in both prose and poetry, would consist of some two thousand or more volumes, with new works appearing every day. About 100 periodicals, some devoted to the spread of Esperanto and others to the production of literary matter, are supported by the Esperantists of the world. Most of these appear monthly; and a goodly number of them contain several score of pages each of Esperanto matter.

There is an international scientific review in the new Esperanto, and various magazines devoted to the interests of different religious bodies and economic and social movements. Those who are so eagerly relating themselves to fellow-thinkers throughout the world by this ready means of intercommunication have completely forgotten that Esperanto is called an artificial language. It is marvelously constructed along natural lines of language development, and so far from being fixed or crystallized that it lends itself most readily to as rapid development as required by human needs.

It ought not to be necessary to add that Esperanto is offered and used as an auxiliary language for international and not for domestic purposes. It aims not to supplant but to build up the existing tongues by liberating their users from the necessity of neglecting their mother tongue in the endeavor to master the different complicated linguistic systems of other peoples. Especially does it come as savior to the small but valuable languages now in danger of being abandoned because of their inutility outside a limited area. Friends of the Gaelic revival, for example, should rejoice in Esperanto as relieving them from the necessity of the sacrifices now demanded of those who would return to the use of their beautiful language.

The simplicity of Esperanto renders it easy of acquisition, and its flexibility adapts it marvelously to the task of interpreting national idioms to alien understandings. It is built on precisely the lines advocated by Mr. Spaulding, utilizing almost exclusively the "living material" found in the existing international roots. The "artificiality" consists simply in facilitating comprehension, and relieving the strain on the memory, by adopting strictly phonetic spelling, by the use of uniform endings which enable the parts of speech to be instantly recognized, and by the adoption of convenient affixes, most of which correspond to those actually in use in other languages, to allow the expression of any number of relations in connection with the mastery of a single root. The whole grammar is summed up in sixteen simple rules, which an ordinarily active mind can muster in less than an hour. As thousands can testify with abundant enthusiasm, a living international language is no longer a mere desideratum nor a pleasant dream, but a tangible reality, being utilized from day to day by a constantly increasing number of men and women of every race and tongue. Mr. Spaulding is most cordially invited to acquaint himself with the Esperanto movement, as it really is, and to discover its value by personal observation and experience.

James F. Morton, Jr.
New York, Jan. 19

Published: January 29, 1911

The Universal Alphabet

To the Editor of The New York Times:

Referring to the letter of Thomas H. Wheeless, in your issue of the 17th inst., under the caption, "Would Literally Abolish War," I would state that precisely such an alphabet as he suggests is now in actual and practical use in a language understood throughout the whole civilized world. In this language are printed and regularly circulated more than fifty monthly periodicals, embracing every branch of literature, from the most abstruse scientific problems to the latest joke; it has a library of more than one hundred volumes, mostly translations of standard works in many languages, and a few originally written in this language. The name of this language is Esperanto. Should any of your readers wish for more information on this subject he will receive it by addressing the General Secretary of the Esperanto Association of North America, Washington, D. C.

S. W. T.
Brooklyn, March 20, 1911

Published: March 22, 1911

New York Literary Notes

...

A new edition of Rhodes's "English Esperanto Dictionary" is being issued by Fleming H. Revell Co. It contains over 550 pages and includes a vocabulary of geographical and personal names, international roots, etc. It aims to be a complete working handbook of Esperanto. New popular editions of the Rev. F. B. Meyer's "Expositions of Biblical Characters" are announced.

...

Published: April 9, 1911

New Phonetic Language

Frenchman Invents Lightning Communication by Means of Elemental Sounds

PARIS, June 16. — A student of phonetics and philology, Mr. J. M. Chappaz, of Mleussy, in the Haute Savole, asserts that, like the chemist who has reduced compounds to elements, he has reduced all spoken words of civilized languages to their elemental sounds and by those sounds he purposes to invent a method of rapid communication hitherto unknown. He writes of the proposed invention to a Paris paper as follows:

"An instantaneous language, consisting of a new phonetic method got up by forty-three polyglot professors of divers countries, enabling all the inhabitants of the world to pronounce, read, write, spell, print, lithograph, telegraph, type, and telephone on the spot all local, National, Colonial, and international languages, including Esperanto, with their pure accent and without having studied them, and to understand and speak these languages infinitely more quickly and more correctly than by the ordinary methods."

In explaining this miraculous invention, the author says that is based on the principle of "reproducing the same sound by one and the same letter in all languages in which it occurs. He asserts that the forty-three polyglot professors have discovered that the sounds in all the languages in the world are reduced to forty-five, and consequently all that is required is to represent these forty-five sounds by forty-five separate symbols, composing a universal alphabet.

Published: June 25, 1911

New York Literary Notes

...

An edition in Esperanto of Trine's "In Tune with the Infinite" will be published in this country in September. The translator is Frederik Skeel-Giørling. Thomas Y. Crowell & Co. also announce two additions to their "First Folio Shakespeare," the two parts of "Henry IV.," edited by Charlotte Porter, and Crowell's Astor edition of Irving's "Astoria," appropriate to the one hundredth anniversary of the founding of Astoria, and the Lewis and Clarke Centennial, which takes place this year.

...

Published: July 23, 1911

ESPERANTISTS DINE ON STUFITA KAPONO

One Who Had Been Breaking Stone with Sinclair Too Tired to Speak at the Festeno.

GOOD REPORT FROM CHINA

Where the Boy Finds New World Language Easier Than His Own—An Open Meeting To-night.

La festeno de la Kunveno de la esperantista Asocio de Norda Ameriko was held last night in one of the private dining rooms of the Broadway Central Hotel. In plain English this means that the 'Esperanto Association of America, which is holding a convention in New York, had its annual dinner last night. About sixty

Esperantists Dine on Stufita Kapono

One Who Had Been Breaking Stone with Sinclair Too Tired to Speak at the Festeno

Good Report from China

Where the Boy Finds New World Language Easier Than His Own— An Open Meeting To-night

La festeno de la Kunveno de la Esperantista Asocio de Norda Ameriko was held last night in one of the private dining rooms of the Broadway Central Hotel. In plain English this means that the Esperanto Association of America, which is holding a convention in New York, had its annual dinner last night. About sixty members of the association were at the afternoon meeting and at least one more came to the dinner.

The one more was Donald Stephens, who had been serving eighteen hours in a Delaware jail because he played baseball on Sunday with Upton Sinclair and several others. Just as soon as he got out of jail yesterday afternoon he took a fast train to New York and got to the Broadway Central in time to be called upon for a speech. He excused himself, however, in Esperanto, saying that he had been pounding stone all day, and that was about all he cared to attempt for the time being.

The menu of the evening was printed in the world language, and follows:

MENUO.
Ostroj
Rafanetoj
Esperanto-Supo El Pizoj
Blufiŝo Gratenita, Laŭ La Sepa
Glaciligitaj Kukumoj, Terpomoj Kun Petrozelo
Lumbaĵo Delikata, Kun Fungoj
Oranĝa Akvoglaciaĵo Zamenhofa

Stufita Kapono Kun Kresoj
Novaj Fizoj
Batatoj
Salato Laŭ La Nov-Jorka Federacio
E. A. De N.A. Kremglaciaĵo
Kukoj Laŭ La Fundamento
Kongresa Kafo

After the waiter had served this exciting repast, the toastmaster, Edwin C. Reed of New York made a short speech extolling the merits of Esperanto. He was followed by James F. Morton, the Rev. Dr. Hubbard of China, who told what Esperanto was doing and could do for the Chinese boy, who never could learn the Chinese alphabet; Donald Stevens, Charles B. Wells, J. D. Houlman of Pittsburg, and Secretary Heller of the New York Society. Part of the speeches were made in English and part in Esperanto. At National conventions, it was explained, a National language is used for the benefit of the new members.

Many of those at the dinner are on their way to attend the seventh international convention of Esperantists to be held at Antwerp Aug. 20-27. The President of the National society is John Barrett, the Director General of the Pan-American Bureau at Washington. The convention will continue to-day and to-night there will be an open meeting at the Broadway Central, to which anybody who is interested in learning about Esperanto may come.

Published: August 3, 1911

1,700 Esperantists Meet

Sixty American Delegates — Alfonso Honors Inventor of Esperanto

ANTWERP, Aug. 21.—Sixty American delegates were present when the International Esperanto Congress opened its seventh annual convention here to-day. Fifteen nations were officially represented. The American Departments of State, War, and Commerce are represented respectively by Edwin C. Reed, Secretary of the Esperanto Association of North America; Dr. H. W. Yemans, Vice President of the American Association, and E. C. Kokeloy. Dr. Yemans, who was President of the sixth congress, held in Washington last year, opened the convention.

One of the striking features of to-day's session was the ovation accorded by the 1,700 delegates to Dr. Ludwig L. Zamenhof of Poland, the inventor of Esperanto, when the Spanish Consul presented to him on behalf of King Alfonso the Cross of the Order of Isabella.

The delegates were informed to-day that some fifty men of the Antwerp Police Force speak Esperanto.

Published: August 22, 1911

Honor Esperanto Founder

100 Students Draw Dr. Zamenhof Through Streets in a Carriage

ANTWERP, Aug. 25.—Edwin C. Reed, Secretary of the Esperanto Association of North America, was the only American elected to-day as a member of the International Esperanto Commission for the organization of a permanent body of Esperantists.

The seventh annual Esperanto Congress, which had been in session here for five days, came to an end to-night with a brilliant ball, at which the delegates wore their National costumes. Dr. Ludwig L. Zamenhof of Holland*, the inventor of Esperanto, was drawn through the streets in an open carriage by 100 students.

Published: August 26, 1911

* One of the many factual errors in the newspaper.

Government is Investigating Fake Universities

Degrees Given Practically for a Few Dollars—Institutions That Sound Big on Paper but Shrink on Investigation—The Oriental University's Odd Curriculum

...

The Oriental University is described in the catalogue as affiliated with many educational institutions in various parts of the world, including Solomon's Temple University (Inc.,) at Jerusalem, and the Latent Light Culture Institute, Tinnevelly Bridge, India.

...

The faculty presents a lengthy and imposing list, and includes a Professor of Theologic Symbolics, a Professor of Odontology, Bacteriology, Psycho-Therapy, and French and South American Languages, and also a Professor of Aviation and Bahaism. The last is also Assistant Professor of Common and Equity Law. There are eight "extraordinary professors," one of whom teaches political economy and Esperanto.
...

Published: August 27, 1911

Slinclair Now Shuns Publicity

...

WILMINGTON, Del., Aug. 29—Upton Sinclair declares he is humiliated by the publicity given his divorce suit.
...

Prof. Hetzel, an educator of Philadelphia, who lives in the Arden Colony, to-day asked Sinclair to make an address before the Esperanto Club of Arden at its meeting next Sunday.

"My Esperanto is bad," replied Upton. "Besides, I think it is time for me to stop talking."

The meeting will be in conjunction with a celebration of the birthday anniversary of Henry George.

...

Published: August 30, 1911

Condemn Russian Officer

Capt. Postnikoff of General Staff Sentenced for Selling Secret Documents

ST. PETERSBURG, Sept. 8. — A military court at a private sitting today tried and sentenced to eight years' penal servitude and a loss of his rights Capt. Postnikoff of the General Staff. The charge against him was selling secret documents to agents of three powers.

Capt. Postnikoff was President of the Universal League of Peace and the Russian Esperanto League. He frequently traveled abroad, and for a time sojourned in the United States. The case was oddly connected with recent sensational trials. The witnesses included Baron von Ungern Sternburg, former correspondent in St. Petersburg of the semi-official Austro-Hungarian news agency, who was sentenced to four years' imprisonment last November for delivering secret documents to a foreign state, and Mlle. Muse Zikke, a sister of the widow of Count Vassilli Bouturlin, who was poisoned by Dr. Pantchenko in 1910.

As a result of the conviction of Capt. Postnikoff the Government has closed the Esperanto League, which it declared to be a convenient screen for international spies.

Published: September 9, 1911

CONDEMN RUSSIAN OFFICER.

Capt. Postnikoff of General Staff Sentenced for Selling Secret Documents.

ST. PETERSBURG, Sept. 8.—A military court at a private sitting to-day tried and sentenced to eight years' penal servitude and a loss of his rights Capt. Postnikoff of the General Staff. The charge against him was selling secret documents to agents of three powers.

Capt. Postnikoff was President of the Universal League of Peace and the Russian Esperanto League. He frequently traveled abroad, and for a time sojourned in the United States. The case was oddly connected with recent sensational trials. The witnesses included Baron de Ungern Sternburg, former correspondent in St. Petersburg of the semi-official Austro-Hungarian news agency, who was sentenced to four years' imprisonment last November for delivering secret documents to a foreign state, and Mlle. Muse Zikke, a sister of the widow of Count Vassilli Bouturlin, who was poisoned by Dr. Pantchenko in 1910.

As a result of the conviction of Capt. Postnikoff the Government has closed the Esperanto League, which it declared to be a convenient screen for international spies.

"Vacuous Spelling Boards"

Lukewarm, They Are Not Ardent for Radical Phonetic Reform

To the Editor of The New York Times:

The amiable and judicious commentary of your correspondent, Mr. Scott, in yesterday's TIMES give me an opportunity to make a few observations, by your courtesy, upon the same subject. In my judgment your correspondent is quite right in calling both the English and American reform spelling boards "vacuous"; quite right, too, in saying that "English spelling is going to be changed; that it must be changed in accordance with knowledge and reason." He is quite right, also, in intimating that neither board is pursuing the work of reform of English spelling along correct or scientific lines. They have no system of procedure, no basis of a proper system in phonetics upon which to predicate a reform that shall endure for ages. Their policy consists of trimming the language of a few of its incongruous and excrementatious growths, as one trims a hedge or lops off unsightly branches. This procedure has its uses, of course, but, as Mr. Scott intimates, it does not meet the occasion, the great and crying need of the times.

What is this great need? The radical, fundamental need of the great and global English language, the most comprehensive and the grandest system of human speech, is a phonetic alphabet. The alphabet has no proper system of phonetics—of vowelization—such as exists in nature. And until such a system is constructed and applied, the labors of spelling and pronouncing boards must be in vain, or, at least, will fall short of their expectations.

The distinguished Schleyer, the author of Volapuk, nearly half a century since formulated a system of phonetics in his artificial language. The studies in the same direction of Dr. Zamenhof came later in Esperanto, and later still those of Sapwnov, a Bulgarian scholar, who, we make bold to say, has advanced a well-nigh perfect system of vowelization of the English alphabet and pronunciation based upon it. M. Sapwnov's system has not yet reached the public, but it is in course of publication. It has been my privilege to examine the manuscript of his work, which it is a pleasure to commend.

David Allyn Gorton, M. D.
Brooklyn, Sept. 13, 1911

Published: September 16, 1911

Suffrage Protagonists

Aboard the steamship Minnehaha, in yesterday from London, was Mrs. Forbes-Robertson Hale, niece of Forbes-Robertson, the actor, and wife of an American. ...

... Dr. and Mrs. H. W. Yemans were among the passengers. Dr. Yemans is an army surgeon and has been, by appointment of President Taft, a delegate of the American Red Cross to the Esperanto Congress at Antwerp. He was also the army representative, by appointment of the Secretary of War, and presided at the opening of Congress. There were 1,800 delegates present, and great enthusiasm existed in Europe, he said, for the adoption of a universal language. America, he added, felt the need of such a language less than Europe. He lectured on the subject on shipboard. ...

Published: October 10, 1911

Baby to Talk in Esperanto

Only the "Universal" Language to be Taught to Buetler Child

Special to The New York Times.

DETROIT, Mich., Dec. 29. — A girl baby which was born to-day to Mrs. John Conrad Buetler of Detroit will be educated to speak only Esperanto. Mr. Buetler is one of the leaders in America of the so-called universal language. He and his wife use it exclusively when conversing together.

Mr. Buetler is 58 years old. Mrs. Buetler is much younger, and is his second wife. It is twenty-two years since his last child was born to him. He is proprietor of the Randolph Hotel in Detroit.

Published: December 30, 1911

52 New Cornell Students

Brother of President Madero of Mexico Returns to College

Special to The New York Times.

ITHACA, N. Y., Feb. 17—Instruction for the second term began on Monday morning. On Saturday of last week fifty-two new students registered, among them Evaristo Madero, a brother of the President of Mexico. Madero was in the university last year, but left when the revolution started in Mexico.

...

Twenty undergraduates have formed a class for the study of Esperanto.

...

Published: February 18, 1912

Writes Book at the Age of Nine

The amazing accomplishments of a little Pennsylvania girl who has published three volumes, one in Esperanto, will be told in an interesting story in TO-MORROW'S SUNDAY TIMES.

Published: February 24, 1912

Child Prodigy: A Poet and Story Writer at Nine

Winifred Sackville Stoner, Jr., Dashes Off Verses in Esperanto, Too, and Is the Author of Three Published Books—Not a Prodigy, Says Her Mother, Merely the Result of Proper Training.

Winifred Sackville Stoner, Jr., 9 years old, speaks, writes, and understands several languages. She has written and had published

three books — one of verse, one of prose, and one in Esperanto. She plays compositions of the old masters on the piano. She whistles like a tomboy. She is mischievous. She disobeys her mother. She leaves doors open. She is splendidly healthy.

At the same time she has opposed skilled players at chess, she speaks Japanese verse, she scans Virgil correctly, and has a mind and thought perfectly attuned to rhythm and meter. Also, she never has attended a school of any description.

...

Her progress was as follows:
Age 1. — She could walk, talk, recite Tennyson's "Crossing the Bar," and scan from Virgil.

Age 2. — She could read in English and speak French.

Age 3. — She was able to write on the typewriter, and began to write original rhymes.

Age 5. — Traveled with her mother to various Chautauqua assemblies in the United States and spoke in behalf of Esperanto.

Age 6. — Wrote rhymes for magazines and newspapers, and received a silver medal from St. Nicholas Magazine for verses.

Age 7. — Became a chess player and published her first book entitled "Jingles."

Age 8. — Published her second book, "Patrino Anserino," or Mother Goose in Esperanto; was able to speak in eight languages, and demonstrated a remarkable knowledge of history, Latin, literature, geography, physiology, and rhetoric.

...

Here are some excerpts from Winifred's first book of jingles, now out of print:

...

An Esperanto Poem Plain to All

Written for Prof. Machloski, Princeton University.

Hundido krias — "Bow-wow-wow!"
Katido krias — "Meow-meow-meow!"
Bovido krias — "Moo-moo-moo!"
Kolombo krias — "Coo-coo-coo!"
Ŝafido krias — "Baa-baa-baa!"
Infano krias — "Ma-ma-ma!"

...

Published: February 25, 1912

Our Consul Tells Value of Esperanto

It's a Great Asset to Those Obliged to Use Foreign Languages, Diederich Says

"Keys" Now Obtainable

These Make It Possible for Those of Different Nationalities to Communicate with Little Trouble

In making a report to the Government on the last International Esperanto Congress held in Antwerp, United States Consul General Henry W. Diederich, stationed at this Belgian port, gives it as his opinion that a knowledge of Esperanto is an invaluable asset to one whose work requires the use of foreign languages.

The countries represented at the congress were the United States, Nicaragua, Belgium, Brazil, Chile, China, Guatemala, Hungary, Norway, Persia, Roumania, Russia, and Spain. Those who went to it from America were Edwin C. Reed, Secretary of the Esperanto Association of North America; Dr. H. W. Yemans, U. S. A., and E. C. McKelvey, as official representatives of the United States Government.

"The local Esperanto Society, of which Dr. Van der Biest is President," says Mr. Diederich in his official report, "made all arrangements for the reception of the congress at Antwerp, and the Royal Athenaeum, (Government Boys' High School,) was placed at its disposal to be used as headquarters. To the great satisfaction of the organizers and to the surprise of the committee there were 1,722 members enrolled at the opening session. During the last days of the convention others arrived, and at its close the enrollment was over 1,800. The congress was attended by 375 official delegates, holding 1,073 votes, representing 26,280 Esperantists.

"During the meetings personal experiences in the practice of Esperanto were discussed, many of which were conclusive in their demonstration of the utility of the language. Attention was called

OUR CONSUL TELLS VALUE OF ESPERANTO

It's a Great Asset to Those Obliged to Use Foreign Languages, Diederich Says.

"KEYS" NOW OBTAINABLE

These Make It Possible for Those of Different Nationalities to Communicate with Little Trouble.

In making a report to the Government on the last International Esperanto Congress held in Antwerp, United States Consul General Henry W. Diederich, stationed at this Belgian port, gives it as his opinion that a knowledge of Esperanto is an invaluable asset to one whose work requires the use of foreign languages.

to the method now adopted by the Esperantists for corresponding with foreigners whose language they can not write. Esperanto keys, costing one cent each and weighing one-half ounce, are published in the different languages, so that if, for instance, an American Esperantist desires to communicate by letter with a Russian who does not understand English, he purchases a Russian Esperanto key which he incloses in his letter written in Esperanto. With the aid of this key the Russian is enabled to translate the letter without difficulty. Keys are now ready in English, Welsh, German, French, Italian, Swedish, Spanish, Danish, Portuguese, Hungarian, Finnish, Polish, Roumanian, Dutch, and Catalan.

"Esperantists state that the merits of their language have been recognized by such eminent authorities as Prof. Max Mueller, Count Leo Tolstoi, and others. It has quietly and without ostentation conquered all obstacles and spread over the whole world. Its grammar has been translated into twenty-eight languages and dialects, and nearly twenty monthly journals are devoted to its propaganda. Its aim is not to displace existing idioms, but to be, as the Esperantists put it, a second language for all. It has shown, by practical demonstration, its humanitarian advantages when employed by the Red Cross, and it was with this particularly in view that the War Department at Washington delegated Dr. Yemans, who also represented the American Red Cross Society.

"It was the opinion of many who watched the labors of the congress that the study of Esperanto should be adopted by official school boards. Having examined carefully the Esperanto grammar, I am prepared to assert that a knowledge of Esperanto must be an invaluable asset to anyone whose work necessitates the use of foreign languages. While the Belgian authorities have not yet decided how far to encourage the new movement, private enterprise has undertaken the spreading of Esperanto and classes are now accessible to all."

Published: March 11, 1912

The Esperantists' Effort

To the Editor of The New York Times:

Because of the interest and discussion aroused by the introduction of House Resolution 220 into the United States House of Representatives by the Hon. Richard Bartholdt, the Esperanto Association of North America is going to distribute free one million copies of "A Glimpse of Esperanto," a pamphlet outlining the purpose of the international language and giving a general synopsis of the grammar. This will be sent to any of your readers sending name, address, and stamp to The Esperanto office, Washington, D. C.

House Resolution 220 reads:

Resolved, That the Committee on Education be and the same is hereby authorized and directed to cause an investigation to be made by the Committee on Education, or a sub-committee thereof, touching the practicability of the study of Esperanto as an auxiliary language and a means of facilitating the social and commercial intercourse of the people of the United States and those of other countries, the committee to submit its report at the second session of the Sixty-second Congress.

This resolution, passed by the House of Representatives, is now before the Committee on Education.

Edwin C. Reed
General Secretary, Esperanto Association of North America
Washington, D. C., March 9, 1912

Published: March 17, 1912

Esperanto Visit for Hedwig Reicher

Hedwig Reicher, who recently closed her season with the Drama Players of Chicago, will sail on the Amerika on Thursday for Berlin.

Later she will go to Vienna for the Ibsen festival, at which her father will appear, and then she will visit Crakow to be present at the International Esperanto Convention. Miss Reicher appeared in the first Esperanto play produced at the International Congress in Dresden in 1908, and since then she has been present at each of the international sessions. She will return to America in September to appear here in a play chosen from the répertoire of the Drama Players.

Published: May 13, 1912

An Opera in Esperanto

Special Cable to THE NEW YORK TIMES.

BERLIN, Sept. 9.—"Col. Chabert," which Andreas Dippel's Chicago Opera Company will introduce in America in the coming season, has been translated into Esperanto by the well-known Esperantist, Grabowsky. It is said to be the first operatic work put into the "universal language."

Published: September 10, 1912

Chemists Aroused by Tutton's Feat

Sir William Ramsay Trusts the Announcement That Molecules Are Made Visible

Others Suspend Judgment

Congress Adjourns After Defeating Resolution to Adopt Esperanto as an Official Language

The Eighth International Congress of Applied Chemistry, which has been in session since Sept. 4, came to an end yesterday noon with a business meeting in the Great Hall of the College of the City of New York, and there Dr. William H. Nichols, President of the eighth congress, handed the gavel to Dr. Paul T. Walden of Riga, Russia, who will preside when the ninth congress will meet in St. Petersburg in 1915. ...

...

Sir William Ramsay, the dean of all chemists, said that he had read of the discoveries in THE TIMES, and that he was greatly pleased by the news. ...

...

A debate over a resolution asking for the adoption by the congress of Esperanto as one of the official languages of future congresses resulted in the defeat of the resolution, Sir William leading the fight. His method was a cunning one, for he would not allow the resolution to come to a vote, substituting instead a motion that the consideration of the resolution be deferred to the 1915 congress.

"It would be premature to decide on Esperanto now," declared Sir William. "I don't deem it fair that the vote should be taken here in America, where the majority of the congress are Americans. In 1915 the vote can be taken under entirely different circumstances and under very fair circumstances."

...

Published: September 14, 1912

Rebuff to Esperantists

French Telegraph Department Refuses to Recognize New Language

By Marconi Transatlantic Wireless Telegraph to The New York Times

PARIS, Sept. 24. — An attempt having been made to have Esperanto admitted in telegraphic usage on the same footing as other languages, the French Postal and Telegraph Department has given an adverse decision.

The transmission of international messages in Esperanto will continue under the same tariff as for code and cipher messages.

Published: September 25, 1912

Last of Volapuk

Can We Esperanto English Into Sane Speech?

By Richard Whiteing
(From The Pall Mall Gazette)

The inventor of Volapuk goes to his grave a disappointed man. The old priest, Martin Schleyer, has just died at Constance, and virtually he takes his new language with him to the grave—killed by Esperanto.

It was in the nature of the case. How could anybody have hoped for finality in artificial language of all things in the world? Latin and Greek were the Volapuk and the Esperanto of the Renascence; we know what happened to them as living tongues. Where they no longer corresponded in their set and unchangeable forms to the needs and the ways of thinking of living men they had to go. But, having once lived, their august remains make excellent building material for the newer structures. Many a precious morsel of them is an inset of modern speech, just as the Roman temple in decay comes in exceedingly handy for the causeway or the cathedral. Volapuk never was alive, and it was no more than make-believe when people professed to have performed the feat of thinking, loving, hating, and joking in it. The whole thing, with its clumsy apparatus of congresses, handbooks, lexicons, and uncouth attempts at literature by policemen and others, faded away into nothingness until the time came for a repetition of the profitless experiment in Esperanto.

The failure is once more inevitable. For while these barbarous jargons are so many attempts to abolish Babel, they can but add to its confusion with their everlasting "one more." Nature and history take a long time to make a single language even for a race; but now that one may be turned out in a day and a night we shall soon have them by the thousand. Languages of this sort made by machinery can never hope to enjoy more than the favor of a moment. True speech of man is not made at all—it grows. All that the machinists can do is to cut a path through the prodigalities of a natural growth. It is made in court and camp, in battlefield and storm, in hall and bower, not for these places; and its grammar and its dictionaries come only as a second thought. Its great shapers are not the hands and brains of a pedant, but the love song, the woman's prattle to her child, the fairy story, the great oration, the tale told by the pilgrim on his way to the shrine—all the things that fashion at the same time the human soul. Words are deeds, in fact, in spite of the foolish saying that tries to put this great truth to shame with a negative.

Volapuk, it seems, came in the night, in vision, to a man who had gone to sleep with scraps of "fifty languages, which had confused his waking thoughts," in his brain. Such a cargo must have threatened nightmare, with insanity to follow; but instead it brought a vision of the new tongue in orderly array. "He rose from his bed and recorded his language on a simple sheet of notepaper," and so the monster was born. Such a succès (d'estime) was, of course, too tempting, and soon other precious schemes of the same sort came into the field with Herr Zamenhoff's Esperanto (a professor this time) as a survival of the fittest to catch the crowd. It had every note of the non-natural from the start. It barred idioms—the most vital thing in all languages—and it offered a worthless substitute for every spontaneous growth. It was easy-going. "Filo" was son, "filino" was daughter (no doubt with due acknowledgements to the Latin group,) and then came "bofilo" for a son-in-law, which none of these would ever have consented to take into the family. How inexpressibly dreary! But there was a lower deep—the drop into poetry, with Tennyson for the victim:

> Flow down, cold rivulet, to the sea,
> Thy tribute wave deliver;
> No more by thee my steps shall be,
> For ever and for ever.

Esperantoed into

> Fluu riveret', al maro vi,
> Tributecon redononta;
> Ne plu ĉe vi repasos mi,
> En tempo la venonta.

There was no harm in it as an exercise to verbal gymnastics — say, as a dancing master's memories of Mistral — but why couldn't they leave it alone?

Who wants it, when we already have perfection in hand? We need but a wise choice among the living languages for a second and universal one to be taught to every child. French, German, or English would do; and French already has some customary rights of possession which may entitle it to the choice. There it is, a thing of life, fashioned by centuries and by countless labors to every need of man, and with its glorious literature at the back of it as a thing beyond price. The chosen language, which ever it is, should be taught by natives as a living tongue — in the board schools quite as much as at Eton, where, if half we hear is true, it is hardly taught at all. With this at his tongue's end every man would be an initiate of a certain freemasonry of speech which would carry him 'round the world.

What has Volapuk or Esperanto, or any other of the breed of folly and presumption, to set against this? It must ever be a language without common pronunciation, for since it has no authoritative standard, it will infallibly catch the local peculiarity everywhere, and will be as unintelligible as "English as She Is Spoke" to the race at large. It can have no literature, for who could use for such a purpose a lingo which prides itself on having but one word for one thing, when you want at least a dozen words for everything as its different shades of significance catch the light of the mind. Fancy a Stevenson or a Ruskin so restricted, and where would our literature be?

Published: November 3, 1912

On Esperanto

Volapuk Is Nothing More Than an Artificial Flower

New York Times Saturday Review of Books:

My attention has been called to an article in your Nov. 3 issue, entitled "Last of Volapuk," with the request that I answer the same.

The desirability of an international means of communication is admitted by Mr. Richard Whiteing in this article, and the suggestion made that one of the prominent living languages be chosen. This is manifestly impossible. The Frenchman, German, Italian, Spaniard, or Englishman would readily consent to the selection of a living language, provided it were his own which were chosen. Let them get together to select the most worthy of the five, and on which one would they agree? Assuming that a choice was finally made, what proportion of people of a moderate degree of education throughout the world, many of them past the school age, could master the chosen language for purposes of written or verbal intercommunication? And yet, this is the class of people which is to-day using Esperanto like a native language:

Like Volapuk, Esperanto is an artificial language, but more skillfully created. Volapuk is like an artificial flower, made of gaudy and inharmonious fragments of various material, not even constructed in the semblance of a natural flower. On the other hand, Esperanto is delicately constructed from bits of many natural flowers, carefully selected with a view to harmony, and so skillfully put together that the design of the maker is easily recognized and admired by the impartial critic.

Esperanto is made up of root words common to many languages, and its sounds are such that they may be learned and accurately imitated by members of any of the various language groups. The ingenious introduction of a limited number of prefixes and suffixes multiplies each root word many times, and the possibility of still further increasing the vocabulary by skillful word building makes it possible to obtain an unlimited number of words from comparatively few roots. The paucity of words is only apparent and does not restrict the expression of the most delicate shades of meaning, as is fully evidenced by the already extensive Esperanto literature. It is true that Esperanto has no idiom, but this does not by any means indicate that it bars expression of poetic thought and in such unmistakable language that it is equally evident to all nations, regardless of local idiom. Is this a disadvantage?

There is no pidgin Esperanto nor Esperanto brogue. In the eight international congresses already held people speaking many languages and dialects have conversed freely together in Esperanto, and it has been impossible to distinguish one nationality from another by any marked variation of pronunciation. This is a fact. Esperanto has a standard of pronunciation and it has no local peculiarities.

The writer goes on to speak of the "free masonry of speech" which would exist, once his natural language had ben selected. Right here he unconsciously touches on a side of Esperanto which more than anything else tends to insure its permanence. There is among Esperantists a spirit of fraternity infinitely stronger than that of any oath-bound organization, and this spirit of fraternity has created a new nationalism, as broad as the limits of the earth and as firm as the rocks of Gibraltar. The language is one in which it is possible to "love," "joke," exchange opinions and ideas, but not to "hate." Esperantism and hatred are incompatible.

Esperanto has existed for more than twenty-five years, and is being used to-day by thousands of people throughout the world and as freely as a living language. It is being taught in the schools of many European countries as well as on this side of the Atlantic. It has something like a hundred periodical publications, distributed throughout the world. It has a literature of many hundred volumes, original and translated, and the number is increasing today by almost geometric proportions.

These are but a few facts concerning the moribund language. I should like to go into my personal experience with Esperanto during the last seven years and tell of the value of close relation with men of my own profession in Russia, France, Spain, Brazil, Italy, and elsewhere, but this would make too long a story. Were the predicted obsequies of Esperanto to take place to-morrow its past value to me would repay tenfold the comparatively short time given to learning the language. It is safe to say that my experience is not unique.

C. H. Fessenden, Chairman
Examination Committee
Esperanto Association of North America

Published: November 24, 1912

At the City College

Last Thursday morning Edmond Privat spoke to the French students in French on Edmond Rostand. At 12 o'clock in the Great Hall he addressed the entire student body on the International Student Club movement. He spoke of the success of the various universities in establishing branches of a large international association of student societies in this country. He talked also of Esperanto and its possible means of facilitating communication among the various chapters.

Published: May 4, 1913

Posthumous Book by Ferrer Reveals His Ideals

Only Volume Written by the Founder of the Modern School in Spain Tells for the First Time the Origin of the System of Education for Which He Was Executed

Francisco Ferrer y Guardia was shot in the trenches of the Montjuich Fortress at Barcelona on Oct. 12, 1909. Instantly there was an uproar in the world of thinking men and women. Conservative opinion accepted and approved the decision of the military council that had found him guilty of "being the head of the insurrection" which had, a few months before, plunged the Province of Barcelona into civil war. Revolutionary opinion declared that his trial had been irregular, his conviction illegal, and that he was innocent of the charges brought against him.

Advanced thinkers all over the world did honor to his memory in various ways. His essays and portraits were spread broadcast. A statue was erected to his memory in Paris, a medal was struck in honor of his work, and in Europe and America Francisco Ferrer Associations were inaugurated. The man was proclaimed a martyr.

...

His Vindication.

Broken in health but determined in mind and spirit he passed the Summer of 1908 in the Pyrenees. There he wrote the book which is now published for the first time, adding to it from time to time, even down to the last days of his life. All in all it reveals the man as he really was—his aims, his ambitions, and his ideals—as nothing else. Moreover, it is a vindication.

One word of caution: Where Ferrer speaks of "existing schools" he means, of course, the schools of Spain; when he talks of "ruling powers" he has in mind the politicians of Spain; when he denounces "superstition" it is the superstition of Spain that he denounces, where nearly 70 per cent. of the population could then neither read nor write.

Ferrer describes at length how he became convinced that the "existing schools" were all wrong, and the advantage that might be gained by applying to them some of the elements that he found in the English, French, and German elementary schools until gradually he evolved a new system. He then sets forth his programme and demonstrates the advisability of co-education not only for the sexes but also for the classes. He gives a chapter on "School Hygiene" which reveals the fact that he had been in correspondence with American educators.

...

The more he submitted his plan to the educators whom he consulted the more he became convinced that he must alone map out his work. Although he gathered valuable hints from many, all seemed to lack universality. The language of his school would have been Esperanto if proficient teachers could have been had to impart a knowledge of it. The first draft of his programme reads as follows:

The mission of the Modern School is to secure that the boys and girls who are entrusted to it shall become well instructed, truthful, just, and free from all prejudice.

...

Published: June 15, 1913

1,100 Esperantists Meet

Twenty-three Nations Represented at the Berne Congress

BERNE, Aug. 24.—The Ninth International Esperanto Congress opened here to-day with 1,100 delegates present, representing twenty-three nations. Twelve American representatives of both sexes marched behind the American flag in the opening procession.

Dr. Ludwig L. Zamenhof, inventor of Esperanto, received a gold medal in commemoration of the twenty-fifth anniversary of the language.

Published: August 25, 1913

Beiliss Almost Ignored at Trial

His Name Not Once Mentioned in the Course of Wednesday's Long Session

Strain Causes Collapse

Prisoner Breaks Down—More Evidence Apparently Implicating Vera Teheberiak Is Given

KIEFF, Oct. 23.—When the trial of Mendel Beiliss, accused of the murder of the boy Yushinsky in March, 1911, reopened this morning, the prisoner's counsel called the attention of the Presiding Judge to the fact that, although the court sat yesterday from early in the morning until midnight, the prisoner's name had not been mentioned even once. Counsel asked the President to put this on record, and he consented to do so.

...

Esperantists of the World Protest

Through the medium of Esperanto, a worldwide protest against the so-called "ritual murder" trial at Kieff has been launched. The protest originated in Bohemia, with the adoption there of a resolution by 136 lawyers and public officials. A copy of this resolution, translated into Esperanto, has been mailed to every council of Esperantists in the world. New York Esperantists yesterday embodied it in a petition to Senator Root requesting him to place the protest before the Senate.

Published: October 24, 1913

POLICE STUDY ESPERANTO.

Paris Officials Hope to Aid Foreigners Through Universal Language.

Special Cable to THE NEW YORK TIMES.

PARIS, March 7.—Several French Police Commisaries and other officials have begun to study Esperanto. M. Mouton, who is the head of the Criminal Investigation Department, takes lessons three times a week from an Inspector who is proficient in that universal language. Police Inspector Miguière was the first French policeman to take up Esperanto, with a view to introducing it on the force.

It is hoped that the city will soon have Esperanto-speaking policemen on service in the streets, where it is believed they might frequently be able to help foreigners.

Police Studie Esperanto

Paris Officials Hope to Aid Foreigners Through Universal Language

Special Cable to THE NEW YORK TIMES

PARIS, March 7.—Several French Police Commissaries and other officials have begun to study Esperanto. M. Mouton, who is the head of the Criminal Investigation Department, takes lessons three times a week from an Inspector who is proficient in that universal language. Police Inspector Miguière was the first French policeman to take up Esperanto, with a view to introducing it on the force.

It is hoped that the city will soon have Esperanto-speaking policemen on service in the streets, where it is believed they might frequently be able to help foreigners.

Published: March 8, 1914

Discuss World Unity

Electricity, Says Humphrey, Thus Far is the Greatest Agent

What is called a "Preliminary World Unity Conference," to continue until April 27, was opened last night at the Daily Temple in East Thirty-second Street. Andrew B. Humphrey, ex-President of the Republican Club, now General Secretary of the Peace and Arbitration League, spoke on the "Present World Peace Movement," James F. Morton, associate editor of The Truth Seeker, read a paper on "Esperanto" as a world language, Dr. Ira S. Wile of the Board of Education spoke of "Brotherhood in the Education of Children," and Miss Elizabeth Knopf, director of the temple, on "World Unity."

...

"Esperanto is no longer a fad, but is of practical use," said Mr. Morton. "Contrary to a mistaken impression, it is not intended to supersede the language of any nation; it is designed to provide a means of communication with all nations, an international language, a neutral language, one that will draw the peoples of all nations closer together and tend toward world peace."

Published: April 13, 1914

Preparations for Celebration of Century of Peace between England and America

Prospects for European Travel

Cheaper Rates, Better Accommodations, and More Extended and Varied Itineraries Seem to be the Season's Features

This year the tourist contemplating Europe is confronted by the paradox that, while keepers in most of the centres abroad anticipate an unusually prosperous season, steamship agents in New York, after consulting similar data, are not so enthusiastic.

The latter were told last week that the hotel keepers even expected to surpass the great touring Summer of 1910 — the year of "The Passion Play" at Oberammergau — when it is estimated nearly 200,000 sight-seeing Americans crossed the Atlantic, and that word had gone forth from London, Paris, Berlin, and even Vienna that visitors must engage rooms a month in advance or find themselves homeless on arriving at their destinations.

...

Aside from the Anglo-American Peace Exposition at Shepherd's Bush, London, there are to be several attractions not only in London but also on the Continent which are inviting without much fuss more or less organized bodies of tourists — the Congress of the Salvation Army, and those of surgeons and dentists in London, several pilgrimages to Lourdes, the Berne National Swiss Exposition, the Esperanto Convention in Paris, the Cologne Fair, &c. — and those bodies will probably form a large bulk of the human cargo this Summer. Moreover,

...

Published: April 26, 1914

Many College Men Now Among Police

Lawyers, Doctors, Dentists, and Teachers Winning Their Way in Blue and Brass

Career for the Educated

Men of Polish and Refinement Find Good Berths— Big Changes in Fifteen Years

...

A striking example of the educated man on the force is Lieut. George H. Quackenbos, who is interpreter at Police Headquarters. He is the son of the late Prof. Quackenbos, who held the chair of Latin and Greek at Harvard for fifteen years. Lieut. Quackenbos was born in Chicago in 1867, and was prepared for college by his father. When he was 11 years old he had been pretty much through the Latin and Greek classics. He was graduated from Washington University, and in 1889 received the degree of Doctor of Medicine from New York University. He taught at St. Francis Xavier's College, at the Weingart Institute, and at Seton Hall, South Orange. He taught in these institutions ancient and modern languages, rhetoric and higher mathematics. He speaks six languages, including Esperanto; knows the deaf and dumb language, and has interpreted this language when mutes have visited Headquarters. He makes all the foreign translations for the department. Lieut. Quackenbos is also a telegrapher. ...

Published: June 21, 1914

Glynn Names Esperantist

First New York Delegate Will Attend Paris Convention

For the first time the State of New York has a delegate to the tenth International Esperanto Congress to be held in Paris the ten days beginning Aug. 2.

Abraham S. Arnold, General Secretary of the Southern New York Division of the Esperanto Association of North America, yesterday received from Gov. Glynn authorization to attend the congress and make a report to the Governor. Mr. Arnold is a lawyer at 27 William Street and a Columbia graduate of the class of 1910.

New York is the sixth State in the nation to have a delegate to the Esperanto congress, the others being Massachusetts, Louisiana, North Carolina, South Carolina, and Illinois. There will be 6,000 delegates in Paris from eighty-five countries. Paris has appropriated 100,000 francs for the entertainment of the delegates.

Published: July 21, 1914

Esperanto for Police

Paris Chief Will Reward Those Who Can Speak It

Special Cable to THE NEW YORK TIMES.

PARIS, July 25.—Policemen speaking Esperanto is the latest innovation of Chief of Police Hennion, who is sparing no effort to modernize the Paris police force.

Seizing the opportunity afforded by the International Esperanto Congress here between Aug. 2 and 10, he recently issued an edict that policemen holding an Esperantist certificate should be distinguished by a green star embroidered on the left sleeve and be detailed for service in the Grand Boulevards and other localities where tourists were likely to gather.

Several sessions of the Esperantist Congress will be devoted to police interests, especially as regards international co-operation.

Other features of the congress, which it is expected will be attended by fully 3,000 Esperantists, including about forty from the United States and the Philippines, will comprise amateur performances in the Esperanto language of Molière's "George Dandin," Prof. Richard's "Mort de Socrate," and an act from "Promotions," by Tristan Bernard.

Published: July 26, 1914

City Brevities

...

Books and magazines printed in Esperanto will be on exhibition tomorrow, Tuesday, and Wednesday, from 7 to 10 P. M., at the Labor Temple, Fourteenth Street and Second Avenue. ...

...

Published: March 14, 1915

Through Siberia

Dr. Nansen's Timely Contribution to Geographical Knowledge

Through Siberia, the Land of the Future, By Fridtjof Nansen. Translated by Arthur G. Chater. Illustrated. New York: Frederick A. Stokes Company. $5.

...

At Yeniseisk, a town of 12,000 inhabitants and 1,000 timber houses—without a single sawmill, everything being sawn by hand power—Dr. Nansen began a series of festive receptions that lasted pretty well across Siberia. He could not talk a word of Russian, but had to make a long address before the boys' school. He spoke in English, of which his hearers did not understand a word; but his friend, Vostrotin, translated, and the boys got a holiday. Then the Mayor and corporation had to give a big lunch with hours of speeches in fluent Russian, praising the guests in words he could not understand, and ending with an address in Esperanto by the school Principal, who was the only soul in the room who understood it.

...

Published: March 28, 1915

The Linguistic Winifred

How Much Japanese Does the Wunderkind Really Know?

To the Editor of The New York Times:

Has it occurred to any one to test the child Winifred Stoner, for whom her mother makes such remarkable claims? The claims of the lecturer seem to have been taken for granted without any trial.

At the first lecture a number of small children were brought upon the stage, and the lecturer would have them repeat after her several words which meant "cow," "pig," &c., in Chinese; "goodbye" and "good morning" in Japanese, "Twinkle, twinkle, little star" in Latin, and a few in Esperanto. They would repeat these after her—though there were some whose lips did not move at all—just as they might say "eeny meeny meiny mo," and there is no certainty that in ten minutes after they could have repeated any of the words or told one kind from the other. After each attempt the lecturer would say with beaming complacency, "There you see, they speak Japanese," or Chinese, or Esperanto, as the case might be. But if Miss Winifred Stoner, the accomplished daughter, speaks her twelve languages only on that basis, she has not added much to the world's stock of knowledge.

Then, geography was supposed to be taught by giving each child a small globe and singing in rhymes some fact connected with a place pointed out on it. Thus:

> To Tasmania we will go
> Because they never there have snow.
> To Tasmania we will fly
> Because the wheat grows eight feet high.

Here is an idea, of course, but as Tasmania is not the only place where they don't have snow, what is to prevent Tasmania from being jumbled up pretty soon with a lot of other places? Furthermore, the number of rhymes is quite limited and the number of places is very great. How are you going to get enough to go around? If you must repeat the same ones, the mixing up process soon begins. Furthermore, there are many mothers who cannot rhyme at all, even in such an elementary way as above.

Note, that if you must teach the geographical fact by locomotion, you run out of words expressing locomotion in very short order. As you have to make your fact suit your rhyme also, should we not be driven to this, for example:

> Out to Pittsburgh let us scoot,
> Where the air is mostly soot.
> From Rock Island let us skip
> For there's the great receivership.

E. X. Porter
New York, May 1, 1915

Published: May 4, 1915

Usonia is Logical

A Suggestion That Esperanto Will Supply Our National Name

To the Editor of The New York Times:

It is both illogical and impertinent for the inhabitants of the United States of America to seize upon the name Americans for themselves. Any one who is a resident of any part of North or South America is an American. But if it is sad to be a man without a country it is also awkward to belong to a country which cannot furnish its inhabitants with a name. United Statesians would not be a very aesthetic designation, and besides, at any moment there may be United States in South America. In any such case the thing to do is to resort to the international auxiliary language which we shall all be presently familiar with—Esperanto, or, better, the Reformed Esperanto of Ostwald, Jespersen, and Couturat. In this language inherent difficulties have been labored over by expert philologists and for the most part logically solved. In both forms of Esperanto, the primitive and the reformed, the word for an inhabitant of the United States of North America is Usona, which, for use in the English language, might become Usonian.

The name of the country itself (since in this perfect language nouns are characterized by all ending in "o") is Usono. In this case Usonian readily suggests U. S. A., (or U. S. N. A.,) but if any one can think of anything better, more appropriate, or more artistic, the committee, of which M. Couturat, Paris, is head, will, I am sure, be ready to receive suggestions. They have already adopted at my request the independent words matro and femino in lieu of using for mother, woman, the feminine derivatives of patro, viro, namely, patrino and virino, which is what the regular rule would require. The word homo is, of course, reserved for man in the sense of a human being.

Christine Ladd Franklin
Columbia University, New York, July 7, 1915

Published: July 12, 1915

USONIA IS LOGICAL.

A Suggestion That Esperanto Will Supply Our National Name.

To the Editor of The New York Times:

It is both illogical and impertinent for the inhabitants of the United States of America to seize upon the name Americans for themselves. Any one who is a resident of any part of North or South America is an American. But if it is sad to be a man without a country it is also awkward to belong to a country which cannot furnish its inhabitants with a name. United Statesians would not be a very aesthetic designation, and besides, at any moment there may be United States in South America. In any such case the thing to do is to resort to the international auxiliary language which we shall all be presently familiar with—Esperanto, or, better, the Reformed Esperanto of Ostwald, Jesperson, and Conturat. In this language inherent difficulties have been labored over by expert philologists and for the most part logically solved. In both forms of Esperanto, the primitive and the reformed, the word for an inhabitant of the United States of North America is Usona, which, for use in the English language, might become Usonian.

The name of the country itself (since in

Universal Ro

The long confusion of post-Babelian speech is to end at last. Not from the ivory, but the horn, gate speeds the millennial dream. Even in the iron bosom of war stirs the breath of Universal Brotherhood:

> For now the deep, dense plumes of night are thinned
> Surely with glimmering of the winnowing wind
> Whose feet are fledged with morning.

For how can the earth sons be brothers till they are one in language? The Rev. Edward P. Foster of Marietta, Ohio, a graduate of the college of that city, a postgraduate of Yale, Leipsic, Berlin, has been struck with the international dangers of the diversity of speech. How can the different nations get one another's point of view unless they have a common medium of expression? The commercial and social advantages of such a medium are obvious. Imagine the perplexities of an Ostiak or a Urabunna trying to order "beef and" in a New York beanery.

Every language but one's own is as obscure to most of us as Basque or Etruscan. Mr. Foster starts fresh. He creates a globe lingo, Ro. Other experiments have failed. Mr. Foster is the editor of World Speech, "a Monthly Magazine of Word-Wide Interests." You can learn a lot of Ro in an hour. This morning's lesson is in verbs. A Ro verb begins with "E." They are divided into three classes, like railroad trains on the Continent:

They affirm, deny, or interrogate. Ro uses the initial "e" for the affirmative verb, "ye" for emphasis or euphony, "ne" for the negative, and "we" for the interrogative verbs. Ro indicates mood and tense by the consonant following the "e," thus: "eb," infinitive; "ec," imperative; "ed," pluperfect; "ef," perfect; "ek," imperfect; "el," present; "em," future; "et," future perfect. Verbs are further subdivided into five classes by the vowel following these consonants, thus: "eba," neuter, affirms state or condition; "ebe," intransitive, middle voice, action confined to the subject; "ebi," transitive, active voice; "ebo," passive, tells what is done to the subject of the verb; "ebu," potential mood.

This is as simple as Etruscan. Any child ought to be able to learn it in less than twice the lifetime of Old Parr. Then the potentialities of the Ro potential are marvelous. You use certain consonants in place of the English auxiliary verbs: "b," may; "c" probable; "f," seems; "k," can, and so on. Add the five vowels, mix, you have the whole conjugation. For example: "Eduba," had been possibly; "educa," had been probable; "edufa," had seemed. See?

Don't you sleep well? Plaster your memory with a little Ro:

Ebab — to exist; ebnab — to be non-existent; ebeb — to come into being; ne-beb — not to come into being; ebneb — to go out of existence; ebib — to create, to make exist; ebnib — to annihilate; ebob — to be created; nebob — not to be created; ebnob — to be annihilated; Ecab! — Exist! Ecnab! — Be non-existent! Eceb! — Come into being! Ecneb ! — Cease to be! Ecib! — Create! Necib! — Do not create! Ecnib! — Annihilate! Ecob! — Let be created! Ecnob! — Let be annihilated! Ecnob whoever loves not this strange, sweet world language. Take a piece home:

Fefab el femab. — That which has existed is that which will exist. — Awi eteb tlav felab etneb? — What will have come into existence when that which now exists will have passed away? Felulab wekuseb? — Should that which may exist come into existence? Fefab wedusab? — Should that have existed which has existed? Fenefukob neluknob, ud feluknob nedukob. — That which cannot have been created cannot be annihilated, and that which can be annihilated could not have been created. "Carthage elumnob": Carthage must be destroyed. So must Volapük and Esperanto. Simple, sensuous, passionate Ro recalls the Miltonian definition, so much admired by Arnold, of the essentials of poetry. Ecnib, ecob! The frogs have talked Ro from the first. Here's a short familiar Ro dialogue: "Paw el ad?" "How are you?" "Abi lica," "All right." If Ro is not abi lica, we don't know right from wrong. "Why to our green, unknowing youth, was this loveliest of tongues denied?"

Published: October 3, 1915

> **Esperanto in the Bronx.**
>
> *To the Editor of The New York Times:*
>
> Permit me to thank and congratulate you for your true and humorous editorial in Sunday's paper in reference to the so-called international language Ro.
>
> The very fact of one's inability to get one's tongue around such sentences and word formations as are characteristic of Ro precludes the possibility of its ever being very widely accepted. Fortunately, however, the international language idea is by no means destined to share the fate of Ro; and it may be interesting to your readers to know that Esperanto has been steadily gaining ground for the last twenty-five years, and that it has never been more "alive" than at the present moment.
>
> CRESTON C. COIGNE,
> Secretary The Bronx Esperanto Society.
> Bronx, Oct. 4, 1915.

Esperanto in the Bronx

To the Editor of The New York Times:

Permit me to thank and congratulate you for your true and humorous editorial in Sunday's paper in reference to the so-called international language Ro.

The very fact of one's inability to get one's tongue around such sentences and word formations as are characteristic of Ro precludes the possibility of its ever being very widely accepted. Fortunately, however, the international language idea is by no means destined to share the fate of Ro; and it may be interesting to your readers to know that Esperanto has been steadily gaining ground for the last twenty-five years, and that it has never been more "alive" than at the present moment.

Creston C. Coigne, Secretary The Bronx Esperanto Society
Bronx, Oct. 4, 1915

Published: October 8, 1915

Bayonne Reformed Spelling

The Jersey town of Bayonne broke from its prosperous seclusion last Summer and produced riots that made a Sheriff famous. Today Bayonne shows a startled world a strike against orthography, a riot of cacographers. After no small or intolerant study of spellings irregular but great, we feel almost a personal affection for the genius of The Advance Sheet of Bayonne, edited "in the interest of" religious and political advancement "and orthographical reform" by the lady to whom we owe this entire and perfect chrysolite:

> It iz very fien four the anahrkist tue preech pursunal integriti; and it iz veri fien foar the "socialist" tue preech soashal ekspeediensi; but soashal justis which purmits boath, iz graiter than eether.
> Soashal justis feedz the hungri, heelz the sik, kloathz the naiked, wiepz awai teerz, and kasts out devilz; and if wee pahrtaik ov eni pursunal injustis it shal bie noa meenz hurt us.

Respectfully dedicated to Colonel Roosevelt and Mr. George W. Perkins. Forever float The Advance Sheet! It is good to see the consonants and vowels taking a day off and memorably punching the noddles of poor tame orthodox spellers. Would that old Noah Webster, somewhat of a gypsy grammarian and orthographer, could see this Bayonne shindy. The Advance Sheet deals in Esperanto shorthand, but the Bayonne "scientific phonetic spelling" "iz moar fahr reeching."

Published: February 27, 1916

A Strong Language

Professor A. J. Weaver doesn't go far enough when he writes to our thrice-prized contemporary, World-Speech, of the Buckeye Marietta: "What an uplift to the world if Ro could be established and made universal!"

Ro, which is Ro for "language," is the universal tongue on which the Rev. Edward P. Foster has labored so long and fruitfully. Compared with it, Volapük is monkey chatter and Esperanto the stirring of a Romance spoon in a Latin salad bowl. It is the simplest and most profoundly philosophical of speeches. The initial letter of each word shows what group of ideas it belongs to. S for sensibilities; T for time words, and so through the alphabet. It is an index language. It is a catalogue. It is an ocean sea of alliteration. And its sound is as of the frogs of Aristophanes or any industrious bullfroggery. For example, "uq" begets words of similarity. Such words as "uqa uq," as like as: "uqna uq," as unlike as, express not only the lyric mood of the bullfrog, but his "plump" and "kerchunk" into his pool. They weave into their passionate web of harmonies an indefinable undertone which recalls somewhat the sound made by a stone "skipped" over and under the surface of a pond by a small boy expert in the art now or formerly called "cutting an egg."

But this excursion in melodious noise doesn't help us to practice the literature that FOSTER speaks. Here is a Monday lesson, indicated for commuters and good New Yorkers: "Weka uza in dusac tiktag uz aci ek rit?" — "Were there as many at church yesterday as you anticipated?" Uplift the world? Why, Ro is strong enough to unleash the dogstar from the Great Dog and spill Cassiopeia from her chair.

Published: March 13, 1916

Obituary Notes

...

Miss Emeline Howard Mann, a writer, of Philadelphia, died on Saturday at her home there, in her seventieth year. She was a daughter of the late Colonel William B. Mann, and was one of the first to take up the study of Esperanto.

...

Published: April 10, 1916

Folly of a New Tongue

People Will Not Adopt a Language Having No Established Literature

To the Editor of The New York Times:

There are several reasons which seem to have been overlooked why no new language that people will use can be created. Also, why no common language for use in writing by peoples of different tongues can be made successful. I will treat the last proposition first.

To begin, different languages have different laws, idioms, and usages, which always make languages difficult to acquire. If it was merely difference in words it might be easy to arrange a common medium for different nations. But their grammars are different. Thus the Russian and most Slavonic languages have no article, definite or indefinite. It would be difficult for those people to use any devised literary medium with an article. They would almost instinctively use the new medium in the Russian way, which would make it hard for people of other tongues to understand. Then, again, if such a tongue were devised without an article, it would be hard for people accustomed to its use to write the language. Then, again, most languages (except English) have what are called reflexive verbs, that is, verbs used in connection with some reflexive pronoun. People speaking languages with such verbs would find it awkward to use a medium without them. People having languages like the English (without such forms) would find it difficult to use such forms properly, so as to make the meaning understood.

It would seem from this that it would be impossible to form a universal medium of intercourse, even for writing, that could be successful. It will explain the little success of so-called Volapuk, Esperanto, and the like.

But there are strong reasons why no new language can ever be adopted by civilized man, (or uncivilized, for that matter,) and why the only language that can ever displace the others and become universal must be some language now spoken, and with a standard literature. It seems strange it has not been considered; people must have a literature. No language can be kept pure without literary standards. Besides, it is something every people will have. They will not dispense with it. The literature of one language can rarely be translated into another and have any force or interest, or in fact be literature at all. Put into another tongue it, in most cases, ceases to be literature, and becomes dull and uninteresting. The reasons can easily be conceived. Different languages have different usages and idioms. The poetry is nearly always lost by translation. Rarely can a poem of one language be paraphrased in another and be anything like the original.

People must have a deep and impressive literature of some sort, if for no other reason than to keep the language pure. They will not turn to any language that has none, because they cannot take any literature with them. A literature, to be of any force or have any influence, must be in the original tongue. For that reason no new languages can be formed in these days either, by a mixture of tongues or by the devices or scholars. Any brogue or "lingo" formed by people of different languages now, as the English was formed about six hundred years ago, would only be "vulgar" and would be condemned in advance. No literature could be brought to it, and people would not wait for it to develop one. Therefore the nations will have to choose some language that already has an established literature for the universal language.

A. Y. Smith
Louisville, Ky., July 11, 1916

Published: July 20, 1916

Esperanto Defended

Its Merits and Success as an International Language

To the Editor of The New York Times:

The argument of A. Y. Smith against the possibility of creating an auxiliary language for international use reminds me forcibly of the lawyer who, being sent for to affect the release of somebody under arrest, cited to the man behind the bars authority after authority that his arrest had been absolutely impossible and even unthinkable.

The continued use of Esperanto by peoples from every land and clime certainly disproves Mr. Smith's main contention, and the fact that the two writers who, next to Dr. Zamenhof, are considered the best stylists in Esperanto literature, Kabe and Grabowsky, are Poles, shatters his labored argument that because "the Russian and most Slavonic languages have no article, definite or indefinite, it would be difficult for those people to use any devised literary medium with an article, and they would almost instinctively use the Russian way, which would make it hard for peoples of other tongues to understand." Considered as groups, the Russians seem to take to Esperanto with greater ease than to their own language.

I myself, born in Russia, found the article the least difficult to tackle in my struggle with the English language. It was the spelling, so arbitrary and contradictory, as related to the sounds of the vowels in the worlds bread, break, breach, that I found most vexatious and disconcerting. In Esperanto each sound is represented by one letter only, and each letter has only one sound. Then, the difficulty of placing the accent on the right syllable, so tantalizing in English, is wholly done away with in Esperanto, for the accent is always on the penult. Again, there are no such things in Esperanto as mute letters. It is absolutely impossible to make mistakes of spelling in that language.

His argument that, since every language must have a literature, therefore Esperanto is doomed to failure, is not a strong one. If I have not misread history, it is not literature that gives life to language; rather it is language which gives birth to literature. In other words, although I am no farmer, I dare say that it is not the apples that sustain the apple tree, but rather it is the apple tree which brings forth the apples. However, having produced in less than three decades of its existence something like 2,500 works, covering all the branches of literary endeavor, Esperanto may modestly say: "I am doing pretty well, thank you."

I am sure that the writer of that letter never examined this language at all, for everybody that does so has nothing but good to say about it. I would advise Mr. Smith to give it a trial.

Joseph Silbernik
New York, July 21, 1916

Published: July 24, 1916

The Mission of Esperanto

To the Editor of The New York Times:

This letter is written to refute the arguments of A. Y. Smith, writing in your esteemed paper on the "folly" of a new tongue. Mr. Smith makes the common mistake of thinking that Esperanto is designed to supplant national languages. This is not true. Esperanto is designed to supplement them. So there is no need that it should have a literature.

Mr. Smith speaks the truth when he says "different languages have different laws, idioms, and usages, which always make languages difficult to acquire." It is well-nigh impossible for one person to gain a thorough speaking knowledge of the representative national languages. But one can (it has been done) acquire a thorough knowledge of a language which combines the logical and easy usages of all. Moreover — and I know whereof I speak — no matter how idiomatically written by a native of one country, Esperanto is always intelligible to a brother Esperantist of another nationality, so long as elementary clearness is preserved.

As for the "little success" of Esperanto, I would say that its growth since its inception is admitted to have been marvelous.

P. Lewinson, Jr.
New York, July 20, 1916

Published: July 26, 1916

The Allies of the Future

A Meditation on the Second Anniversary of the Beginning of the Great War in Europe

By Professor Hugo Muensterberg, of Harvard University

Only one way seems open — a might must be established which is stronger than the right of self-defense. We must be able to compel the unruly nation by militant power to wait a year at the gates of the arena. This is the program of the League to Enforce Peace, with the "Enforce" printed red in the title. Will it really bring us salvation?

…

The League to Enforce Peace is like the league for the use of Esperanto. This, too, was invented in order to harmonize the nations of the globe. Their common mistake is to fancy that in the world of history an artificial abstract construction can replace that which has grown organically. The linguistic forms of a nation's expression and the emotional forms of its friendly or hostile behavior cannot be created in a philological or juristic laboratory; they have to grow in free historical development. The mere abstract formula for international war obligations, treating each case after the same logical pattern, must remain a failure. It will always be brought to nothing by the organic alliances which are held together by the self-conscious will and the historic interests of great nations. Does this suggest that no outer force exists which can keep order in this unruly world? Certainly not. It does mean only that such a force can never be created by a mechanical prescription with paragraphs fit for every case, but that the power to enforce peace must come from a true living alliance of nations physically strong enough to discourage every enemy and morally strong enough to win the faith of the world.

...

Published: July 30, 1916

Language Purity

Why Not Have a Commission to Recommend Various Changes?

To the Editor of The New York Times:

The letter of A. Y. Smith, headed "Folly of a New Tongue," assumes that it is imperative "to keep the language pure." What does it mean to keep a language pure? Evidently, to guard it against change; to hold it rigid; to bring its evolution to an end.

Heretofore all languages, except the classical dead languages, by gradual change have gone through a process of evolution. The purists seem to have been most successful in preventing change with Chinese, which was fixed in the monosyllabic stage of development and held there. The result is a monotonous language with an impoverished vocabulary.

English was once in a very plastic condition in which change was rapid, taking place apparently by accident and without conscious volition. Now, however, the English speaking population numbers 160.000.000 people, distributed over a large part of the world, and is held so closely to a fixed standard by daily reading of printed matter that the natural evolution of the language seems to have come practically to an end.

If, at this time, English had reached the goal of perfection, this condition might be satisfactory; but it is plain that the language has crystallized in its present form, not by reason of its perfection, but because of circumstances which are quite unrelated to its merit. The question arises whether it may not be well to consider the desirability of artificial changes in the language, since natural change, of unknown and irresponsible origin, is at an end. It is suggested that an academy or commission might be chosen—fairly representing the users of English in all lands—with power to recommend, from time to time, changes or innovations in the language. The use of new constructions, words, or forms would, of course, not be obligatory upon any one, but would have the sanction of authority. If the changes had real merit they would probably, in time, come into general use. If not, they would pass into oblivion.

Mr. Smith objects to Esperanto because Russians have no article; but Russians can learn French, which has articles. He asserts that because artificial languages start with no literature "they can never be adopted." But all literatures were young once. It may be well to view with suspicion the claims of artificial languages to merit, but it is just possible that the artificial language idea may be sound. Therefore it seems wise to tolerate artificial languages long enough for a fair trial. Even we who are inclined to expect failure may consistently encourage those who are willing to take the pains to experiment.

Jonathan Holden
Pleasantville, N. Y., July 20, 1916

Published: July 31, 1916

How to Send Mail to Prisoners of War

New York, Dec. 1, 1916
To the Editor of The New York Times:

In an article published in The Times of Sept. 6 I have stated briefly what is being done by the Swiss Post Office to help the communications by mail between the war prisoners and their families. What had impelled me to write that article was that shortly after I arrived here from Switzerland I began to receive inquiries from my compatriots in this country, who asked me how they could send parcels to their relatives in captivity; how they could find them; how they could help them. Besides, I knew from personal experience that the problem of communications with war prisoners was a complex one; different Post Offices in this country had more than once refused to accept from me letters to prisoners of war free of charge.

Following the publication of my article I received a number of letters on that subject, among others one from Mr. Creston C. Coigne, Secretary of the Greater New York Esperanto Society. Mr. Coigne informed me that he had been all the time sending letters, books, and magazines to a Belgian soldier interned in Holland, and that before commencing his correspondence he "made inquiries at the Foreign Department of the New York Post Office and at the Pennsylvania Terminal Station, and at both places was informed that no postage was required on mail to a prisoner of war or an interned soldier.

"I think," Mr. Coigne continued, "your trouble has consisted in coming into contact with an uninformed postmaster who was ignorant of the fact that the American Government is just as generous as her 'elder sister' in making sacrifices for the suffering folks in the Old World. There are several Esperantists in New York City who are now corresponding in the international language with prisoners of war, who could support the statements I have made in this letter."

...

And therefore, although most unwilling to displease the esteemed Secretary of the Esperanto Society, I have to conclude with the same appeal with which I concluded my first article: "Let the great American Union follow the example set by her elder sister, the Swiss Union, and make it possible to people in this country to relieve the situation of their relatives who are in captivity, by sending parcel post packages free of postage."

Published: December 10, 1916

AUTHOR OF ESPERANTO DIES

Dr. Ludwig Zamenhof's Book Was Hailed as 'Language Hope for Peace'

AMSTERDAM, Monday, April 16.— Dr. Ludwig Zamenhof, inventor of Esperanto, died yesterday at Warsaw, according to advices received here.

Dr. Zamenhof was born in Bielostok in 1856. He published his first book in the then new language called Espeanto in 1887. It succeeded Volpük as an international auxiliary language, and it was hailed as the "Language Hope for International Peace."

Dr. Zamenhof chose the roots of Esperanto from existing languages, mainly the European languages. The phonology of his language is said to be very simple. - There are 2,642 roots in Dr. Zamenhof's language. Esperanto was taken up in many countries.

Dr. Zamenhof came here in 1910 to attend an Esperanto congress in Washington. An effort was made to get President Roosevelt to take up Esperanto, but he was then busy advocating simplified spelling and nothing came of the Esperantist appeal.

Author of Esperanto Dies

Dr. Ludwig Zamenhof's Book Was Hailed as 'Language Hope for Peace'

AMSTERDAM. Monday, April 16. — Dr. Ludwig Zamenhof, inventor of Esperanto, died yesterday at Warsaw, according to advices received here.

Dr. Zamenhof was born in Bielostok in 1856. He published his first book in the then new language called Esperanto in 1887. It succeeded Volpük as an international auxiliary language, and it was hailed as the "Language Hope for International Peace."

Dr. Zamenhof chose the roots of Esperanto from existing languages, mainly the European languages. The phonology of his language is said to be very simple. There are 2,642 roots in Dr. Zamenhof's language. Esperanto was taken up in many countries.

Dr. Zamenhof came here in 1910 to attend an Esperanto congress in Washington. An effort was made to get President Roosevelt to take up Esperanto, but he was then busy advocating simplified spelling and nothing came of the Esperantist appeal.

Published: April 16, 1917

In the Current Week

Today

...

Dr. Ludwig L. Zamenhof, the founder of Esperanto, will be honored by speakers at a meeting of the Public Forum of the Church of the Ascension in the evening.

...

Published: May 27, 1917

This Week's Free Lectures

...

Sunday

Esperanto, in Memory of Dr. Ludwig L. Zamenhof, founder of Esperanto. Talks by the Rev. Percy Stickney Grant, Professor D. O. S. Lowell, James F.Morton, Henry W. Fisher, Rufus W. Powell. Public Forum, Inc., Church of Ascension, 10th St. and 5th Av., 8:15 P. M.

...

Published: May 27, 1917

Felix Moscheles, Painter

London, Dec. 24. — Felix Moscheles, the painter, died at Tunbridge Wells on Saturday. He was born in London Feb. 8, 1823, a son of Ignaz Moscheles, a composer, and godson of Felix Mendelssohn. His artistic education he received in Antwerp and Paris, where his early pictures were exhibited. He had been President of the International Arbitration and Peace Association, and also President of the London Esperanto Club.

Published: December 25, 1917

Record of 1917 in Chronology and Statistics

...

Entrance of the United States Into the War, the Withdrawal of Russia, and the Groping for Peace Have Discounted the Year's Fighting.

...

Prominent Persons Dead

...

Dr. Ludwig Zamenhof, inventor of Esperanto, the universal language, 58 years old, April 15.

...

Published: December 30, 1917

Letters to The Times on War Topics and Other Subjects of Public Interest

For Ido and "Usona"

To the Editor of The New York Times:

Our international relations are destined to be so close after this war has come to an end that it will be quite impossible for us to get on without a common medium of exchange in language as well as in money and in weights and measures. In the case of language, it must be carefully borne in mind that no giving up of a country's own speech is involved; all that is required is a medium of communication with the foreigner — the Russian, the Japanese, the Turk, the Italian, the Frenchman. Instead of learning half a dozen languages, or more, imperfectly, one has only to learn a single one in order to be able to speak fluently with the forty and more nationalities that the commercial man, the scientist, the artists, the international lawyer, the statesman, the diplomatist will hereafter be forced to have dealings with. Already before the war it was an absurdity for a member of an international scientific congress to have to hear a paper read first in English, German, or Italian and then read over again in French, and in the end to have only half understood it, unless its language happened to be his own. When it came to the discussion of papers — the real reason for the holding of the congress — the foreigner, of whatever nation, was out of it altogether. Science would have progressed more than it has done if it had not been for the handicap of many languages.

For purposes of ready, exact, convenient intercourse among foreigners an international synthetic language is indispensable. I am constantly told that such a language wold lack the poetic quality which attaches to speech that one has learned at one's mother's knee. Of course it would; one cannot have everything. But this artificial language is not meant as a substitute for one's native tongue, but only as an auxiliary to it. It will lack patriotic associations; it is intended especially for international purposes. It seizes upon the best words and the most effective and most reasonable grammatical forms of all the existing languages, and out of these it constructs a language which lacks instinctiveness. It is true, but which is far from being without artistic beauty of its own. In fact, it is nothing less than a keen intellectual pleasure to make acquaintance with the best of these made languages—that is, with Ido, not Esperanto. Esperanto is far too Slavic in its vocabulary and far too Teutonic in its grammar, but Ido, the more modern, and improved, form—devised in connection with the International Congress of Philosophy, Paris, 1900—comes very near to perfection. In face of a crying need, this language (or a better one, if such be provided,) is sure to be adopted in course of time, for those purposes for which it is intended; but if not, it will always remain a brilliant example of what can be done in the way of artificial language construction.

Usona (or Usonia) is an incident in this coming world language, but it deserves more speedy currency than the rest of it, on account of the fact that few people are really satisfied with our clinging to either America or Yankeedom as our only name when we are fighting in France shoulder to shoulder with the Canadians and with our own Southerners. Those who think that either of these two neighbors of ours—of us Northerners, that is—is satisfied with our grasping ways in the matter of a name are only those who have never talked with them about the matter. It is not for them to make complaint, of course, especially in this moment of world stress, but it is a good time for the swashbuckling "Americana" to show consideration for the more modest inhabitants of all of America outside of the United States.

As a matter of fact, the name Usona (of very easy construction, to be sure,) was first proposed by a Canadian, James P. Murray of Toronto, in 1885. It was thoroughly discussed, both pro and con, in The Nation (among other places) in March, 1916. And at the time of The Hague Conference, when the "Americans" first claimed their name—being unwilling, it is said, to come in for seats in the rear of the hall with the U's and the V's—Sir Edward Grey (as he was then) urged upon us, in a speech delivered in London, the name Usona, but, of course, without undue insistence.

Your editorial article maintains that there is "something wrong" about Usona, (Usonia,) but without pointing out what it is. The English regularly speak of an A. D. C. when they mean an aide de camp. To one who sees these letters for the first time they look very wrong, for the reason that the capital "D" plays a much more important rôle than fits the modest de of the real phrase. So in the synthetic word Usonia, it is a pity that the accent has to fall on the "o," the letter which stands for the unimportant word "of" of the real name. This is a blemish, I admit, but it seems to be an unavoidable one. A writer in The Boston Herald has, indeed, suggested dropping the "o" altogether and using simply "Usna" for our new auxiliary name, and perhaps this might be the better plan. All that I insist upon is that the anomaly of being a country without a name should be brought to an end, now that we are hoping to play a great and a magnanimous part in the reconstruction of a world set free from a domination-loving Prussia.

Christine Ladd Franklin
Columbia University, July 18, 1918

Published: July 20, 1918

Sees World League Our Godsent Duty

Dr. Wilton Merle Smith Says Senate Criticism Is a Discredit to America

Defends Russian Jews

Dr. Wise Quotes Kerensky to Show Majority Are Anti-Bolshevist

...

The Peace Conference should cultivate a universal language, declared Dr. S. Edward Young at a Polish meeting in the Bedford Presbyterian Church, Brooklyn, last night. Some language or device of the allied nations — Esperanto or what not — that will enable them to talk together when they come together, should be adopted, he said. "After a century and a quarter, Canada is still almost two nations along the bilingual lines of French and English," he added. "The Slavic language has always been a more vital unity than any of the empires or political divisions into which it has been broken. With the tongue go countless affinities and prejudices that may be intangible enough; but they affect the blood and the soul of men. Let the Peace Conference call in the linguists and the ethnologists and set them to work at the long, long task of promoting a common utterance and a common literature, and by so much will the diverse peoples of earth approach the era of understanding and hence confidence, which all the international conventions to date seem to have furthered only negligibly."
...

Published: February 24, 1919

Dr. George Macloskie

PRINCETON, Jan. 5. — Dr. George Macloskie, Professor Emeritus of Biology of Princeton University, died here yesterday in his 85th year. From 1875 to 1906 he held the chair of biology. Born in Ireland, he was ordained in the Presbyterian ministry in 1861, and was a pastor of a church in Ballygoney, Ireland, from 1861 to 1872. He wrote "Elementary Botany" and "Flora of Patagonia" and many papers on botany and Esperanto.

Published: January 6, 1920

Exchange of Words

To the Editor of The New York Times:

Referring to your editorial article in last Sunday's TIMES, regarding English words in the French language, it may be interesting to note that the following Russian words have settled comfortably in the King's English: Douma, mir, ukase, pogrom, knout, mujik, zemstvo, Izba, bolshevik, Soviet. I might also mention with Mr. Anderson's approval the word "vodka," which, however, reached the English language long before the passing of the well-known and popular amendment.

Perhaps this interchange of words among the chief European languages points to the possibility of there evolving after a few brief centuries an international jargon to meet the needs and purposes of humanity so incompletely and unsuccessfully served by the Esperanto and other artificial languages.

J. G. Fourman
Special Traffic Agent, Russian Division
New York, March 22, 1920

Published: April 3, 1920

An Alsatian's Language Problem

To the Editor of The New York Times:

I wish to correct a statement in a letter in THE TIMES by stating that Esperanto is not a jargon but a language which has a fixed grammar, known to be better than that of any existing national language. It is simple and clear in spelling, reading, writing, dictation, singing and talking and practical in its use whether for business, scientific or political transactions.

My concern has been using Esperanto for several years in business and entertains correspondence with nearly all countries. For thirty years I know French, for eight English, making still many mistakes in using both languages. I cannot clearly pronounce such words as: World, worth, earth, though, thought, nor can I make any differentiation in pronouncing the words hidden place and hidden plays. As to French, I serve you with this sentence: "Si six scies scient six cyprès combien de scies scient soixante-six cyprès!" I am an Alsatian and I don't want you to pronounce the German words Hecht, Pfeife, Pfruende, Zwetschkenknoedel, because you could never do it! Yet an Esperantist would be able with the Esperanto letters to pronounce them better than any one else. Any Englishman having learned Esperanto is able to pronounce the words Pripet, Cerna, Trieste, Fiume, Bukarest, Jugoslavia, Czechoslovakia, Ukrainia, Moskva, Petrograd, Zara, Spalato, Dubrovnik, Sarajevo, Cetinje, Vladivostok, Vladikavkaz, Blagoviestchensk, etc.

Esperanto is in fact a living language, spoken among its admirers and in international congresses, where more than forty-five nationalities have met.

H. E. Lempertz
New York, April 5, 1920

Published: April 9, 1920

ESPERANTO SPREADING FAST

Universal Language Compulsory in Schools of Several Countries.

According to delegates to the Thirteenth Annual Congress of the Esperanto Association of North America, which opened yesterday in the Bahai Library, 415 Madison Avenue, the universal tongue is spreading fast. Edward S. Payson of Boston presided and the address of welcome was delivered by Miss Cora L. Butler, President of the New York Esperanto Association.

The annual report disclosed that the so-called universal language had been made compulsory in the schools of Russia about a month ago and that it is either compulsory or optional in the schools of Hungary, Jugoslavia, Czechoslovakia, Saxony, Serbia and in many cities. Among the latter are Barcelona, Amsterdam, Grenoble and Lille. The congress will continue until tomorrow.

Esperanto Spreading Fast

Universal Language Compulsory in Schools of Several Countries

According to delegates to the Thirteenth Annual Congress of the Esperanto Association of North America, which opened yesterday in the Bahá'í Library, 415 Madison Avenue, the universal tongue is spreading fast. Edward S. Payson of Boston presided and the address of welcome was delivered by Miss Cora L. Butler, President of the New York Esperanto Association.

The annual report disclosed that the so-called universal language had been made compulsory in the schools of Russia about a month ago and that it is either compulsory or optional in the schools of Hungary, Jugoslavia, Czechoslovakia, Saxony, Serbia and in many cities. Among the latter are Barcelona, Amsterdam, Grenoble and Lille. The congress will continue until tomorrow.

Published: July 23, 1920

Hold Esperanto Congress

Speeches in Same Language Made by Delegates of Many Countries

Special Cable to THE NEW YORK TIMES

THE HAGUE, Aug. 10. — The Hague is becoming the meeting place of international congresses which follow fast one upon another. At the International Esperanto conference which held its opening ceremony yesterday in the old Knights' Hall seldom used except for the opening of Parliament, there were almost 400 delegates, representing every conceivable country and including America's representative, Mr. Trost.

Speeches were made in Esperanto by delegates from practically every country. The Italian delegates' speech was greeted with great applause, although he has known Esperanto only six months. The Hague Burgomaster Patyn who welcomed the congress, referred to the great difficulty two of the world's greatest statesmen, Wilson and Orlando, had in understanding each other.

At today's congress many new points were discussed and a program arranged for the following congresses which will be resumed

Wednesday. The President of the congress read a telegram from Sir Eric Drummond, expressing his regret at being unable to represent the League, owing to the San Sebastian meeting.

Published: August 11, 1920

League Assembly Ends: Delegates Praise Its Work

By EDWIN L. JAMES
Special Cable to THE NEW YORK TIMES

GENEVA, Dec. 18 (By telephone to Paris). — The first Assembly of the League of Nations adjourned tonight after five weeks' work. It will meet again the first Monday in September, 1921.

At the closing session today M. Hymans, President of the Assembly, and M. Motta, President of the Swiss Republic, and the Assembly's host, made congratulatory speeches stating that the work done by the Assembly had made the League a living, working organization.

...

A number of pet projects have met with disaster, yet there are few, if any, delegates who remained for the entire Assembly who will leave dissatisfied with the work of that body.

Esperanto fell a victim to a sharp assault by Gabriel Hanotaux when the committee reported in favor of an expression by the Assembly with the object of encouraging the general teaching of Esperanto in the public schools with a view to making it eventually an international language and the language of the League. After a debate the Assembly voted against the proposal.

...

Published: December 19, 1920

Paris Business Men Would Use Esperanto

Chamber of Commerce Committee Finds It Useful as a Code in International Trade

By Wireless to THE NEW YORK TIMES.

PARIS, Feb. 15.—The Paris Chamber of Commerce has taken the initiative in instituting Esperanto classes in all their commercial schools so that students can learn for commercial purposes an auxiliary international language. Before taking this step the chamber appointed a committee to inquire into the real usefulness of Esperanto, and among other tests they made was to translate a large number of business letters into Esperanto and then back into French. It was found that the sense of the letters was in no way lost.

The committee recommended that Chambers of Commerce in other countries should be asked to institute similar classes in the language invented by Dr. Zamenhof, which they are convinced will enable international business to be carried on without error and with much greater dispatch and cheapness than when translators into half a dozen languages have to be employed. The ease with which Esperanto can be learned and its accuracy in translation were regarded as its two principal recommendations above other artificial languages. For business purposes it is regarded as by far the clearest and richest in expression and easy to translate.

Some of the texts submitted to the test were such that the slightest mistake would completely change the meaning, but Esperanto was found to meet all requirements. M. André Baudet, Chairman of the committee on whose recommendation it was decided to open the classes, describes Esperanto as rather an international code than as a language.

"It won't revolutionize the world," he said, "and there is no likelihood that it will take the place of any language, but, just like a telegraphic code or a system of stenography, it can be useful to every people and aid enormously in international business."

Published: February 16, 1921

New German Foreign Minister

To the Editor of The New York Times:

It may interest your readers to learn that Dr. Friedrich Rosen, whose appointment as Foreign Minister in the German Cabinet is the subject of so much comment in Berlin and Paris, is, on his mother's side, a member of the Moscheles family, prominent for generations in the musical and artistic centres of Europe. His grandfather, Ignaz Moscheles, in his time the most brilliant virtuoso in the field, had a lifelong friendship with Mendelssohn. When asked to take the lad Felix as a pupil, he said: "If he wishes to take a hint from me as to anything new to him, he can do so, but he stands in no need of lessons." In 1916 Ignaz's son, Felix (a godson of Mendelssohn), was still living in London, where he had been President and Chairman of the International Arbitration and Peace Association, as well as President of the London Esperanto Club. This well-known artist's pictures have been exhibited in the chief galleries of London and Paris.

It has seldom been my fortune to meet a man so versatile in culture as Dr. Friedrich Rosen, whom I saw intimately when he was Vice Consul in Beirut and Consul General in Jerusalem. Having passed his boyhood in the Holy City, he retained a free use of the Arabic vernacular without a trace of foreign accent. He is, I understand, also at home in Persian, as he is, of course, in French and English, and I know not how many other European languages. He has his share of the family love of music, and his wife — also a grandchild of Moscheles — was, at the time I knew her, a pianist of unusual competence. Apart from his almost world-wide experience and knowledge of political affairs, his dignified charm of manner should render him an admirable Foreign Minister.

Frederick Jones Bliss
New Haven, May 25, 1921

[Unfortunately, it must be added that Dr. Rosen's diverse talents were put to a somewhat unhappy use in 1905 and 1906, when he was the Kaiser's chief instrument in Morocco. The type of diplomacy there exhibited is hardly the sort of thing that will make friends for the German Republic. — Editor Times.]

Published: June 5, 1921

Schooner Esperanto Sinks Again

HALIFAX, N. S., July 11. — A meagre message received here from Sable Island today said the Gloucester fishing schooner Esperanto, which was raised for the third time yesterday had gone down again. Pontoons had given way twice previously when it was thought the schooner was safely afloat. The Esperanto, winner of the international fisherman's race off this port last Fall, foundered off Sable Island when returning from the Banks several weeks ago.

Published: July 12, 1921

Schooner Esperanto Sinks Again.

HALIFAX, N. S., July 11.—A meagre message received here from Sable Island today said the Gloucester fishing schooner Esperanto, which was raised for the third time yesterday had gone down again. Pontoons had given way twice previously when it was thought the schooner was safely afloat. The Esperanto, winner of the international fisherman's race off this port last Fall, foundered off Sable Island when returning from the Banks several weeks ago.

Advocate Esperanto as World Language

Thirteen League Delegates Introduce Resolution in Favor of Its Adoption

The question of an international language is coming more and more to the front within the League of Nations, according to information received by the League of Nations News Bureau. The matter has been definitely brought before the Assembly by a resolution introduced by thirteen delegates, and there is every reason to believe, the bureau says, that this resolution will be passed.

The signers of the resolution are Lord Robert Cecil, representing South Africa; Professor Jonnesco of Rumania, Emir Zoka-ed-Dowleh of Persia, Senator La Fontaine of Belgium, Dr. Benes of Czechoslovakia, Dr. Restrepo of Colombia, Tsai Fou-tang of China, Mr. Enckell of Finland, Bishop Noli of Albania, M. Adatci of Japan, Dr. Escalante of Venezuela, Maharaja Khengarji of Kutch, India, and Professor Askenazy of Poland.

The resolution reads as follows:

"The League of Nations, recognizing that linguistic difficulties form a barrier to direct relations between the peoples, and that it is urgently necessary to find a remedy which may contribute to goodwill between nations, follows with interest the endeavors made by several members of the League to introduce the teaching in schools of the international language Esperanto; hopes that this system of education may spread throughout the world, so that children of all countries may, in the future, know at least two languages, that of their country and another, which may serve as a simple and easy method of international communication; requests the Secretariat to prepare for the next Assembly a report on the results obtained in this field."

Published: October 2, 1921

In the Current Week

...

Dr. M. J. Plese will lecture on the use of Esperanto under the auspices of the Esperanto Institution at Omar Khayyam Restaurant, 34 West Thirty-fifth Street, at 8 P. M.

...

Published: October 9, 1921

A "Lingvo" for All?

To the Editor of The New York Times:

In answer to Mr. Arthur Elliott Sproul's letter of the 15th inst., I can assure him that English, however much we would like it, has no right to claim to be the second language to all, for it is the hardest language a foreigner could rightly spell or pronounce. Besides that, the language is very unclear, as, for instance, "laughter" and "slaughter" are so similarly written and so differently pronounced. What about needle, needles and needless, and pair, pare and pear, &c.? For this reason we who speak English must be more tolerant toward the larger part of humanity, who cannot speak English.

We surely will favor French before German, Spanish, Russian, Arabic or Japanese.

French is a second language to the diplomats, but it can never be the second language to business men and working men, for both of them are too busy to lose efforts and time in studying languages, and then when they have acquired some knowledge in them to talk with foreign accent, as this is the case with French, German, Russian and any other national language.

The schools are teaching English, French and Spanish, Latin, Greek and Hebrew, and let every one select his own second language.

The real second language must be simple, easy and regular, and has been already introduced in the schools of Brazil, Saxony, Bulgaria, Finland, Czechoslovakia and Russia. We simply must follow it, like our Chamber of Commerce and the other similar institutions of London, Paris and Tokio, &c. The Red Cross, the Boy Scouts of different countries and so many other organizations have taken hold of it, and therefore every individual should think on the language of brotherhood of man and buy a grammar of Esperanto, the second language to all!

Esperanto estas lingvo pli simpla ol angle au france!

H. E. Lempertz
New York, Sept. 18, 1921

Published: October 11, 1921

Foster Common Language*

League of Nations Considers Adoption of Esperanto

The question of an international language is coming more and more to the front within the League of Nations, according to information received by the League of Nations News Bureau. The matter has been definitely brought before the Assembly by a resolution introduced by thirteen delegates, and there is every reason to believe that this resolution will be passed. The signers of the resolution are Lord Robert Cecil, representing South Africa; Professor Jonnesco of Rumania, Emir Zoka-ed-Dowleh of Persia, Senator La Fontaine of Belgium, Dr. Benes of Czechoslovakia, Dr. Restrepo of Columbia, Tsai Fou-Tang of China, Mr. Enckell of Finland, Bishop Noli of Albania, M. Adatci of Japan, Dr. Escalante of Venezuela, Maharao Khengarji of Kutch, India, and Professor Askenazy of Poland. The resolution reads as follows:

FOSTER COMMON LANGUAGE

League of Nations Considers Adoption of Esperanto.

The question of an international language is coming more and more to the front within the League of Nations, according to information received by the League of Nations News Bureau. The matter has been definitely brought before the Assembly by a resolution introduced by thirteen delegates, and there is every reason to believe that this resolution will be passed. The signers of the resolution are Lord Robert Cecil, representing South Africa; Professor Jonnesco of Rumania, Emir Zoka-ed-Dowleh of Persia, Senator La Fontaine of Belgium, Dr. Denes of Czechoslovakia, Dr. Restepo of Columbia, Tsai Fou-Tang of China, M. Eackell of Finland, Bishop Noll of Albania, M. Adatci of Japan, Dr. Escalante of Venezuela, Maharao Khengarji of Kutch, India, and Professor Askenazu of Poland. The resolution reads as follows:

"The League of Nations, recognizing that linguistic difficulties form a barrier to direct relations between the peoples, that it is urgently necessary to find a remedy which may contribute to good will between nations follows with interest the endeavors made by several members of the League to introduce the teaching in schools of the international language, Esperanto; hopes that this system of education may spread throughout the world so that children of all countries may, in the future, know at least two languages, that of their country and another, which may serve as a simple and easy method of international communication; requests the secretariat to prepare for the next Assembly a report on the results obtained in this field."

At the thirteenth universal Esperanto

"The League of Nations, recognizing that linguistic difficulties form a barrier to direct relations between the peoples, that it is urgently necessary to find a remedy which may contribute to good will between nations follows with interest the endeavors made by several members of the League to introduce the teaching in schools of the international language, Esperanto; hopes that this system of education may spread throughout the world so that children of all countries may, in the future, know at least two languages, that of their country and another, which may serve as a simple and easy method of international communication; requests the secretariat to prepare for the next Assembly a report on the results obtained in the field."

At the thirteenth universal Esperanto congress, held in Geneva the beginning of August, the League was represented by Dr. Nitobe of the Bureau Section, who addressed the congress and later reported to the Council on the proceedings. While in session the congress sent a telegram to the League which said: "Thirteenth universal Esperanto congress with 2,000 delegates from forty nations respectfully asks the League to recommend gradual introduction of Esperanto teaching in the schools of her members in order to help popular education in ideals of the League."

Published: October 16, 1921

*The first two paragraphs of this article are identical to "Advocate Esperanto as World Language" (October 2, 1991) on page 223.

In the Current Week

...

There will be a peace memorial dinner of the Esperanto Institute at Omar Khayyam Restaurant, 34 West Thirty-fifth Street, at 8 P. M.

...

Published: November 6, 1921

In the Current Week

...

Saturday

Esperanto Instituto will meet in honor of Dr. L. L. Zamenhof, the founder of Esperanto, at the Omar Khayyam restaurant, 34 West Thirty-fifth Street, at 7:30 P.M.

...

Published: December 4, 1921

In the Current Week

...

Esperanto will be illustrated in addresses and songs at a dinner of the Harmonio, at 68 East Eleventh Street, beginning at 7:30 P. M.

...

Published: January 8, 1922

A Political Observatory

David Jayne Hill, once our Minister to Switzerland, speaks of that country as "an admirable observatory from which to study other nations" because of its geographical location. But M. Fatio, one of the most distinguished citizens of Geneva, just returning to Europe after a visit to a number of our colleges and universities, speaks of another advantage which Geneva has for such observation. The beautiful city is the seat of twenty-six international institutions, social, political, educational, moral, religious and humanitarian. Moreover, according to M. Fatio, fifty-seven assemblies and congresses of an international character were held in Geneva during the year 1920-1921, all the way from a miners' convention to a world assembly of faith and order, and from a convention on the opium traffic to one on Esperanto. It might better be called not an observatory but a laboratory, with admirable and exceptional clinical facilities in politics, economics and morals.

...

Published: April 2, 1922

Pope Tells of His Interrest

Will Do All in His Power to Contribute to Conference's Success

GENOA, April 9 (Associated Press).—The municipality of San Remo has received word from Rome that Pope Pius, in accepting olive branches sent from San Remo on the occasion of Palm Sunday, said:

"I will do all in my power to contribute to the success of the Genoa conference, for the pacification of the world and the restoration of economic conditions in Europe."

The Society of Esperanto of Genoa has addressed a message to the economic conference, greeting the delegates as "pillars of the world" and welcoming them to the city of Columbus and Mazzini, saying that humanity awaits from the conference peace, fraternity and progress.

Scores of manifestos have been received from other organizations, including the Fascisti, who conclude their pronouncement by instructing their members to observe strict discipline and avoid demonstrations of approbation as well as of disapproval, and expressing the hope that the conference will pass in perfect tranquility.

Published: April 10, 1922

In the Current Week

...

"Esperanto's Future" will be the subject of a lecture and songs at a meeting of the Esperanto Instituto at the Green Witch Restaurant, 68 East Eleventh Street, beginning at 8 P. M.

...

Published: May 7, 1922

Bilingual

The lesson which the author and Academician, Maurice Donnay, learned during his recent visit to America is that it is necessary for his countrymen to know English. It is only so, he intimates, that Frenchmen and Americans will be able to reach a better understanding of each other. He refrains from adding, except in a very courteous intimation concerning our American unfamiliarity with French literature, that he has also found out that it is desirable for us to learn French. This we are probably doing now much more widely than the French are learning English. Very few even of the cultured Academicians speak English. But with all their passionate desire to have their own language appreciated, the French must not, says Donnay, "hold any illusions as to its universality." Two-thirds of the civilized world is now speaking English.

It is not likely, despite the continuing spread of English, that any national language will be immediately—that is, short of a half century—accepted as a universal second language. And this, says a responsible body of American scholars, is too long for the world's need. It is therefore proposed by them that Latin—"the only universal language that the world has ever had"—the language of lettered Europe for a thousand years, should meanwhile be chosen as the universal auxiliary language for the use of statesmen, scientists and business men. This would necessitate its being taught as a living language; but, with so many teachers of Latin already in the schools of the civilized countries, it should be much easier to accomplish this than to find competent teachers of Esperanto, or some other artificial language, and add it to the already overcrowded school curriculum.

Meanwhile, it would be a great advance toward international understanding if we were to widen our acquaintance with French, which must be for most people of English speech the second language, even if Latin becomes an auxiliary tongue and if Donnay and his countrymen were to learn to speak and write English as well as Chevrillon, the nephew of Taine, who with Donnay represented the French Academy at the Molière celebration in America. The Times presents in another column an article by this distinguished liaison scholar, illustrating incidentally the advantage of being bilingual.

Published: May 24, 1922

Former Service Man Shot Dead by Nurse

Woman in Kansas City Then Shoots Herself, Explaining Her Acts

KANSAS CITY, Mo., June 3.—A romance which sprang from the war and mutual interest in Esperanto, the international language, ended tragically to-day for Frank W. Anderson, floor manager in a local department store, and Peggy Marie L. Beal, a nurse, of Dayton, Ohio.

Patrolmen, responding to a call from a hotel, were directed to a room where guests heard two shots, and found Anderson dead on a bed, with a bullet wound in the back of his head. Lying on the floor with a bullet hole in her left breast was Miss Beal, clad in her nightrobe. Beside her was a revolver. The police expressed the belief that the "eternal triangle" was the motive.

On the dresser was a novel with a page turned down at an illustration portraying a woman dancer, dagger in hand, standing over the prostrate form of a man. Miss Beal was sent to a hospital, where her condition was reported critical tonight.

Officers said Anderson and Miss Beal had lived at the hotel as husband and wife since Wednesday and for a week previous had lived at another address. The woman came here about ten days ago, they said, from Springfield, where for five months she had been a nurse.

Anderson had met Miss Beal while a Lieutenant in the Signal Corps and she was a nurse in the East. A courtship sprang up between the couple in an Eastern hospital. Their letters contained frequent passages in Esperanto. After the war Anderson worked in St. Louis, coming here three months ago.

Anderson was shot in the back of the head as he was lying on his side, officers said. He was 33 years old, according to an application for work filed with the store where he was employed. He also stated on the application blank that he was married. His wife is believed to be in St. Louis.

A note written by the nurse was found in the room by the police. It read:

"My name is Peggy Beal. I am 29 years of age. I live in Springfield, Ill. I came to Kansas City with the intention of marrying Frank Warren Anderson. When I arrived I met him and we went to the Midwest Hotel together.

"He told me he was married, and that he was not divorced yet. Therefore he could not marry me.

"There is nothing more to tell. I shot him because he brought me here and could not marry me.

"Peggy Beal"

Published: June 4, 1922

In the Current Week

...

Saturday

"Esperanto-Language in Radiography" will be the subject of a meeting of the Esperanto Instituto at the Green Witch Restaurant, 68 East Eleventh Street, at 8 P. M.

...

Published: June 4, 1922

Today's Radio Program

STATION WJZ, NEWARK, N.J.
360-Meter Wave Length.
(Daylight Saving Time)

...

7:30 P.M. — "Esperanto," a suggested radio international language; by James Denson Sawyers.

...

Published: June 19, 1922

Letters to the Times

The Universal Language

Mr. Sproul, in The Times, professes French or English to be the universal language, but neither of these languages will be successful for they are too difficult. There is only one language that can fulfill the requirements of this question and that's Esperanto.

Esperanto being a very simple, although very rich language, everybody can learn it thoroughly in a short time.

I am an Esperantist for fourteen years, French born, and learning English for ten years. After a careful study I can say that I believe that of one hundred English-speaking people learning French, there will be only one successful. Of one hundred Frenchmen learning English there will be only one successful. Of those two hundred learning Esperanto there will be one hundred and fifty successful.

Charles Chomette
New York, July 31, 1922

Published: August 6, 1922

League Activities

Remarkable Record Set Forth of Achievements in Maintaining Peace in Europe and South America—World Court Functioning

By Hamilton Holt

...

What, then, is this League of Nations that Senator Harding said was "already scrapped" and President Harding says now "can have no sanction by us"? I cannot hope in this short paper to bring in review all the things that have been done by the League of Nations and under its auspices since it began its official existence on Jan. 10, 1920, two years and a half ago. Things are happening with such cumulating swiftness that I doubt if any one outside the secretariat at Geneva can keep fully up to date in things accomplished and things projected.

...

Finally, the Assembly refused to approve of Italy's proposal for an impartial international distribution of raw materials, it declined

Senator La Fontaine's plea for the establishment of an international university at Brussels, and it was unwilling to record itself as favoring Esperanto as the international language.

...

Published: August 20, 1922

Need of a Common Speech

The nations comprehend today, as never before, the necessity of a common or universal medium of verbal expression, possessing the richness, but devoid of the difficulties and absurdities of the national languages, and thus, for obvious reasons, we must evolve a universal language, not an artificial language like the Esperanto, which is complicated, incongruous, repellent, whose very alphabet condemns it. The universal language must be based on the noblest common usage of language that the grandest nations of Europe have as an interrelated heritage.

George Du Bois

Published: September 24, 1922

Symposium of Languages

Seekers for a Medium of Universal Speech and a Simplified English

To the Editor of The New York Times:

A great public service is being performed by The Times in so generously opening its columns to a discussion relative to the adoption of a second language for world use. No better proof could be adduced of the need for such a step than the active correspondence that has followed my letter to The Times of July 30. Mr. Du Bois's letter advocates the elimination of the Saxon portion of our language and the substitution therefor of "Latin equivalents or synonyms." I am very far from failing to recognize the high value of Latin. Indeed, it may not be improper for me to state the fact that, some years ago, when wishing to express a certain idea in English, for which no word was then in our dictionaries, I coined one out of Latin, on the spur of the moment, and sent it to print. This word not only found a place in the succeeding editions of our American dictionaries, but was inserted in the Oxford Dictionary. However, I do not feel that the suggestion to make over the English language by the substitution of Latin for Saxon is at all practicable. Whatever language may be chosen for universal "second" use must be adopted "as is," with all its faults. Changes in language come very slowly and they cannot be forced.

After Maurice Donnay, author and Academician, had returned to Paris from his official mission to this country, in May last, he authorized a statement to the effect that "the great lesson" taught him by his visit here was the need for his countrymen to learn to read, write and speak English. And he added, with characteristic courtesy of expression, that he thought many Americans "not sufficiently informed" about the French, and possessed of "perhaps wrong views" concerning the French attitude toward international questions today.

However, as Mr. Du Bois well says:

"There is a tremendous need for a universal language. ... The nations comprehend today, as never before, the necessity of a common or universal medium of verbal expression." That, as I have previously pointed out through the courtesy of The Times, is the main, big fact. It was the fact in the mind of J. Pierpont Morgan when, in June last, he called attention in an authorized statement to the fact that the international bankers, while in session in Paris, had found "a difference between English and French texts of the reference from the Reparation Commission to the bankers' committee" of so important a nature that it "touched the very root of the matter." Yet the two texts were supposed to be identical!

I think there is a character in Charles Reade's novel, "The Cloister and the Hearth," who, after lamenting this very difficulty occasioned by differences in languages, cried passionately: "For what are your barbarous jargons but barriers between men's hearts!" "Barriers between men's hearts" seems, in this period of world travail and discord and misunderstanding, to be particularly worthy of emphasis, in order that such things may be more clearly seen and hence more summarily dealt with.

The facts are undisputed. In view of them, one may well ask: How long is this condition of things to be permitted to endure? And I repeat my wish that our own country might take the lead in calling an international convention to be composed of men of the type of Dr. Eliot of Harvard University, for example—men not only educators but publicists—to meet, and with regard only to the greatest good to the greatest number of mankind to decide as to which one of the existing languages should be fixed upon to be taught in the schools of all countries—side by side, of course, with the languages of those countries. It will be a forward step of incalculable value to the world. When once taken, and its beneficent results become apparent, the cry will go up: Why wasn't it done before? Will our Government now take the initiative by calling an international conference to sweep away, for all time, this "barrier between men's hearts"?

Arthur Elliot Sproul
New York, Sept. 24, 1922

To the Editor of The New York Times:

English is spoken more than any other language, not only for the larger trade, as I said in my letter of Sept. 3, but also for the reason that the American and English flags mean more political liberty and religious tolerance than any other flag or flags. These factors have already made the use of English more "universal" practically, and its use will continue increasing for generations to come; in the meantime, these factors will be foremost in human progress, and that even without making any change in this language as it is now.

Moreover, the Anglo-Saxon race is naturally becoming more artistic; and, realizing that the purer the language the more refining will be our tastes and aims, I venture the belief that America will sooner or later have an Academy of Languages to help make English as perfect as possible. True progress will be made, not by the radical change as Mr. George Du Bois suggests in his letter of Sept. 10, but by the line of least resistance, recognizing that a language, any language, being a human work of art will never be perfect, but subject always to a higher degree of perfection.

R. Da Torre
New York, Sept. 25, 1922

To the Editor of The New York Times:

Mr. Du Bois's characterization of Esperanto as "complicated, incongruous, repellant," I disagree with. The only solution is in the use of an artificial language and Esperanto practically fills the requirements. Esperanto words are based primarily on the commonest usage of the several most widely used languages and the grammatical rules are few, simple and not subject to exceptions; there are no irregularities. It is most similar to Spanish in its being regular, sonorous and having every letter sounded. It is very easy to learn even for an adult. Its method of forming parts of speech co-related in meaning from a single root word makes its flexibility and perspicuity enormous.

It is hopeless to try and make a universal language out of English because in doing it "the structure is liable to fall to pieces," as Mr. Du Bois says. So why not use a real artificial language already beyond its period of incubation, one which already has thousands of users and which already has some distinctive literature, and not try to breathe life into the disconnected fragments of some national language.

G. E. Hoeft
Queens, N. Y., Sept. 25, 1922

To the Editor of The New York Times:

It is emphatically incorrect to class Esperanto as an artificial language. Less than 5 per cent. of the root words of the language are of artificial origin, the rest being taken from the living Occidental languages, making the vocabulary of the language already recognizable in almost its entirety to most natives of the Western European languages. Mr. Du Bois in a recent letter says: "The universal language must be based on the noblest common usage of language that the grandest nations of Europe have as an interrelated heritage." A disciple of Dr. Zamenhof, not having read the preceding portion of Mr. Du Bois's letter, could easily believe these last words were written by a fervent advocate of Esperanto, for they verily do sound like a worthy tribute to that wonderful language.

On Sunday, Oct. 1, I am going to begin at 12 o'clock noon to instruct a member of the Old Colony Club in the Esperanto language. By midnight that night this man, who will gladly make affidavit that up to that day he has known nothing of Esperanto, will read and write Esperanto easily and will be able to converse with a Portuguese Esperantist now in this city with whom he will only be able to speak in Esperanto.

James Denson Sayers
New York, Sept. 25, 1922

To the Editor of The New York Times:

From one source we have suggestions for purifying English, from others the use of Spanish, or Latin, or the Latinization of English. Why all this attempt at mutilating a perfectly good language like English or Latin when there are other means of a universal tongue more easily arrived at? The means I have in mind is, of course, Esperanto. Although Mr. Du Bois asserts that Esperanto is complicated, incongruous, repellent, with even an alphabet which condemns it, I would venture to say that, possibly due to knowledge of other artificial languages, such as Volapük, which have all the above-mentioned faults, Mr. Du Bois condemns all such projects without fully investigating them.

Esperanto approaches as near perfection as a real language may be. It is not at all complicated, for, being built up in an agglutinative way, but retaining a true inflectional appearance, it only requires learning a simple set of invariable case and tense endings and a few suffixes and prefixes of constant meaning, in order to speak and write the language correctly. And its vocabulary is made up entirely of roots common to all the Indo-European languages, with some slight preference for Latin, so that any educated person can acquire a good vocabulary in a few weeks.

The alphabet of Esperanto, which is our English alphabet without "g" "y" and "w," and employing one accent (the circumflex), is so contrived that all words retain very nearly, if not exactly, the same forms as the French, Latin, English, German or Russian words from which they are derived. Some of the letters may not be sounded as some of us would like to have them, but the majority can find nothing repellent or condemnatory in pronouncing the letters as in the usual modern Continental pronunciation of Latin. ...

Regarding the simplification of English, I might say that although it is comparatively easy to simplify our spelling, the grammar is quite another matter. Schemes for spelling reform are very numerous, and all have some good in them. And yet, although every one sees the need of a reformed spelling, no one actually does anything toward its adoption. In view of this fact, how can any one suppose that the English-speaking people would sanction a "simplification" of their easy, inflectionless and not very irregular grammar, which, indeed, in my opinion, needs no simplification besides the elimination of the possessive case and of "irregular" verbs.

In conclusion let me repeat, in perfect agreement with Mr. Du Bois, that we need a universal, not artificial, language, based on Latin and other Indo-European roots — and, now in disagreement with Mr. Du Bois, that language is Esperanto, "l'Espero de la mondo."

George L. Trager
Rutgers College
Newark, N. J., Sept. 25, 1922

A Common Tongue

To the Editor of The New York Times:

The case with which Asiatics learn pidgin-English and make themselves fairly intelligible by its use is a strong indication that a less uncouth and more efficient language might readily be worked out along somewhat similar but more scientific lines. A tremendous advantage of such a language over one purely artificial is that one who has learned it is well on the way to acquiring something still better — a real language with perhaps the greatest literature in the world.

E. C. Frost
Baltimore, Md., Sept. 23, 1922

To the Editor of The New York Times:

English is an imperfect language. Its irregular pronunciation and the innumerable exceptions to its grammatical rules are but some of the proofs of this assertion. This imperfection is, however, not derogatory to the language, for there is not and never has been a perfect language. But that which is derogatory is the attempt of certain grammarians to feign explanations of difficult points by either repeating irrelevant statements of other grammarians or making equally irrelevant statements of their own. Indeed, many grammarians seem entirely to forget that they cannot indiscriminately make rules, though they may seem to fit the case exactly, without making them conform to the testimony which philology bears in speaking of the natural development of languages throughout the ages. Let us examine some of the explanations which put English grammarians into a dilemma.

A writer on English grammar has lately confronted the public with this startling piece of information: "In writing we must be guided by instinct, not logic." Now language is one of the offsprings of the intellect, and the intellect presupposes correct reasoning, or logic. Hence in speaking on this one point at least the esteemed writer must find himself in a logical difficulty. And if, indeed, instinct be the criterion by which we are to write, then why employ professors, intelligent beings, to teach us our language? A parrot, which is guided to a far greater degree by instinct than is man, would, according to this writer's reasoning, make a far better teacher. But the survey of language development in general seems to justify the conclusion that we are still far from founding chairs of languages for parrots.

The "shall and will" discussion is also a linguistic curiosity. The usual explanation is this: Use "shall" for the first person and "will" for the others. Then occasionally follows this naïve statement: In questions, if you expect the answer "will," use "will"; if you expect the answer "shall," use "shall." This is subterfuge. To the question, "Will you?" (or as some would have it, "Shall you") either answer, "I shall" or "I will" may be given, though, of course, with different meanings. In order, therefore, to ask this question correctly it becomes necessary for the speaker to divine correctly just which answer will be given. Philology has as yet discovered no such system of prognostication, and so those who wish to speak correctly need not yet supply themselves with a ouija board.

The potential mode is a mere step-child of English grammarians. It is not a real off-spring of our grammar. It is in fact no mode at all. In Greek the potential was considered a mere phase of the indicative and of the optative modes. The very fact that we speak of a potential indicative and a potential optative is already sufficient proof that potential is not a mode. The potential most probably entered the Greek through influence of the Semitic languages in which each verb may have a vast number of conjugations, each having a different shade of meaning. This system is, however, entirely foreign to all the Indo-European tongues. Then, too, the particles and peculiar construction which made it necessary for the ancient Greeks to distinguish potential verbs have passed away with the Greek and there is no reason why their spirits should be permitted to haunt our language. If we must have a potential mode, because certain verbs express potentiality, why not have a mode of motion, since many verbs express that also? And if English grammarians cannot bear to part from the potential, let them at least stop calling it a mode.

The English subjunctive is undoubtedly a vast ocean of shipwrecked hopes. In order, however, to avoid its difficulties grammarians will make the most adroit and at the same time incorrect statements. I shall consider but one such. It is to be found generally just after the student has been initiated into the mysteries of the word "may." What could be easier than to say: ... "Now that you know how to use the word "may" you can at one stroke learn the use of the word "might." It is simply the past of "may." This explanation is adroit and helps to smooth the way wonderfully — for grammarians, but not for the student. We know that if we are asked the question, "Will you do it?" we may answer correctly, "Yes, I may do it." But we may also answer with equal correctness, but with a different meaning, "Oh, I might do it." In both answers the tense is the same and both refer to the future, but that which is different is the amount of certainty. When we say "I may do it," we indicate that it is possible and probable that we do it; when we say "I might do it," we indicate that it is possible but improbable that we do it. The difference between these two words is, therefore, one of degree of certitude and not one of tense. This view can be defended even against the argument that "may" always becomes "might" in a change from the direct to the indirect discourse, for if the statement were uncertain in the direct form, it is but natural that it take a less certain form in the indirect.

George F. Kronenberger
Brooklyn, N. Y., Sept. 25, 1922

Published: October 1, 1922

Learnes Esperanto Quickly

Student Studies Rules and Converses in 7 Hours, Says Teacher

As evidence of the simplicity of Esperanto as an international language, J. D. Sayers, in a statement, gave details of an unusual experiment which he said never before was made in America, though it has often been recorded in Europe.

He said:

"The extreme simplicity of the international language is proved by its being taught to a new student sufficiently within a few hours to enable the student to converse intelligibly with a foreign Esperantist with whom conversation is only possible in Esperanto. The student is Charles B. Foley of 2 Arnold Court, Bristol, Conn., member of the Old Colony Club of this city. Beginning the study of the language at 1 o'clock, Mr. Foley was taught the sixteen grammatical rules and given a short rehearsal in the vocabulary and at 8 o'clock was introduced to Carlo Rhombus, a Portuguese Esperantist who is visiting the city.

"A slow but entirely intelligible conversation between the two was carried on for two or three hours. Mr. Foley expressed great astonishment at the ease with which he acquired conversational knowledge of the language."

Mr. Sayers announced that classes in Esperanto will soon be opened in the free night schools.

Published: October 2, 1922

"Oh, Shade of Euripides!"

In an editorial article with this reproachful title *The Morning Post of London* reproves Professor Gilbert Murray, translator in verse of Euripides, surpasser of Way and E. P. Coleridge in the difficult task of Englishing the works of the great Greek and "modern" maker of "romantic drama," for championing Esperanto before the Assembly of the League of Nations. Dizzy himself couldn't have been more fluent in assailing the proposed artificial tongue of international intercourse:

> Even an endless chain of interpreters is better than this pallid tongue which has no past, no memories, no rich, terrible and beautiful associations, which has been taught by no mothers and lisped by no babes, which has never been loved and made immortal by the poets, for whose song and meaning and music men have never died and have gone gladly to battle.

This is more romantic than Euripides ever was, but what has it to do with the case? Esperanto may or may not be the tongue out of a hundred made-up international tongues proposed since the time of Bishop Wilkins and Leibniz, but, whatever its faults or merits, it is not suggested as the vehicle of poets and orators in great literary movements and monuments. When the Greeks bought dyes in Tyre or tin in the Cassiterides they probably didn't employ the grand tragedy manner and language of Aeschylus and Sophocles or the "romantic" manner of Euripides. They had some sort of "pidgin-English," Hobson-Jobson, Chinook, or "Bostonese," as the language of commercial barter used to be called in the Northwest, just as the English colonists at the time of the Revolution were known to the French of Illinois and Indiana and to the Algonquin tribes as "Bostonians."

The American interest in this matter is considerable. With every effort, the majority of Americans, particularly those with "special advantages," will never learn to speak French. In most of our schools and colleges it is taught, and probably always will be taught, really as a dead language—something you read, if you're lucky, but don't speak and pronounce save in the manner of "a Spanish cow." The contest between French and English as to which shall be the international language, that ceased to exist when spoken Latin died in the seventeenth century, isn't likely to be decided in favor of either. The Russians are not innumerous. The Mohammedans, speakers of many languages, are becoming a more and more important part of this little world. In spite of famines and inundations the Chinese may be conceived as yet populating the world. A common denominator of language may or may not be possible, but that it must be artificial is evident; that it can have nothing to do with the literary expression of various nations that may or may not condescend to speak it is even more evident.

A Connecticut man in this city learned to converse slowly but intelligibly in Esperanto in seven hours. Doubtless he had a gift and genius for learning a language quickly, just as some people have for catching the pronunciation of French; but if any considerable number of people can learn Esperanto in anything like a reasonable time, it ought to be the international language. The only doubt is if any great number of people will take the trouble to learn any artificial language. Whatever such language comes to have international currency will be a matter of convenience; and the shades of Euripides, Shakespeare, Molière, Dante and Edgar Lee Masters won't have to turn a bit shadier in consequence.

Published: October 8, 1922

In the Current Week

...

"Esperanto, the Language for Radio-phonography," address by J. D. Sayers, Esperanto Institute, The Green Witch Restaurant, 68 West Eleventh Street, 8 P. M.

...

Published: October 15, 1922

Brief Extracts From Letters From Readers of The Times

Easy Esperanto

... I recall a meeting of the Esperantists at Cambridge, England, in the Summer of 1907, when I called on Professor J. E. B. Mayor, the editor of Juvenal, and found him preparing a speech in Esperanto to be delivered that evening. He told me he had made his first acquaintance with the language that week.

James H. Dillard
Charlottesville, Va., Oct. 10, 1922

Published: October 15, 1922

Labor Office Kept Busy

Increasing interest in the work of the International Labor Office of the League of Nations is shown by a report from Geneva that the monthly average of letters received during the first half of 1922 was 1,428, against 1,299 in 1921 and 835 in 1920. Nineteen languages, including Esperanto, were used in the correspondence.

Published: November 12, 1922

International Languages

To the Editor of The New York Times:

The interesting article by Dr. John D. Prince, in your issue of Nov. 5,* despite certain slight errors of fact and its concluding "counsel of despair," deserves the serious attention of all who are concerned with the promotion of a closer understanding among the people of the earth. Many years of study of the principal classic and modern languages, and more than a dozen years of attention to the international language movement, may entitle the writer to a moment's consideration in the expression of some grounds for dissenting from the principal conclusions of Dr. Prince.

Dr. Prince misses much of the point of the movement for an international language through too close an attention to merely academic considerations. Hence the demand, lying at the bottom of his whole discussion, that a language proposed for international usage shall overqualify. Unless we can have theoretical perfection, we must continue to endure the present chaos and reject every project offering substantial help to overcome its increasingly realized disadvantages.

The discussion of the various forms of sign language, pidgin English and bêche de mer scarcely needs much comment. These expedients are extremely useful as stopgaps where nothing better exists, but their limitations are obvious. Only concrete and highly practical subjects can be adequately discussed in any of them. They are crude and inharmonious in the last degree. Complex technical topics on the one hand and anything of a literary nature on the other are impossible of expression by them. Yet these ingenious systems of overcoming linguistic barriers in a rough way are of great value as showing the usefulness of even a crude type of international language, and as testifying to the immense need of a general means of communication among the peoples. If the barbarous tribes of the Pacific islands can learn and use a rude international language surely the more developed races of the earth can have little difficulty in adopting and using a better one. It is astonishing if the ignorant Solomon Islanders are to communicate without difficulty with neighboring tribes and with the white men by use of an artificial language, while the intelligent civilized races are to gaze hopelessly at one another across their frontier and to reject a simple means of rendering conversation possible and easy. When four of the leading representatives of the greatest nations of earth meet** to determine in a measure the fate of the world, and it is found that they have no common language in which to express themselves, Wilson speaking only English and Orlando only Italian, we are certainly face to face with a condition demanding a remedy.

Just before the war no less than one hundred international congresses were being held each year, besides many special international gatherings for every conceivable purpose. In every case except one the work was delayed or hindered by the difficulty, often amounting to impossibility, of mutual understanding, and the time and expense required for oral translations and the preparation of reports in several languages was in all cases a serious handicap. In many instances, serious disputes were occasioned by inaccurate ore disputed translations and by quarrels in the congresses over the languages to be officially used. The enormous total loss by reason of this preposterous friction, due to the single cause of the lack of an international language, is beyond calculation.

The one group of congresses which escaped all this difficulty was that of the men and women from all lands who met at the international Esperanto congresses. At one of these, attended by the writer, held in Antwerp in 1911, more than 1,800 delegates were registered, representing nearly every civilized country, Occidental or Oriental, on earth. Not a word was publicly spoken throughout the week of the congress in any language except Esperanto. Not only debates and parliamentary discussions, covering an immense variety of topics, engaged the attention of the congress, but separate group conventions were held by different professional bodies and by advocates of varying creeds or movements.

This was the seventh of a series of similar congresses which continued unbroken up to the war, and have now been resumed with equal success. A comparison of these results with the difficulties and limitations of the old-style congress where a diversity of language maintains a constant barrier among many of the delegates, demonstrates beyond all cavil the advantages of the progressive idea of utilizing an international language which really serves the purpose, even if theorizing philologists are able to find academic objections to it.

Dr. Prince mentions Volapük, with Esperanto, Ido and Neutral, as types of proposed international languages. He might have included 200 or more earlier experiments, now forgotten, and the fifty or so that have been offered since Esperanto became known, such as Dilpok, Spokit, Nov-Latin, Europal, Esperantida, Universal and Ro. A vital difference between Esperanto and all its would-be rivals is the fact that it alone is in actual and widespread use, and has created not only a propaganda in its own behalf but a world-wide and constantly growing movement. Whether Ido or any other project has some trifling advantages in structure is of minor consequence. The outstanding fact is that Esperanto does the work of the international language, does it well, and has not only won but held the support of an overwhelming majority of those who are persistently active in the international language movement. To scrap it now for something else would be to destroy coincidence in the whole idea and to give the movement a setback from which it would be extremely slow in recovering. These considerations are entirely apart from the fact that the alleged improvements of Ido are by no means universally accepted as such by those best qualified to judge. Ido itself comes under strong fire by the adherents of Esperantida, Europal and other projects. The friends of an international language in the main therefore wisely cling to Esperanto, not as theoretically perfect, but as amply qualified to do all the important work of an international language and as having the logical right of way. Only by such a concentration of effort can any stability be assured.

Dr. Prince's strictures on the Esperanto grammar are few and slight. It is true that English and one or two other national languages get along without the accusative. An international language, however, is intended for all peoples. The natural word-order varies largely in different languages, and the use of the accusative makes for complete clarity, no matter what order of words is followed by persons who find it easier and more natural to speak and write as the thought would flow in their own tongue. For so great an advantage the learning of one simple principle is a ridiculously small price to pay. It is peculiar to find Dr. Prince objecting to a uniform definite article, in direct antagonism to his own argument on the accusative. This admirable feature of the English language, to mention no other, secures clearness without complexity, and is open to no serious objection on any ground, Dr. Prince's view that it is "offensive" to users of the Romance tongues being quite without basis. His only other objection to the grammar of Esperanto is that there is too much of it. This is most extraordinary and would lead the reader to imagine that the Esperanto grammar is highly complex and requires the mastery of many rules. Hence it is not amiss to state that this grammar consists of only sixteen very simple rules, and has no exceptions or irregularities.

An international language is not desirable as a mere instrument of mechanical perfection, but as a medium to be continuously used. If changes in Esperanto are desirable, to make it a more efficient agency, there is precisely one time for such changes. Let an international commission, representing the nations of the civilized world, prepare its recommendations, that the result of its labors may be accepted by all leading Governments, and the international language adopted may be officialized and put in the schools of all nations. If the language thus recommended and adopted involves such changes from the present Esperanto as to constitute an entire transformation of the same, it will be of little consequence, since Esperanto will then have fulfilled its purpose, and its successor will be permanently established. Until that time, Esperantists are confident that they can best serve this cause of an international language by continuing to demonstrate on the widest possible scale the practicability and utility of such a language. The past achievements of Esperanto are such as to guarantee the success of such a course.

James F. Morton Jr.
New York, Nov. 14, 1922

Published: November 26, 1922

* The article by Mr. Prince could not be retrieved.
** The World War I peace negotiations in Versailles (1919) with David Lloyd George, Georges Clemenceau, Woodrow Wilson, and Vittorio Emanuele Orlando.

Leters to the Editor

The Language Question

I have been studying painstakingly the 300 years' history of the problem of an auxiliary language for twenty years. The auxiliary international language must be absolutely neutral and extremely easy to learn, to write and to speak. These two requirements exclude all natural languages.

The claims of great practical successes by the adherents of any one system, even if they were true, will not help that system in the least as shown by the example of Volapük. A daily paper is not the place for exposing the defects of Esperanto which render it unfit for the rôle of an international language. Only two important faults of Esperanto may be mentioned briefly because laymen will easily understand them. The international language must not contain types that cannot be printed everywhere. Esperanto has five peculiar letters foreign to any natural language. The sound of the international language must not be disagreeable. The sound of Esperanto is nothing short of repugnant, due to the extreme frequency of the sibilants, and to almost unpronounceable combinations of letters.

Because of these two defects alone, which are not the most important ones, comparative texts of other artificial languages and Esperanto are shunned by its adherents. All that they offer in defense of Esperanto's defectiveness are claims of practical successes.

Dr. Max Talmey
New York, Nov. 29, 1922

A Language Convention

In a letter from James F. Morton Jr., respecting an international language, he makes a plea for the use of Esperanto. Some of us think otherwise, preferring a choice of either English or French. The time for merely academic discussion is past. The time for action is here. Will our Government call an international convention, without delay, to consider the facts and to act upon them? At the end, a vote could be taken that would be approved by the intelligence of mankind; and, being so approved, there is no conceivable bar to the prompt realization of one of the greatest forward steps toward international progress and harmony that the world has ever seen.

Arthur Elliot Sproul
New York, Nov. 27, 1922

The Mission of Esperanto

I read with pleasure the letter of James F. Morton Jr. on "International Languages." The Esperanto movement is the most beautiful of all movements, for it aims to spread confidence and friendship among all human beings by giving them a means of contact and understanding; hatred shall disappear the day people will know each other more.

Charles Chomette
New York, Nov. 28, 1922

...

Published: December 3, 1922

Esperanto In Far East

Esperanto is being taught in twenty-three institutions for higher education in Japan, and in Tokio there are special courses in that language for teachers, according to reports recently received here. In China Esperanto is being taught in five cities.

Published: December 3, 1922

In the Current Week

...

Esperanto Institute, lecture, "Dr. Zamenhoff's Memorial for Esperanto." Gonfarone's, 40 West Eighth Street, 8 P. M.

...

Published: December 10, 1922

Excerpts from Letters

Observations and Comments of Many Men of Many Minds Upon a Variety of Current Topics of General Interest

Use of Esperanto

Among your letters on the international auxiliary language I read the statements made by Mr. James F. Morton Jr., Mr. Chaumette and several others, who favor Esperanto. As to Mr. Sproul's idea of voting for English or French, he may be assured that 99% of the English-speaking people of England, United States, Australia and Canada will vote for English, while 99% of my countrymen in France and French-speaking people of Belgium, Switzerland and

Canada will vote for French! This would never solve the question of adopting an auxiliary international language, for French or English are national languages. Now, let us give the Frenchman and the Englishman the same chances as the Italian, Russian, German, Chinese, Hindoo and Spaniard. Such chance can only be given by adopting a language made for that purpose! Latin and Greek, obsolete languages, are only good for a student of philology and impractical for business transaction, traveling or information service; and let us not forget the workman, who works today in this country, tomorrow in another!

There are three languages in existence, i.e., Esperanto, Yido and Esperantido. The first one is being taught in very many schools of Finland, Czechoslovakia, Bulgaria, Hungary, England, France, Russia, Brazil, Germany, Switzerland, Italy and other countries. It has been recognized and is in use by Chambers of Commerce, London, Paris, Yokohoma, Vienna, Reichenberg, and the State of New York, Washington and Los Angeles. It is being used by the annual great fairs of Paris, Frankfurt a. M., Leipzig, Praha, Reichenberg, Barcelona, Padova, Rio de Janeiro, &c. It has been discussed by the League of Nations with support of several countries and among them China, Japan, India, Persia, Czechoslovakia, Italy, Jugoslavia, &c. An Englishman, Sir Robert Cecil, was the main speaker in favor of Esperanto at the League. Professor Gilbert Murray of Oxford University, in the commission of the League, was a propounder of Esperanto. There is no city on the globe, where there are not to be found people speaking the Esperanto language.

Pierre Baville
New York, Dec. 6, 1922

...

Published: December 10, 1922

Index
of Personal Names

Adatci, Minéitciro (Adachi, Mineichirō) – 223, 225
Adler, Felix – 42
Aeschylus – 246
Alden, W. L. (Mr.) – 16, 24, 27, 29, 30, 31, 35, 36
Alfonso XIII, King of Spain – 158, 159
Ali Kuli Kahn (Ali Qoli Khan?) – 138
Anderson, Frank Warren – 231, 232
Archdeacon, Ernest – 134
Aristophanes – 199
Arnhold, J. (Mr.) – 138
Arnold – 196
Arnold, Abraham S. – 189
Askenazy, Szymon – 223, 225
Auerbach, R. – 120
Avellanus, Arcadius – 71, 72, 73, 74, 75, 76, 78, 82, 88
Baker, Arthur – 114, 132
Baptista Mello Souza, João – 143
Barrett, John – 137, 141, 143, 144, 158
Bartholdt, Richard – 172
Baudet, André – 220
Bauer, George – 1-7, 13
Baville, Pierre – 255
Beal, Peggy Marie L. – 231, 232
Beaufront, Louis de – 102, 107, 120, 122
Bebel, August – 57
Beiliss, Mendel – 184
Bein, Kazimierz (Kabe) – 202
Bell, Alexander Melville – 1-7
Beneš, Edvard – 223, 225
Bernard, Tristan – 148, 149, 190
Bianchini, Giacomo – 137
Birdwood, George – 27, 28
Bliss, Frederick Jones – 221
Boirac, Émile – 122, 126
Bois, George du – 235, 236, 238, 239, 240, 241
Bonbright, W. P. – 90
Bouturlin, Vassili (Count) – 161
Brainerd, Mary Olivia — 44
Brashear, John Alfred – 70

Bréal, Michel Jules Alfred – 112
Bryant, Edward W. – 31
Buckner – 136
Buetler (Mrs.) – 165
Buetler, John Conrad – 165
Bullen, George W. – 46
Butler, Cora L. – 218
Bye, Raymond T. – 143
Caglieris, Marie – 61
Cannon, Joseph Gurney – 134
Carnegie, Andrew – 70, 130, 134, 146
Cary, Edward – 126
Cecil, Robert – 223, 225, 255
Chappaz, J. M. (Mr.) – 154
Chater, Arthur G. – 190
Chevrillon, André – 231
Chomette, Charles – 234, 253
Church, W. L. – 143
Clarke, Herbert Morrison – 146
Cohen, Rebecca – 136
Coigne, Creston C. – 198, 207
Coleridge, E. P. – 245
Cornet (Mr.) – 47
Couturat, Louis – 28, 29, 53, 80, 120, 193
Cox, George – 52, 54, 77, 91, 93
Dana, Charles L. – 71, 72
Dante Alighieri – 57, 246
Diederich, Henry W. – 169
Dillard, James – 247
Dillard, James H. – 247
Dizzy (may refer to Benjamin Disraeli) – 245
Donnay, Charles Maurice – 230, 231, 236
Doro, Marie – 70
Dreyfus, Alfred – 29
Drummond, Sir Eric – 219
E. D. F. – 23
Edison, Carroll E. – 37
Edison, Thomas A. – 114
Edward VII, King of the United Kingdom – 115

Eliot (may refer to Thomas Stearns Eliot) – 237
Ellis, Alexander John – 4
Ellis, John – 34
Enckell, Carl – 223, 225
Escalante, Diogenes – 223, 225
Euripides – 245, 246
Fatio, M. (Mr.) – 228
Ferrer y Guardia, Francisco – 181, 182, 183
Fessenden, C. H. – 180
Fisher, Henry W. – 108, 109, 210
Foley, Charles, B. – 244, 245
Forbes-Robertson Hale (Mrs) – 164
Forman, Henry James – 52, 71
Foster, Edward Powell – 106, 195, 199
Fourman, J. G. – 215
FR. – 29
Franklin, Christine Ladd – 193, 213
Frederick August of Saxony, King of Saxony – 97, 117, 130
Freedman, Leo – 147
Freidenker – 18
French, Edwin Davis – 44, 45
Frohman, Charles – 68, 70
Frost, E. C. – 241
Geillon (Mr.) – 122
George, Henry – 161
Glynn, Martin H.
Gorton, David Allyn – 164
Gouin, François – 89
Grabowski, Antoni – 77, 173, 202
Grant Percy Stickney – 210
Grey, Sir Edward – 213
Griffith, C. S. – 50
Gubernatis, (Mr.) di – 19
Guesnet, L. M. de – 120
H. G. P. – 26, 36
Hale, Albert – 139
Hall, Hershel S. – 143
Hamerschlag, Arthur Arton – 70
Hanotaux, Gabriel – 219

Harding, Warren Gamaliel – 234
Harger, J. R. – 120
Harris, Herbert – 132
Harvey, George – 47, 53, 55, 71, 81, 120, 121
Hayashi Tadasu – 99
Hearn, John Ed. – 112, 127
Heller – 158
Henderson, George – J. 3
Hennion, Célestin – 189
Hetzel, Henry William – 160
Higgs, Esther – 143
Highboard (Mr.) – 39
Hill, David Jayne – 228
Hoeft, G. E. – 239
Hoffman, Paul F. – 137, 140
Holden, Jonathan – 206
Holt, Hamilton – 234
Homan, Paul – 144
Houlman, J. D. – 158
Howells, William Dean – 47
Hubbard, (Mr.) – 158
Hughes, Charles Evans – 114
Humphrey, Andrew B. – 186
Hunt, Theodore W. – 125
Husband, R. Wellington – 77, 90, 91, 93
Hutchinson, M. (Miss) – 138
Hymans, Paul – 219
Ionescu, Take (Jonnesco) – 223, 225
Jackson, Andrew – 134, 135
James, Edwin L. – 219
Jaurès, Jean – 57
Javal, Emile – 37, 38
Jespersen, Otto – 76, 93, 104, 193
Jonnesco (Ionescu, Take) – 223, 225
Kangas, Andrew – 59, 96, 102, 104, 107, 108, 109, 121
Khengarji III of Kutch (Maharajdhiraj Mirza Maharao Sri Khengarji III Sawai Bahadur) – 223, 225
King, Henry D. – 124
Kipling, Rudyard – 16, 42, 77

Knopf, Elizabeth –186
Kofman, Abram – 77
Kokeloy, E. C. – 159
Kronenberger, George F. — 244
La Fontaine, Henri – 223, 225
La Harte, Rose – 43
Lacey (Mr.) – 46
Lawrence, Annie – 26
Leau, Léopold – 28, 29, 34, 80
Leibniz, Gottfried Wilhelm – 245
Lemperly, Paul – 44
Lempertz, H. E. – 216, 225
Leskien, August – 77, 93
Lewinson Jr., P. – 204
Lewis, William A. – 74, 77, 92
Lincoln, Abraham – 134, 135, 143
Liptay (Mr.) – 22
Longfellow, Henry Wadsworth – 77
Loomis, Charles Battell – 125
Lott, Julius — 22
Lowell, D. O. S. – 71, 122, 210
Machloski (Mr.) – 168
Macloskie, George – 214
Madero, Evaristo – 166
Malone (Judge) – 136
Mann, Emeline Howard – 200
Mann, William – 138
Mann, William B. – 200
March, F. A. – 6
Martin, Henrietta – 138
Mason, John – 69
Masters, Edgar Lee – 246
Matthews, Brander – 42
Mayor, John Eyton Bickersteth – 247
McCall, Samuel W. – 135
McKelvey, E. C. – 169
Mendelssohn, Felix – 210, 221
Meyer, F. B. (Mr.) – 154
Meyer, O. H. – 120

Meyer, P. L. – 120
Michaux, Alfred – 100
Miguière (Mr.) – 186
Molee, Elias — 19
Molière (Jean-Baptiste Poquelin) – 126, 190, 231, 246
Montt, Pedro – 143
Morgan, John Pierpont – 236
Morton, James F. – 153, 158, 186, 187, 210, 248-252, 253, 254
Morton, Martha – 128
Moscheles, Felix – 15, 54, 122, 210, 221
Moscheles, Ignaz – 210, 221
Motta, Giuseppe– 219
Mouton (Mr.) –186
Mueller, Max – 171
Muensterberg, Hug – 204
Murphy, C. M. – 95
Murphy, Myles – 75
Murray, Gilbert – 245, 255
Murray, Gilbert – 245, 255
Murray, James P. – 213
Nansen, Fridtjof – 190, 191
Nasi (Mr.) – 18
Nichols, Ernest Fox – 134
Nichols, William H. – 174
Nitobe Inazo – 226
Noli, Fan S. – 223, 225
Norman, Henry James – 81
North, Olive – 43
O'Connor, J. C. (Mr.) – 15, 19, 21, 46
O'Meara (Mr.) – 11
Orlando, Vittorio Emanuele – 218, 249
Ostwald, Friedrich Wilhelm – 51, 193
Page, Curtis H. – 126
Pantchenko (Mr.) – 161
Payson, Edward S. – 218
Perkins, George W. – 198
Philander C. Knox – 132
Phillips, Walter P. – 5
Pius XI, Pope – 229

Plese, M.J. – 224
Pollen, John – 122, 131, 132, 138
Porter, E. X. – 192
Postnikoff (Postnikov), Aleksandr Aleksejeviĉ – 161
Powell, Rufus W. – 210
Pratley, Harry H. – 113
Prince, John D. – 248, 250, 251
Privat, Edmond – 60, 61, 66, 67, 69, 71, 95, 180
Quackenbos, George H. – 188
Rathbun, Frank H. – 73, 76, 93, 94
Reade, Charles – 237
Reed, Edwin C. – 124, 132, 138, 141, 158, 159, 169, 172
Reicher, Emanuel – 129
Reicher, Hedwig – 97, 128, 130, 172, 173
Reid, E. C. (Mr.) – 144
Restrepo, Antonio José) – 223, 225
Reusch, Augusta – 111
Revell, Fleming H. – 46, 58, 62, 67, 69, 95, 111, 154
Rhodes, Joseph – 58, 95, 111, 154
Rhodes, S. (Mrs.) – 114
Rhombus, Carlo – 245
Richard (Mr.) – 190
Riecher, Manuel – 69
Robbie, James – 143
Roosevelt, Theodore – 40, 41, 45, 49, 66, 134, 198, 209
Root, Elihu (United States Secretary of State) – 52
Rosen, Friedrich – 221
Rosenberger, Waldemar (Woldemar, Voldemar) – 17, 18, 23
Rostand, Edmond – 180
Roy, Gustave – 66
Rummede – 103
S. W. T. – 154
Samenhof, L. – cf. Zamenhof
Sapwnov (Mr.) – 163
Sayers, James Denson – 239, 244, 245, 247
Sayers, James Denson – 239, 244, 245, 247
Schaeffer, F. (Miss) – 138
Schleyer, Johann Martin – 1-7, 14, 17, 19, 23, 163, 175
Schubert, B. F. – 144

Sebert, Hippolyte – 122
Shakespeare, William – 25, 36, 47, 88, 155, 246
Sharpe, Richard – 138
Silbernik, Joseph – 147, 203
Silver, Bennett C. – 136
Sinclair, Upton – 157, 160
Skeel-Giørling, Frederik – 155
Smiley, James L. – 137, 140
Smith, A.Y. – 200-206
Smith, Wilton Merle – 214
Solas (Father) – 137
Sophocles – 246
Spaulding, Wayland – 151, 153
Sprague, Charles E. – 3, 4, 6, 13
Sprague, Charles E. – 3, 4, 6, 14
Sproul, Arthur Elliott – 224, 233, 237, 253, 254
Stead, William (W. T.) – 15, 24, 25, 26, 62
Stephens, Donald – 157
Sterrett, W. E. – 81
Stevens, Donald – 158
Stoner, Jr., Winifred Sackville – 166, 191, 192
Straub, Paul H. – 97
Strutton, Henry J. – 120
Swivelbrain, H. Percy – 68
Taft, William Howard – 124, 164
Taine, Hippolyte – 231
Talmey, Max – 40, 62, 64, 65, 100, 121, 123, 124, 253
Tamara (Mademoiselle; aka "The Russian Nightingale") – 38
Teheberiak, Vera – 184
Tennyson, Alfred – 176-177
Tiard, Marcelle – 138
Tolstoy (Tolstoi), Lev Nikolayevich (Leo) – 30, 89, 97, 171
Torre, R. Da – 238
Trager, George L. – 241
Trine, R. W. – 155
Trost (Mr.) – 218
Tsai Fou-Tang (Tsai Fu Tang) – 223, 225
Twain, Mark – 47, 145
Ungern Sternburg, Baron von – 161

Van der Biest-Andelhof, Amatus – 169
Vandervelde, Emile – 57
Vincent, George Edgar – 81
Vogel, Leo – 67
Vogler, W. A. – 143
W. J. P. – 80, 91, 100, 105, 110
Walden, Paul T. – 174
Walker, J. Charles – 61
Warnier, Georges – 144
Way, Arthur Sanders – 245
Weaver, A. J. (Mr.) – 199
Webster, Daniel – 135
Webster, Noah – 198-199
Wells, Charles B. – 158
Wheeless, Thomas – 153
White, Andrew D. – 130, 131
Whitehouse, Cope – 40
Whiteing, Richard – 175, 178
Wile, Ira – 186
Wilhelm II, King of Prussia – 117
Wilkins, John – 245
Wilson, James – 41
Wilson, Woodrow – 218, 249
Winkelmann, Sergius – 138
Wishard, G. W. – 33, 34
Work, John H. – 128
Wu Tingfang (Ting-fang) – 115, 116
Yemans, H. W. – 141, 159, 164, 169, 171
Yemens, H. (Mr.) – 144
Young S. Edward – 214
Yushinsky (boy) – 184
Zamenhof, L. L. (Zamenhoff, Samenhof) – 9, 10, 11, 13, 15, 17, 21, 22, 31, 32, 52, 57, 58, 59, 71, 76, 77, 78, 80, 90, 93, 94, 95, 97, 101, 104, 109, 110, 112, 119, 137, 138, 139, 141, 143, 159, 163, 176, 183, 202, 209, 210, 211, 220, 228, 239, 254
Zamenhof, Lidia – 138
Zangwill (Mr.) – 36
Zikke, Muse – 161
Zoka-ed-Dowleh, Emir – 223, 225
Zola, Emile – 29

For Further Reading
Short Bibliography

Wells, John C. 2010. *English-Esperanto-English Dictionary*. New York: Mondial.

Korzhenkov, Aleksander. 2010. *Zamenhof. The Life, Works and Ideas of the Author of Esperanto*. Ed. by Humphrey Tonkin. Translated by Ian M. Richmond. New York: Mondial.

Blanke, Detlev. 2009. *Causes of the relative success of Esperanto*. Language Problems & Language Planning 33/3:251-266.

Okrent, Arika. 2009. *In the Land of Invented Languages*. New York: Spiegel & Grau.

Sutton, Geoffrey. 2008. Concise Encyclopedia of the Original Literature of Esperanto. New York: Mondial.

Lins, Ulrich. 2008. Esperanto as language and idea in China and Japan. Language Problems & Language Planning 32/1:47-60.

van Dijk, Ziko. 2008. *La Asocio: Skizoj kaj studoj pri la historio de Universala Esperanto-Asocio*. Antverpeno: Flandra Esperanto-Ligo.

Minnaja, Carlo. 2007. *L'Esperanto in Italia: alla ricerca della democrazia linguistica*. Padova: Poligrafo.

Conley, Tim & Stephen Cain. 2006. *Encyclopedia of Fictional and Fantastic Languages*. Westport CT & London: Greenwood.

Wennergren, Bertilo. 2005. *Plena manlibro de Esperanta gramatiko*. El Cerrito CA: Esperanto League for North America.

Blanke, Detlev. 2003. *Interlinguistics and Esperanto studies: Paths to the scholarly literature*. Language Problems & Language Planning 27/2:155-192.

Schubert, Klaus, ed. 2002. *Planned Languages: From Concept to Reality*. Brussels: Hogeschool voor Wetenschap en Kunst.

Duc Goninaz, Michel, and others. 2002. *La nova plena ilustrita vortaro de Esperanto*. Paris: SAT.

Fiedler, Sabine. 1999. *Plansprache und Phraseologie: Empirische Untersuchungen zu reproduziertem Sprachmaterial im Esperanto.* Frankfurt/M. et. al.: Peter Lang.

Tonkin, Humphrey (Ed.). 1997. *Esperanto, Interlinguistics, and Planned Language.* Lanham-New York-Oxford: University Press of America / Rotterdam-Hartford: Center for Research and Documentation on World Language Problems.

Tonkin, H. 1996. *Language hierarchy at the United Nations.* in: Sylvie Léger, ed. *Vers un agenda linguistique: Regard futuriste sur les Nations Unies / Towards a Language Agenda: Futurist Outlook on the United Nations.* Ottawa: Canadian Centre for Linguistic Rights, University of Ottawa. 3-28.

Eco, Umberto. 1995. *The Search for the Perfect Language.* Translated by James Fentress. Oxford & Cambridge MA: Blackwell.

Piron, Claude. 1994. *Le Défi des langues. Du gâchis au bon sens.* Paris: L'Harmattan.

Richmond, Ian, ed. 1993. *Aspects of Internationalism: Language and Culture.* Lanham MD: University Press of America.

Janton, Pierre. 1993. *Esperanto. Language, Literature, and Community.* Ed. by Humphrey Tonkin. Translated by Humphrey Tonkin, Jane Edwards and Karen Johnson-Weiner. Albany: State University of New York Press.

Fantini, Alvino E. & Timothy G. Reagan. 1992. *Esperanto and Education: Towards a Research Agenda.* Washington: Esperantic Studies Foundation.

Carlton, Edward. 1990. *Towards a Better Understanding: Esperanto, the Universal Secondary and Intermediary Language.* East Wittering, England: Gooday.

Schubert, Klaus, & Dan Maxwell, ed. 1989. *Interlinguistics: Aspects of the Science of Planned Languages.* Berlin, New York, Amsterdam: Mouton de Gruyter.

Lins, Ulrich. 1988. *Die gefährliche Sprache. Die Verfolgung der Esperantisten unter Hitler und Stalin*. Gerlingen: Bleicher.

Duliĉenko, Aleksandr. 1988. *Esperanto: A unique model for general linguistics*. Language Problems & Language Planning 12:148-151.

Lins, Ulrich. 1986. *The Contribution of the Universal Esperanto Association to World Peace*. Esperanto Documents 37A. Rotterdam: Universala Esperanto-Asocio.

Blanke, Detlev. 1985. *Internationale Plansprachen*. Berlin: Akademie-Verlag.

Tonkin, Humphrey. 1982. *Esperanto in the Service of the United Nations*. Esperanto Documents 27A. Rotterdam: Universala Esperanto-Asocio.

Forster, Peter G. 1982. *The Esperanto Movement*. (Contributions to the Sociology of Languages. 32). The Hague-Paris-New York: Mouton.

Hagler, Margret C. 1970. *The Esperanto-Language as a Literary Medium. A Historical Discussion of Esperanto-Literature 1887-1970 and Stylistic Analysis of translated and Original Esperanto Poetry*. Bloomington: Indiana University.

Short Collection of Internet links on Esperanto

**The links may be accessed directly at
www.mondialbooks.com/nytimes**

General information:

esperanto.net
(esperanto.net/info/index_en.html)

Wikipedia
(en.wikipedia.org/wiki/Esperanto)

Teaching materials and courses:

Lernu!
(en.lernu.net)

NASK (North American Summer Esperanto Institute at the University of California, San Diego (UCSD)
(esperanto.org/nask)

John Wells: English-Esperanto-English Dictionary
(librejo.com/wells-vortaro)

Reta Vortaro (Online Dictionary)
(reta-vortaro.de)

Organizations:

Universal Esperanto Association
(uea.org/info/angla.html)

World Esperanto Youth Organization
(tejo.org/en)

Esperanto USA
(esperanto-usa.org)

Esperanto Association of Britain
(esperanto-gb.org)

Esperanto Association of Southern Africa
(esperanto.za.org/en)

Australian Esperanto Association
(aea.esperanto.org.au)

New Zealand Esperanto Association
(esperanto.org.nz)

Interlinguistics / Esperanto Studies:

Esperantic Studies Foundation
(esperantic.org/en)

Language Problems and Language Planning
(benjamins.com/cgi-bin/t_seriesview.cgi?series=lplp)

Akademio de Esperanto
(akademio-de-esperanto.org);
information in English:
en.wikipedia.org/wiki/Akademio_de_Esperanto

Gesellschaft für Interlinguistik (Society for Interlinguistics)
(interlinguistik-gil.de) – mainly in German; general information in English

Literature:

Akademio Literatura de Esperanto
(everk.it) – only in Esperanto

Concise Encyclopedia of the Original Literature of Esperanto
(librejo.com/enciklopedio)

Originala Literaturo Esperanta
(esperanto.net/literaturo) – only in Esperanto

Esperanto Literature
(en.wikipedia.org/wiki/Esperanto_literature)

Other:

Unesco Resolutions about Esperanto
(e.euroscola.free.fr/unesco-en.htm)

Austrian National Library: Department of Planned Languages and Esperanto Museum
(onb.ac.at/ev/collections/plansprachen.htm)

German Esperanto Library in Aalen (Online Catalog)
(cs.chalmers.se/pub/users/martinw/esperanto/aalen/index_en.html)

www.ingramcontent.com/pod-product-compliance
Lightning Source LLC
Chambersburg PA
CBHW030239170426
43202CB00007B/56